ADVERSARY AND ALLY

ADVERSARY AND ALLY

HOW CHINA SHAPES THE FRONTIER POLITICS OF INDIA AND PAKISTAN

HARRISON AKINS

Columbia University Press
New York

Columbia University Press
Publishers Since 1893
New York Chichester, West Sussex
cup.columbia.edu

Cataloging-in-Publication data is available from the Library of Congress

ISBN 9780231221818 (hardback)
ISBN 9780231221825 (trade paperback)
ISBN 9780231563925 (ebook)
ISBN 9780231564922 (PDF)

LCCN 2025026236

Cover design: Chang Jae Lee
Cover image: © Shutterstock

GPSR Authorized Representative: Easy Access System Europe,
Mustamäe tee 50, 10621 Tallinn, Estonia, gpsr.requests@easproject.com

FOR MARINA, MY LOVE

CONTENTS

PART II. THE ALLY

NOTE ON SOURCING

Regarding the extensive primary source research for this book, *Adversary and Ally* relies exclusively on open-source information and does not utilize any classified information or documents, nor any government documents or information that were leaked to the public or otherwise improperly released. When referencing or discussing various U.S. government documents that contained classified or controlled information, such as intelligence reports or diplomatic cables, this book only uses information and documents that have been formally declassified and publicly released according to official U.S. government policy.

ABBREVIATIONS

AFSPA	Armed Forces (Special Powers) Act
ASEAN	Association of Southeast Asian Nations
BLA	Balochistan Liberation Army
BLF	Balochistan Liberation Front
BNP	Balochistan National Party
BRI	Belt and Road Initiative
BSU	Balochistan States Union
CIA	Central Intelligence Agency
CPEC	China–Pakistan Economic Corridor
CPECA	China–Pakistan Economic Corridor Authority
FDI	foreign direct investment
FIR	first information report
FULRO	Front Unifié de Lutte des Races Opprimées (United Front for the Liberation of Oppressed Races)
FWO	Frontier Works Organization
IB	Intelligence Bureau (India)
ISI	Inter-Services Intelligence (Pakistan)
IFAS	Indian Frontier Administrative Service
LAC	Line of Actual Control
MCC	Metallurgical Corporation of China

MNF	Mizo National Front
MNFF	Mizo National Famine Front
NAP	National Awami Party
NEFA	North-East Frontier Agency
NHTA	Naga Hills–Tuensang Area
NNC	Naga National Council
NWFP	North-West Frontier Province
PLA	People's Liberation Army
PPP	Pakistan People's Party
PRC	People's Republic of China
PSA	Port of Singapore Authority
PTI	Pakistan Tehreek-e-Insaf
RGM	Revolutionary Government of Manipur
RGVs	Regrouped Villages (Nagaland)
UDF	United Democratic Front
UNLF	United National Liberation Front

ADVERSARY AND ALLY

1

ADVERSARY AND ALLY

In the mountainous terrain surrounding India's contested border with China, soldiers from both sides, often only hundreds of feet apart, have faced off for decades, maneuvering for position among the region's peaks as they push and probe the territorial claims of their respective governments. In December 2022, amid rising tensions between the two adversaries, the standoff once again turned violent. An Indian military patrol in the Tawang area of India's northeastern state of Arunachal Pradesh chanced upon a group of Chinese soldiers whom they suspected of encroaching into Indian-claimed territory to "change the status quo" of the border region, according to the Indian defense minister. Wary of the broader ramifications of an exchange of gunfire following a 1996 agreement prohibiting the use of firearms near the border, the two sides clashed with sticks and clubs, leaving several soldiers injured.[1] This incident came in the wake of the June 2020 clash in the Galwan Valley in the Ladakh region, in which twenty soldiers were killed and another seventy-six injured; many were victims of stone throwing, fists, and iron bars, while others were simply pushed to their deaths on the sharp rocks far below the steep ridge they occupied.[2] The ferocity of the hand-to-hand combat, which lasted for hours at high altitude and in near total darkness, was a flashpoint in the long and fraught relationship between India and China as both countries have sought to assert their territorial control along the disputed border over the previous seven decades.

In stark contrast, at the Khunjerab Pass, where the Karakoram Highway connects China and Pakistan, Chinese and Pakistani border guards have been photographed reaching across the international border and holding hands in friendship. Such gestures symbolize the close relationship between these two countries over the past half century.[3] With Pakistan locked in an enduring rivalry with India, and as the United States' support waxes and wanes according to the vicissitudes of US strategic interests, Pakistanis have looked to China as a consistent military and economic partner, an "all-weather ally" for the Islamic Republic.[4]

China's varying engagement with and influence within South Asia, as well as many other regions around the world, have gained greater attention within academic and policy circles in recent years, a product of the Communist state solidifying its position as a leading economic and political power on the world's stage. In his 2017 book *Everything Under the Heavens*, journalist Howard French writes, "China's ultimate goal, however, is not merely to restore a semblance of the region's old order. . . . A larger, more ambitious goal is already edging into view. This ambition, evident from behavior even if still not fully avowed, involves supplanting American power and influence in the region as an irreplaceable steppingstone along the way to becoming a true global power in the twenty-first century."[5]

Following Mao Zedong's death in 1976, Deng Xiaoping, who rose to power in 1978, pursued a series of market-based reforms and transitioned the Communist government's policies away from the stringent revolutionary ideology of Mao and toward economic pragmatism, eventually opening and modernizing the country's economy. Beginning in the 1980s, China began to shift its foreign policy to foster more friendly relations and trade with neighboring countries in support of its domestic economic development. The need to foster rapid economic growth to provide employment opportunities for the world's largest population, protect pensions for an ageing workforce, and address lingering issues of social inequality that can underpin social unrest helped to drive this new policy. China's growing regional economic integration culminated in President Xi Jinping announcing a "Silk Road economic belt" in a September 2013 speech at Kazakhstan's Nazarbayev University. The purpose of this economic belt, President Xi stated, was to "make the economic ties closer, mutual cooperation deeper and space of development broader between the Eurasian countries." He continued, "We should turn the advantage of political relations, the geographical advantage, and the economic complementary advantage into advantages for practical cooperation and for sustainable growth, so as to build a community of interests."[6] The following month, during a visit to Jakarta, President Xi similarly announced a new Maritime Silk Road in a speech to the Indonesian parliament. This initiative was intended to strengthen economic and trade links across the South China Sea and the Indian Ocean.[7]

These announcements laid the basis for China's wide-ranging Belt and Road Initiative (BRI), a global development strategy with the ultimate goal of linking the economies of Asia, Africa, and Europe through land and maritime trading networks.[8] Driven by interlinked domestic and foreign policy objectives, the Chinese government has invested billions in various energy, transportation, and extractive infrastructure projects across South, Central, and Southeast Asia, the Middle East, and Africa. As part of the BRI, China also has sought to develop six economic corridors: the China–Mongolia–Russia Economic Corridor; the New Eurasian Land Bridge; the China–Central Asia–West Asia Economic Corridor; the China–Indochina Peninsula Economic Corridor; the China–Pakistan Economic Corridor; and the China-Myanmar Economic Corridor. In the eyes of China's leadership, these expanding regional economic links under the BRI will operate within the framework of a new global order envisioned and dominated by China and challenging American hegemony.[9]

By early 2023, China had already spent approximately $1 trillion on BRI-related projects, with estimates of the overall costs of the BRI reaching as high as $8 trillion across four continents.[10] This expanding economic integration was further facilitated by new multilateral financial institutions such as the Chinese-initiated Asian Infrastructure Investment Bank, established in January 2016 and now the second-largest multilateral development bank, with 110 member countries as of late 2025. By wielding its economic and political strength through the BRI, China has sought to transform itself from a regional to a global power and economic and political competitor of the United States, with China playing an increasing role in shaping and directing the domestic politics and economies of various countries around the world as a result.[11]

Since China overtook Japan in 2010 as the world's second-largest economy, US political leaders have increasingly pivoted US foreign policy to maintain the United States' global economic dominance and shape international priorities around the growing competition with China. In 2021, US President Joe Biden stated, "China has an overall goal . . . to become the leading country in the world, the wealthiest county in the world, and the most powerful country in the world. That's not going to happen on my watch because the United States is going to continue to grow."[12] The White House's 2022 *National Security Strategy* prioritized outcompeting China as "the only competitor with both the intent to reshape the international order and, increasingly, the economic, diplomatic, military, and technological power to do it."[13] To support this goal, the US government has increasingly focused on the spaces of expanding Chinese reach around the world.[14] In June 2023, Assistant Secretary of State for Energy Resources Geoffrey Pyatt testified before the House Foreign Affairs Committee on the US government's efforts "to strengthen global energy security and counter the PRC's attempts to create economic dependencies and to coerce others through its 'Belt and Road' and similar initiatives."[15] These efforts focused on countering China's growing reach in varied regions around the world such as the Indo-Pacific, Africa, and Latin America, and included supporting new US investments, loan programs, public-private partnerships, and technical assistance through US institutions such as the Export-Import Bank of the United States and the US Development Finance Corporation.

Yet, in its immediate neighborhood, China's influence as a political and economic regional power dates back decades. Chinese actions have helped to shape and direct the domestic politics of nearby states, as both an adversary and an ally, since the early days of postcolonial independence. Within South Asia, soon after the British government's transfer of power in 1947, senior Pakistani and Indian officials faced the challenge of extending the writ of the state over populations and territory in the difficult terrain of distant frontiers that remained largely unadministered under British rule. The legacy of British colonial administration engendered ambiguous, and at times belligerent, relations between center and periphery. As a result, many people within these spaces of contested sovereignty saw the attempts of the newly independent governments to establish control—never a particularly easy task, even in the most conducive of environments—as an outside imposition and thus frequently resisted it. They sought to assert their own, distinct political identities, including by pushing for greater political autonomy or even independence from the newly created states. Government officials quickly grew concerned with the frontier regions on the peripheries of their respective states as early sources of opposition to their rule and the potential for this opposition to spread to other regions, threatening the unity of the new states from within. Therefore, central governments in the region have prioritized the extension of government control and the integration of the periphery into the state. Within both India and Pakistan, government attempts to assert state sovereignty over these border regions often devolved into repressive actions from the center and violent rebellion from the periphery.

This process has not only been a product of the domestic frontier politics defined by the tensions between center and periphery but was exacerbated by the international political environment as well. In China's neighboring states, as I argue here, Beijing's influence on state relations with the periphery has largely occurred in two ways, reflective of two distinct phases in Chinese foreign policy. In its first phase, China's foreign policy under Chairman Mao, the founder of the Chinese Communist Party who led the country from 1949 to his death in 1976, was shaped by an ideological commitment and antipathy to foreign influence born out of a perceived history of humiliation at the hands of various imperial powers, "reactive assertiveness" as the party consolidated power domestically, and the pursuit of territorial security, particularly through establishing control over contested regions on its periphery, such as Tibet.[16] The government's commitment to cultivating ideological allies and pursuing territorial expansionism over regions seen to be rightfully China's frequently inculcated hostile relations with neighboring countries.

During this period, India increasingly perceived China, with its military invasion of Tibet, its repudiation of the international border, and claims on Indian territory, as a military threat, and this in turn spurred on its efforts to integrate the northeastern Assam region into the postcolonial Indian state. Security concerns have long shaped New Delhi's perception of and policies toward the distant northeastern periphery—distant in terms of both geography and culture. After China's October 1950 invasion of Tibet, which pushed the People's Liberation Army right up to the border with India, New Delhi's precarious hold over the Northeast was understood to be a strategic vulnerability. While many scholars have highlighted India and China's friendly relations during the 1950s, senior Indian officials, including India's first prime minister, Jawaharlal Nehru, expressed their apprehension about Chinese expansionism as early as 1950 and the potential Communist influence on antigovernment and secessionist movements that posed a serious threat to the unity of the new country. From the perspective of New Delhi, the intersection between Chinese expansionism and ethnic separatism in the Northeast was a dangerous mix, especially as the two countries increasingly competed for regional influence.[17]

As a result, the Indian government expanded its administrative reach, implemented state-led development projects, and increased the presence of security forces in the underdeveloped northeastern region in order to assert government control. These efforts were made all the more urgent as the Chinese government proved its willingness to back its territorial claims within India's northeastern frontier with military force following Chinese military action against India in 1962. Compounding this problem, a series of separatist insurgencies fighting the expanded presence of the central government erupted within the broader northeastern region through the 1950s and 1960s. Given the adversarial relationship between India and China that culminated in the 1962 war, the militant groups would eventually look to the Chinese government for financial and military support. Concerned with the broader ramifications of the potential loss of its border territory under the looming shadow of the Chinese threat and the fear of Chinese links with anti-state militant groups within the Northeast, Indian officials expanded their plans to extend the government's political hold and bolster the military presence within the restive border region into the 1970s, further exacerbating tensions between center and periphery.

The second phase of Chinese foreign policy began in the 1980s and has been marked by a shift toward economic pragmatism and economic diplomacy. Beginning with the rule of Deng Xiaoping in 1978, China sought to build economic relationships not only in its immediate neighborhood but also in other parts of the world to accelerate the country's economic growth.[18] This continued into the 1990s. In the middle of that decade, Chinese President Jiang Zemin pushed Chinese companies to "go global" and invest, increasing China's commercial presence around the world.[19] This effort to exert international influence and control through economic integration eventually led to Xi Jinping's BRI announcement in 2013. Even before the establishment of the BRI, Pakistan's leaders were already courting Chinese investors. During the 1990s, Pakistan increasingly sought financial support and international investors to help bolster its struggling economy and soon looked to the economically expanding China, which, because of its shared animosity toward India, had long been a key source of military and political support. Over the next two decades, China led and financed a series of development projects throughout Pakistan, including in the western province of Balochistan, which helped to increase the central government's presence to support investments in the energy, transportation, and extractive sectors, such as the Gwadar Port on Balochistan's Arabian coast. The announcement of the China–Pakistan Economic Corridor (CPEC) in 2015, a leading project of China's BRI, has spurred even greater levels of development, with China's total investment in CPEC estimated to eventually reach as high as $62 billion.

Such projects have exacerbated many of the lingering problems between the center and its strategic Western periphery. Following the creation of Pakistan in 1947, the people of Balochistan complained of persistent political marginalization and economic exploitation of the region's natural resources, which has sparked a history of antistate insurgencies. The province has chronically lagged other regions of Pakistan in education, health, and infrastructure development, remaining the poorest of the country's four provinces. The expansion of Chinese-led development during this period has been met with strident opposition from Baloch nationalists, who complained that local voices were not taken into consideration in the planning process and that the projects are not intended to benefit local Baloch communities. They perceive these development efforts as simply a means of consolidating central government control over the periphery. Given the relationship between Pakistan and China, Baloch militant groups quickly saw Chinese targets in Pakistan as part of their domestically focused campaign of violence. As a result, there have been increasing levels of violence against government and military personnel, development projects, and Chinese workers in the region. Under pressure from the Chinese government, the increasing attacks against the project sites and the Chinese workers present at them resulted in the increased militarization of the region, which, in turn, provoked ever higher levels of violence from Baloch militant groups opposed to the presence and actions of the Pakistani military. Thus, Chinese-led development has exacerbated many of the underlying tensions between center and periphery in Pakistan and contributed to the outbreak of antistate violence.

The United States and many other countries contending with China's global rise must remain cognizant of the implications of China's expanding influence, including the potential ramifications from China's impact on domestic political developments around the globe. Such processes have implications for the United States' and other countries' own economic initiatives aimed at countering and competing with China. Sitting along China's southern border, India and Pakistan will remain unavoidably vital to any conversation concerning China's international engagement and a key part of US global strategy to "outcompete" China.

Therefore, laying out the history and context of China's relationship with India and Pakistan and the pathways of influence through different phases of Chinese foreign policy is a useful exercise, particularly for US policymakers seeking to constructively position the United States as an alternative economic and political partner.

CENTER VERSUS PERIPHERY IN SOUTH ASIA

Political leaders inhabiting the centers of power in South Asia have long grappled with the challenge of extending their writ over the various peoples populating the distant frontiers—the mountains, deserts, and forests on the periphery of their claimed territories—that traditionally lay beyond their reach and strongly resisted the intrusion of outside forces. The term "periphery" is used in this book following anthropologist Akbar Ahmed and his conception of the tense relationship between center and periphery.[20] While there were intermittent attempts by the region's historical empires to extend their control, the harsh terrain of the frontier and fiercely guarded independence of its inhabitants frequently kept outside forces at bay. These far-flung regions repelled the process of integration with the state, becoming zones of evasion from the centripetal forces of state formation. Indeed, the periphery, far from a mere geographic descriptor, is defined through this opposition to government control that was often abetted by the difficult terrain of these areas and isolation at states' frontiers, as political ethnographer James Scott has argued.[21] Moreover, rulers of the past often saw little economic return for the high military and administrative costs required to assert political control in these regions, with the result that a "delicate balance" and "uneasy truce" was often forged between the center and periphery, as observed by anthropologist Clifford Geertz.[22] This left peripheral communities largely to govern themselves according to local political and social customs without much outside interference or control.

The introduction and expansion of European colonial rule frequently disrupted this hard-fought yet precarious status quo. In British India, the question of how to handle the problems of its lengthy frontier preoccupied many colonial officials throughout the nineteenth and twentieth centuries, such as George Curzon, the arch-Russophobe viceroy of India from 1899 to 1905. Lord Curzon observed in his 1907 Romanes Lecture at Oxford University that British India's vast frontier contained numerous tribal populations over which the colonial government exercised "no jurisdiction and only the minimum of control; into the territories of some we have so far not even penetrated; but they are on the British side of the dividing line, and cannot be tampered with by any external Power."[23] He continued, "The most arduous struggle in which we have been engaged in India in modern times was waged with Frontier tribes. . . . Think, indeed, of what the Indian Frontier Problems, as it is commonly called, has meant and means; the controversies it has provoked, the passions it has aroused; the reputations that have flashed or faded within its sinister shadow." Stressing the importance of such issues, he concluded, "Frontiers are indeed the razor's edge on which hang suspended the modern issues of war or peace, of life or death to nations."[24]

In response to this transborder threat during the nineteenth and early twentieth centuries, British colonial authorities established a series of defensive buffer regions along India's northern and western borders, ostensibly to stymie Russian advancement and influence as the British government feared that imperial Russia's ultimate aim was to extend its control throughout Asia, thereby threatening the British hold on India.[25] The British government adopted a three-tiered approach to the security of its Indian colony, its "threefold frontier." The first geographical frontier was the political boundaries of the subcontinent over which the British Raj was able to exert direct administrative control. The second consisted of the space between the first frontier's border and a demarcated international border to which the Raj laid territorial claim but over which it was unable to impose its laws or political control from Calcutta (and later New Delhi). This space included the tribal tracts within the hills of India's northeastern frontier, the Pashtun-populated tribal areas of the northwestern frontier lying along the Durand Line with Afghanistan, and tribal regions of the Baloch frontier leading to the Bolan Pass connecting Afghanistan and Balochistan. The third frontier lay beyond India's international borders and consisted of various protectorates—such as Afghanistan, Nepal, and Tibet—that remained independent kingdoms but were cemented to British interests and guarded from foreign influence through various treaty agreements.

Within the second frontier, the British Indian government faced the challenge of keeping the border tribes onside as a buffer region for external defense as well as maintaining law and order in what colonial officials perceived as lawless and violent lands inhabited by "fanatical" tribes, a perspective that informed colonial regulations and governing approaches to the periphery.[26] These "zones of anomaly" were seen as "blank spots in the cultivated vistas of British sovereignty," in the words of anthropologist Kalyanakrishnan Sivaramakrishnan.[27] Given the absence of effective government control in these vast borderlands, any unrest on the frontier, colonial officials feared, could quickly spread and be exploited by outside powers to undermine the British position in South Asia. In the waning years of his tenure as viceroy of British India, Lord Curzon argued that as India's land frontier stretched over 5,700 miles and contained hundreds of different tribes, "a single outbreak at a single point may set entire sections of that frontier ablaze." In his view, such unrest became exponentially more dangerous with "the muffled figures of great European Powers, advancing nearer and nearer, and sometimes finding in these conditions temptations to action that is not in strict accordance with the interests which we are bound to defend."[28]

To protect British interests in border regions without the high costs of introducing direct administration and political control, colonial authorities often relied on indirect rule, an administrative approach that consisted of isolating frontier regions from other parts of the subcontinent and ruling through recognized local elites based in ethnic or communal identities to maintain law and order, all while respecting the tribes' internal autonomy and purposefully keeping the regions under the semi-control of colonial authorities.[29] As historian Benjamin Hopkins argues, British frontier governance focused on "containment and encapsulation."[30] This approach was formalized by the British political officer Robert Sandeman while serving in Balochistan during the 1870s and 1880s. A key aspect to Sandeman's approach to frontier administration was indirect rule through local tribal leaders, providing them financial support, administrative roles, and political recognition that would not only bolster their position among the local population but help align their interests with those of the colonial government. Yet, all the while, they would operate under the threat of British military action. As historian Christian Tripodi describes, "[Sandeman] was determined to revive indigenous political systems, placing power in the hands of effective local leaders and promoting the restoration and maintenance of a system of rule and law that was perfectly suited to that particular region."[31] While the ultimate aim of Sandeman's approach was to create a self-running system, it became reliant on the presence of effective political officers, each serving as the "man on the spot" representing British interests and applying pressure to tribal leaders as needed.[32] Richard Bruce, who served under Sandeman in Balochistan, stressed that Baloch tribal leaders, known as sardars, and *jirgas* (councils of elders) held great influence among the tribes and, if handled correctly, "can be utilised with enormous benefit to the Government and to the good administration of the frontier. . . . They are each and all essential parts in the tribal machine, which requires specially trained officers for its successful working." In Bruce's summation, "it is, I believe, all a question of intelligent management and support judiciously granted."[33] The practices Sandeman developed in Balochistan were subsequently used as a model of frontier governance in other parts of British India, including in the tribal areas to Balochistan's north and on the northeastern frontier of Assam, and it influenced broad British conceptions about frontier spaces and how to approach them. In fact, British officials frequently made explicit comparisons between these frontier regions to guide or justify their actions.[34]

The introduction of some measure of political control, even in an indirect fashion, frequently failed to meet the ideals of frontier administration. In the ideal, such an approach had the added benefit of avoiding costly punitive military expeditions, which were regularly met with violent blowback from local populations. However, as the British government extended its reach into the unadministered tribal areas on its borders, local tribes perceived the extension of any level of government presence as an intrusion into their territory and interference with their autonomy. The practice of raiding into the settled areas and the selective use of violence against symbols of central government presence were often strategic or political responses to and means of delaying any intrusion by the state.[35] The British colonial government at times took the frontier's internal law-and-order matters into its own hands through military interventions before unrest could spill beyond its borders. As a result, the British presence within these border areas was uneven and frequently relied on ad hoc approaches that were often "confused and ineffective."[36]

After gaining independence, the Pakistani and Indian governments inherited territory absent a uniform system of governance and with varying levels of government control exerted across a plethora of administrative units—tribal areas, princely states, and directly administered districts. In his study of subnational conflict and competition within South Asia, political scientist Adnan Naseemullah argues that postcolonial conflict patterns were rooted in how the postcolonial states were constructed, "which was without national coherence at all." He describes modern states in South Asia as "patchwork states," with a "fragmented and diverse character of public institutions at the local level." In Naseemullah's analysis, this diversity in governing institutions and state control inherited from colonial rule shaped "the deep and long-lasting character of state capacity and relationships between state and society, prefiguring how citizens and social groups, including violent actors, engage the state's authority and resources."[37] In their analysis of the construction of state sovereignty in former colonial possessions, Thomas Blom Hansen and Finn Stepputat further argued that

> European states never aimed at governing the colonial territories with the same uniformity and intensity as were applied to their own populations. The emphasis was rarely on forging consent and the creation of a nation-people, and almost exclusively on securing subjection, order, and obedience through performance of paramount sovereign power and suppression of competing authorities. . . . As a result, the

> configurations of *de facto* sovereign power, justice, and order in the postcolonial states were from the outset partial, competing, and unsettled.[38]

These colonial-era challenges laid the foundation for pervasive tensions and even the intermittent eruption of violent conflict between center and periphery following the British withdrawal from the subcontinent. Historian Kyle Gardner argued in his study of the border-making process in India's northern Ladakh region that such challenges "bequeathed to [the Raj's] successor nation-states a conception of political space that made borders objects of existential significance."[39] This set the stage for political and military clashes not only between the center and periphery but between India and Pakistan over their ill-defined borders as both countries sought to define and assert state sovereignty over their strategic frontiers. Both inherited the legacy of British colonial policy toward British India's northwestern and northeastern frontiers, policies that would continue to shape and influence relations between center and periphery following the transfer of power in 1947.[40]

Facing the legacy of British colonial rule's layered and fragmented sovereignty, Indian and Pakistani political leaders in the years leading up to and following independence developed differing conceptions of national identity and belonging, processes that in many ways are still relevant today. While Pakistani and Indian political elites may have viewed the underpinning ideas of the state and belonging differently, their expressions of sovereignty were similar, particularly in response to antistate challenges emanating from the periphery that both newly independent states inherited from British colonial rule. India and Pakistan faced the imperative of extending the writ of the central government over the periphery. The political and territorial claims of the postcolonial state, especially on the frontier, often exceeded the central government's capacity and political will to project its direct control or exert influence over the entirety of the Indian and Pakistani populations. As government officials feared the broader implications of lawlessness or separatism spreading out from the frontier, they faced the challenge of building up state authority, dealing with political rivals within the frontier, and extending administrative control up to the international borders, especially as large swaths of the frontier remained largely autonomous and essentially unadministered.

Ironically, despite emerging from under the thumb of British imperialism, the Indian and Pakistani governments' treatment of their frontier communities carried with it shades of imperial control, a type of internal colonialism, over the diverse ethnicities, cultures, and political identities of the periphery.[41] While debates raged within the corridors of power over how to define the new countries' political identities, the views of the periphery were often excluded from this process, especially as government authorities promoted and projected a single culture and political identity, both domestically and abroad, as a means of supporting the unity of the state and assert their writ in spaces of contested sovereignty, such as the periphery. However, this unifying identity was often based on the characteristics of the dominant population and imposed, often through coercion or even violence, on the state's minorities, rather than consistently and constructively engaging and cooperating with minority communities.[42]

In the face of such efforts, political leaders on the frontier often sought to assert their own distinct identities and protect the region's political autonomy, resisting state penetration into the periphery and government attempts to integrate the region into this centrally dominated cultural and political identity. In many ways, the periphery's identity has been defined in sharp contrast with and in opposition to the culture and politics of the center, creating a deep chasm between the two. The periphery is often imagined as "an internal other," according to South Asian scholar Sanjib Baruah.[43]

In a description of India's northeastern frontier, for instance, Indian journalist Anil Yadav described the popular view of the region as "the most mysterious and neglected part of the country," given its geographic remoteness from the centers of political power in India.[44] "The result," B. K. Nehru, the former governor of several northeastern states during the 1960s and 1970s, and Jawaharlal Nehru's cousin, explained,

> has been a marked lack of knowledge in the rest of the India of the peoples and the problems of that large, potentially rich, naturally beautiful area and of its most attractive people. Large parts of its territory are peopled by tribes who have never been part of the Indian mainstream and who were, under British rule, deliberately kept apart from the rest of the country for reasons both legitimate and illegitimate. . . . The consequence has been a totally insufficient integration of the tribes with the rest of the Indian community, giving rise to dissatisfactions of various kinds which have, in some parts, culminated in insurgencies and insurrections.[45]

In 2021, a Naga poet and politician, Mmhonlumo Kikon, observed this divide between the northeastern periphery and the rest of the country, one that persists to this day. "The Northeast only gets attention when something goes wrong," he stated. "Even long after Independence, the impact of the multiple conflicts on society, which require attention, and the lack of knowledge of the basic geography of the region by many in India are still prevalent. . . . The representation and the mind space we occupy is minimal."[46] Within Pakistan, Akbar Ahmed observed that the conflict between center and periphery was similarly rooted in clashing conceptions of state sovereignty, writing,

> The center's main priority was to consolidate and establish its authority in all its parts. The periphery assumed that its state of semi-independence would be preserved, and that its own unique identity would be left untouched. From the birth of the nation, the divergence in the two points of view began to show, and before long the relationship between the center and periphery fluctuated between a working, if not entirely amicable, partnership and a rupture with attendant conflict.[47]

As a result, this process of integrating the border regions into the state often devolved into violence as the beleaguered periphery ultimately saw little change in its political status in the transition from colonial rule to independence, and government officials saw these regions as hotbeds of antistate resistance.

CHINA AND SOUTH ASIA: "THE SECOND IMAGE REVERSED"

While the study of international relations has traditionally downplayed domestic political processes, scholars have increasingly rejected the division between international and domestic politics posited by realist scholars, instead demonstrating how domestic political constraints can help to determine foreign policy actions, including domestic political costs for foreign policy decisions and other institutional constraints on political leaders' decision-making processes.[48]

International relations scholar Peter Gourevitch flipped this view through his "second image reversed," a concept he developed in a reexamination of the three images theory of realist scholar Kenneth Waltz to argue that the international political system also plays a key role in shaping and influencing states' domestic politics.[49] Economic, political, and security conditions at the international level can influence a state's domestic political development by both generating or limiting opportunities for economic and political processes and affecting internal security dynamics. As conflict has increasingly occurred at the intrastate level in recent decades, several scholars have adopted this theoretical frame to examine how international politics shapes governments' domestic security and conflict behavior.[50] No different from these other international factors, political leaders' perceptions of foreign actors and the international political environment within which they operate not only influence a state's foreign policy but can also impact governments' domestic behavior and policies.

Under both British colonial rule and postcolonial independence in South Asia, international politics have exacerbated the central government's concerns with strategic but poorly administered border regions and influenced state action in the periphery, whether through highlighting the lack of administrative control as a strategic vulnerability of the state or helping to push state presence within the periphery for economic exploitation in support of the country's broader economic growth. The strategic border regions of northeastern India and Balochistan lie at the heart of India's and Pakistan's respective interactions with China, shaping the two countries' perceptions of and policies toward their northern neighbor. While the periphery has consistently served as a space for regional cooperation and conflict, these areas are not empty interstices on the map, simply awaiting the expansion of the state to fill them. The periphery is populated with often little-known populations with their own distinct histories, cultures, and identities. These oft-forgotten edges of empire have been caught up in the vagaries of international politics, with their individual histories and experiences too often lost in the high politics of interstate relations. Yet, it is precisely by understanding China's impact on relations between center and periphery that one can find evidence of China's influence on the domestic politics of its neighboring countries.

By no means is China the only international factor influencing domestic political developments in the Indian and Pakistani frontiers, nor did China cause the internal problems between center and periphery. Since Indian and Pakistani independence in 1947, other international factors have similarly influenced internal politics in varying ways, particularly in strategic frontier areas. For example, during the 1980s in Pakistan, the Soviet invasion of Afghanistan exacerbated General Zia-ul-Haqq's Islamization policies and helped to destabilize tribal governance in Pakistan's border region with Afghanistan. At the same time, the emergent ideological and religious rivalry between Saudi Arabia and Iran also influenced tensions between Pakistan's Shia and Sunni populations.[51] Similarly, after 2001, the US invasion of Afghanistan and broader US-led war on terror altered Pakistani policies and actions toward the Tribal Areas, including the Pakistani military launching a series of counterterrorism operations in the region, which caused further destabilization and contributed to an increase in domestic terrorism within Pakistan.[52] And, then, of course, the long-standing India-Pakistan rivalry, which has resulted in four interstate wars (in 1948, 1965, 1971, and 1999), has had a profound impact on the internal political development and domestic security dynamics of both countries in numerous ways.

This book does not cover the entirety of the complex domestic political development of India and Pakistan or the two countries' wide-ranging foreign entanglements. Rather, it attempts to draw out how political elites representing the "official mind" of both governments have perceived China's influence, how China has influenced and conditioned state engagement with the periphery, and the periphery's response.[53] While the realms of domestic and international politics are inextricably bound with one another, Chinese actions and perceptions of Chinese intentions have overlapped with and accelerated other sources of domestic pressure that have shaped the center's perspective of and policies toward the periphery and the resulting patterns of intrastate conflict. This book, therefore, presents two connected but distinct narratives: the history of the relationship between center and periphery and the history of the Indian and Pakistani governments' interactions with China. It is only by considering this intersection between domestic and international politics that we can understand the dynamic decision-making process of political elites and the resulting impact on relations between center and periphery in India's and Pakistan's respective strategic frontiers.

Despite the looming presence of China within this book's arguments and narrative, this is not necessarily a book about Chinese foreign policy or how Chinese elites understand their foreign policy. It is about neighboring states' perceptions of and engagement with China and how these help to influence and condition the decision-making process in those states. Within international politics, perceptions are not always grounded in fact, and this is particularly apparent when studying individual leaders' decision-making processes. In his study *Perception and Misperception in International Politics*, political scientist Robert Jervis argues that leaders' reliance on preexisting beliefs and previous experiences, including past engagements with counterparts in competing states, acts as a theoretical framework through which they filter and interpret information.[54] As Jervis observes, this framework is a source of common misperceptions within international politics, pushing decision-makers to mistakenly assume coordination among the main actors of an opposing state as part of a unified plan, to overestimate their importance in motivating others' actions, and to assume the opposing side correctly interprets the intentions behind their own actions. He specifically discusses the security dilemma in which any military buildup intended to be defensive is often seen as an act of offensive aggression by a rival state, particularly if there is a history of conflict between the two. This misinterpretation leads to a corresponding military buildup, which in turn is viewed as an act of aggression by the opposing state, and so on, bringing the two states ever closer to open warfare.

In his study of the tumultuous India-Pakistan rivalry over the past seven decades, Christopher Clary further demonstrates how fractured foreign policy authority within a government also can influence leaders' perspectives on foreign policy and perpetuate interstate rivalries. "Veto players"—that is, individuals within a government bureaucracy whose agreement is necessary to change a policy or engage in other kinds of government action—can influence political leaders' decision-making through a variety of means, including by controlling or distorting information, particularly with the flow of information up to senior leadership through military, diplomatic, or intelligence channels, undermining the implementation of particular policies they disagree with, or overtly advocating for riskier behavior. As Clary demonstrates, veto players that pursue hawkish foreign policies, particularly those who cannot be easily removed from their positions, such as in military or intelligence agencies, can create incentives for political leaders to avoid meaningful conciliatory policies and continue risky behavior in relation to interstate rivals, given leaders' concerns with their political survival.[55] Clary argues that "the relationship between resources, threats, and foreign policy is complicated and conditional."[56] In a certain respect, the actual reality of Chinese leaders' intentions toward neighboring states are almost secondary to the core argument examined here. Rather, what matters most is how Indian and Pakistani political leaders, based on their preexisting beliefs about Chinese intentions and under varying domestic political pressures, perceive Chinese actions, not the facts of the situation for which they may not have accurate insights. As Jervis puts it, "Pure empiricism is impossible: facts do not speak for themselves."[57]

As this book further demonstrates, international politics influences not only government officials' perceptions of their domestic security environment but also those of non-state actors. Antistate militant groups have adapted their behavior based on the interplay of international and domestic politics and their perceptions of foreign governments, including their relationship with the central government to which they are opposed. This can include new appeals for international support or target selection within their conflict environments. Scholars have examined the linkages between insurgent groups and external actors, highlighting the importance of examining regional politics to fully understand rebel group behavior and civil war dynamics. States may see an advantage in clandestinely supporting insurgent groups in foreign states, including providing them with an extraterritorial base for their operations, as an alternative to open warfare, particularly within rival states in which past conflicts inform future interactions. While governments face the challenge of limited control over insurgent group behavior, such support can be seen as a less risky or costly means of challenging a rival state and occupying their security resources and attention. Research suggests that moderately strong and centralized insurgent groups are more likely to attract and maintain external support, with such groups more likely to accept such support when they have a clear international constituency such as through religious or ideological connections. Insurgent groups also are more likely to garner external support if the government is engaged in an international rivalry, particularly if the rival is within their immediate neighborhood.[58] Such dynamics have played out in northeastern India, where various ethnic militant groups saw China as a potential source of support for their cause through the 1960s and 1970s, given the Chinese government's adversarial position against India amid the border dispute between both countries. These groups, who frequently embraced Christianity as a key aspect of their political identity, were not easy ideological allies of China's atheist Communist government. Nevertheless, they found common cause in their opposition to the Indian state.

The reverse has been true for antistate militant groups who have seen close allies of the central government as their enemies as well. This situation has played out in Pakistan with Baloch militant groups over the past two decades. Following a brief period of tension due to border issues in the early years of Pakistani independence, China and Pakistan have grown increasingly close. In recent years, Pakistan's political elites have advocated for the importance of developing their relationship with

China, including attracting Chinese support for economic development and infrastructure projects. Given the close relationship between the Pakistani and Chinese governments, and the growing Chinese investment in Pakistan through the China–Pakistan Economic Corridor, Baloch militants have increasingly targeted the Chinese presence in Pakistan as part of their campaigns of violence to challenge the Pakistani state, as they see Chinese support as exacerbating the state presence within and economic exploitation of Balochistan.

This political analysis of northeastern India and Balochistan helps to demonstrate that increased state penetration into the periphery, including when exacerbated by China's international influence, can contribute to instability and violence if the underlying problems between center and periphery are left unresolved. To demonstrate this point, the analysis relies upon the "causal narrative" approach, to use the term of sociologist William Sewell,[59] to illuminate the processes and mechanisms through which India's and Pakistan's differing relationships with China influenced the tensions between center and periphery in both countries during the periods of analysis. Comparative historical scholar James Mahoney writes that the "causal narrative" approach can "validate aggregated cross-case associations by 'breaking apart' variables into constituent sequences of disaggregated events and comparing these disaggregated sequences across cases. The purpose of unpacking aggregated variables through narrative is not only to provide a contextualized description of cases; rather, the goal is to support a cross-case argument at a more disaggregated level."[60] These two case studies focus on disaggregating the process of China's influence in both countries into successive steps linking government officials' perceptions of China with state action in the periphery, as outlined in table 1.1. This approach shows how different engagements at the international level, whether through an adversarial or a cooperative relationship, contribute to increased state presence in the periphery, which in turn bolsters antistate activities given the dynamics of the center-periphery relationship.

While Balochistan and northeastern India have distinct histories, cultures, and historical and contemporary political dynamics, other scholars have recognized the utility of including both frontier regions within

TABLE 1.1 Impact of China's engagement with India and Pakistan

	China-India (1950s–1970s)	China-Pakistan (2000s–2020s)
Nature of relationship	Adversarial	Cooperative
Operationalization of relationship	Dispute (territorial) → Military conflict	Non-territorial mutual support → Economic integration
Impact on peripheral societies	Expanded state presence → Accelerates antistate insurgency	Expanded state presence → Accelerates antistate insurgency
Militant group actions	Attack state targets and pursue Chinese support	Attack both state and Chinese targets

the same study. Historian Thomas Simpson, for instance, argued for the importance of considering British India's western and northeastern frontiers within a single study. Many British officials frequently drew comparisons between the two regions and understood that similar governance and security-related processes were at play in both.[61] In her study of differing state responses to antistate insurgencies in India and Pakistan, Elisabeth Leake similarly argues that both countries "confronted similar challenges in Nagaland and Baluchistan: they have faced resistance to national integration, and their policies towards these regions have been complicated because of their borderlands locations."[62]

By similarly examining Balochistan and northeastern India within this study, one is better able to understand not only the varying efforts to establish and enforce state sovereignty over strategic frontiers following independence but also the influence of China through the two distinct phases of the country's foreign policy. While China was not the cause of these internal problems, which predate the establishment of China's Communist government in 1949, Chinese actions, and, more importantly, senior Pakistani and Indian officials' perceptions of these actions, have influenced and conditioned internal state decisions and in many ways accelerated tensions between center and periphery. The study of these two distinct but intertwined narratives—the central government's interaction with the periphery and the central government's interaction with China—provides a clear demonstration of how international and domestic politics are connected, offering lessons about how to understand the domestic implications of international politics as the globe becomes ever more interconnected. With Western policymakers increasingly anxious about the rise of China as a challenge to American hegemony and their growing concern with political instability emanating from the frontiers of key partner states such as India and Pakistan, this analysis also points to the potential limitations of China's engagement abroad, as it can exacerbate domestic conflicts that inhibit the potential reach of Chinese-led development, not only in Pakistan but in other countries forming a link within the BRI. Yet, this is not intended to sound a clarion call about a supposed Chinese threat. Rather, it is a scholarly examination of perceptions of Chinese foreign policy actions in two of the country's neighboring states and the resulting impact on domestic security issues, demonstrating how international politics can condition domestic political processes, particularly in the context of center-periphery relations. This analysis provides important historical context for those grappling with the spread of Chinese influence.

In recent year, scholars have increasingly examined China's growing global presence, especially through the Belt and Road Initiative, and the Communist state's relationship with surrounding countries within South, Southeast, and Central Asia. Jonathan Hillman's book *The Emperor's New Road: China and the Project of the Century* provides a global overview of the BRI and, within this discussion, focuses broadly on Chinese-Pakistani relations, largely in comparison with Pakistan's strategic relationship with the United States and the history of the failure of US international development efforts over the previous seventy years.[63] In his book *China's Western Horizon: Beijing and the New Geopolitics of Eurasia*, Daniel Markey recognizes the importance of considering domestic politics to understand various states' recent engagement with China, focusing on Pakistan, Kazakhstan, and Iran and those countries' political and economic elites' engagement with Chinese officials. He demonstrates how domestic politics influenced Chinese investment in these three cases, while acknowledging that this can engender domestic political tensions as benefits are unevenly distributed.[64] Andrew Small's *The China–Pakistan Axis: Asia's New Geopolitics* provides a comprehensive overview of the relationship between these two countries, including security, political, and economic relations, in the years before CPEC was announced.[65] Other studies have similarly explored the nature of China's evolving relationships in other regions around the world, including with countries in Southeast Asia, Africa, the Middle East, and Europe.[66]

While many studies of China's increasing international engagement focus on state-to-state relations, *Adversary and Ally* flips this perspective and primarily examines the ways in which engagement with China, as both an adversary and an ally, have influenced how political leaders perceive their domestic security environments within the periphery and the resulting shifts in the policy toward strategic frontier regions. Within northeastern India, there has been increasing scholarly attention on Chinese and Indian engagement in the region and the status of the disputed border. For instance, Berenice Guyot-Rechard's book *Shadow States: India, China and the Himalayas, 1910–1962* further examines the paired efforts of China and India to expand development into Tibet and the Assam region, through the first half of the twentieth century, which contributed to a security dilemma in the area.[67] Bertil Lintner's *Great Game East: India, China, and the Struggle for Asia's Most Volatile Frontier* also discusses India and China relations in the context of the covert actions within northeastern India and western Myanmar, but without exploring the history of the strategic state-building process within the region in the context of governance and development.[68] In *Understanding the India-China Border: The Enduring Threat of War in High Himalaya*, Manoj Joshi also provides an overview of the border dispute up to the present day through a journalistic perspective.[69] *Adversary and Ally* builds and expands on these studies to highlight the importance of considering the interplay between international and domestic politics in the examination of conflict dynamics in the periphery.

The subsequent chapters of this book cover in detail the history of the Indian and Pakistani governments' interactions with China and the resulting impact on their engagement with the periphery through primary source research, including declassified documents from the National Archives of India that provide unique insights into policymakers' perspectives of the periphery as well as their engagement with Chinese officials, and interviews with former government officials, journalists, and scholars from the region. The first part of the book focuses on India, the book's eponymous adversary, from the 1950s through the 1970s. Chapter 2 opens with a history of India's border dispute with China and then examines the India-China relationship from 1950 to 1962, including an overview of policy debates within the Indian government about the nature of the Chinese threat and China's influence on relations between New Delhi and its northeastern periphery in the years following independence. Chapter 3 discusses the 1962 border war between India and China and the resulting impact on India's domestic politics, including antistate militant groups in northeastern India increasingly looking to China for support and training during the 1960s and 1970s.

The second part of the book focuses on Pakistan, the book's eponymous ally, largely from the 2000s through the 2020s. Chapter 4 outlines the long-standing friendship between the Pakistani and Chinese governments and then provides an overview of Chinese investment in Pakistan, particularly the construction of Gwadar Port beginning in the early 2000s and the announcement of CPEC in 2015. Chapter 5 provides an overview of the history of Baloch resistance against the Pakistani government following independence. It then analyzes local Baloch opposition to CPEC and the role that Chinese-led development has played in the antistate violence plaguing Balochistan since 2006. The conclusion provides a summary of the book's main arguments and their potential applicability for understanding China's impact on the periphery within neighboring states in Southeast Asia, including in Vietnam, where the government's conflict with ethnic minorities in the 1970s and 1980s presents a parallel with India's, and Myanmar's growing relationship with China through the development of the China–Myanmar Economic Corridor after 2017, which parallels Pakistan's experience with CPEC. The chapter closes with a discussion of the United States' pivot to Asia and the importance of understanding China's impact on countries' domestic politics amid the growing competition between China and the United States.

I

THE ADVERSARY

2

"ANOTHER GREAT GAME"

India Versus China

The appellation the "Great Game," coined in the 1840s and popularized by Rudyard Kipling in his 1901 novel *Kim*, has been frequently employed to describe the strategic rivalry between the Russian and British Empires in the mountains and steppes of Central Asia through the nineteenth and early twentieth centuries. During this period, the two competing empires sought to extend their political influence and control throughout the region. This now clichéd phrase is often used today to describe the geopolitical struggles between world powers—the United States, Russia, and China, alongside regional rivals Pakistan and India—for economic and political dominance within the same region.[1] Their rivalry has brought the mighty weight of international politics once again to the same remote mountain passes, desert stretches, and villages of Afghanistan, northwestern Pakistan, and their Central Asian neighbors.

No less than the more romanticized and well-known border region lying astride Afghanistan and Pakistan, India's northeastern frontier has played host to strategic rivalries, political intrigue, and tribal conflicts for decades. Bangkok-based journalist Bertil Lintner observed "another Great Game" in the offing at the crossroads of India, Burma, and China. "The rivalry between India and China goes back to the 1950s," he writes. "Spies and agents from both sides have been active in each other's

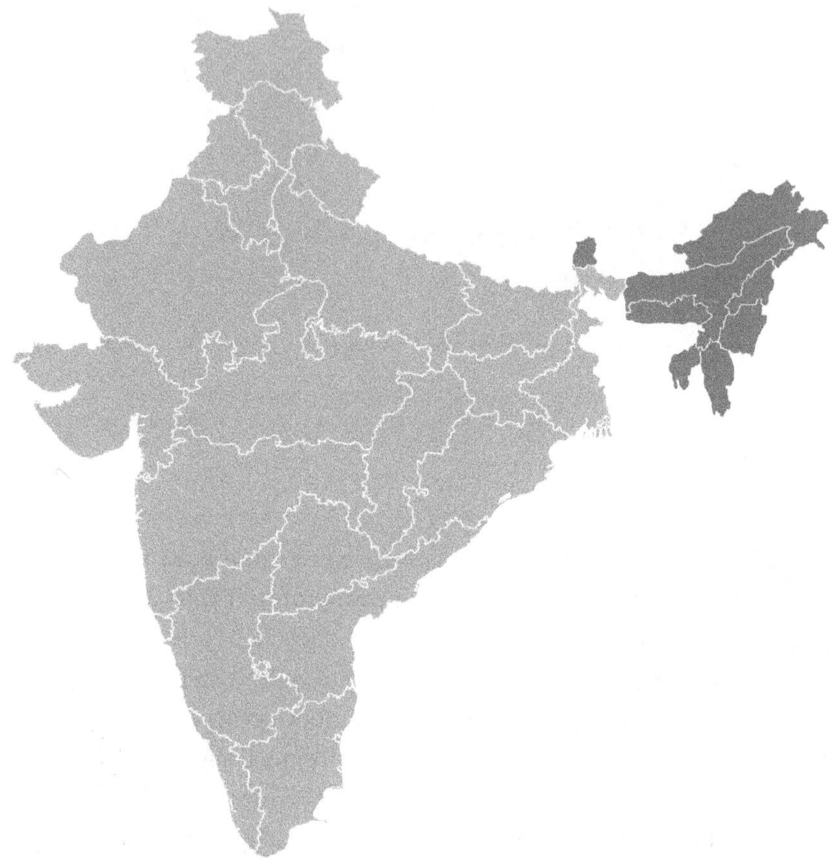

FIGURE 2.1 Northeastern India. (Courtesy of Wikimedia Commons, CC BY-SA 4.0.)

volatile—and disputed—frontier areas for decades."[2] With China's invasion of Tibet in 1950, senior Indian officials viewed New Delhi's precarious hold over the northeastern frontier as a strategic vulnerability as Chinese expansionism pushed the People's Liberation Army right up to the contested border between India and Tibet. Combined with this potential threat, the region also experienced a series of separatist insurgencies beginning in the 1950s, which would eventually draw some support from the Chinese government.

Security concerns have long shaped New Delhi's perception of and policies toward its distant northeastern periphery—distant in terms of both geography and culture. With Muslim-majority East Bengal having joined Pakistan at Partition, before becoming the independent state of Bangladesh in 1971, the northeastern region is geographically connected to "mainland India" by the fourteen-mile-wide Siliguri land corridor, referred to as the "Chicken's Neck" and a "terrifyingly vulnerable artery in India's geography," in the words of one Indian security analyst.[3] This precarious geographic link underscored the importance of securing the government's hold within the region, as it was exposed to being cut off from the rest of the country. Indeed, the process of integrating the northeastern frontier into the postcolonial Indian state would come to be influenced and defined by the intersection of domestic and international politics. The region was plagued by a turbulent history of armed conflict played out in the shadow of its northern neighbor, China, with the divide between internal and external security blurring over time.

From the perspective of New Delhi, this was a dangerous mix. As senior officials grew increasingly wary of Chinese intentions within the region following the Communist takeover in 1949, the Indian government paired the expansion of Chinese control within Tibet with their own efforts to extend India's administrative hold over the restive northeastern border region. This process was made increasingly urgent as the Chinese government laid claim to Indian territory and demonstrated its readiness to back up its claims with military force, as was made abundantly clear by Chinese military actions across the border into India in 1962. At the core of the Indian and Chinese rivalry lay the disputed border running along the crest of the Himalayan mountains, originally demarcated by British and Tibetan officials in the early twentieth century.

BRITISH INDIA, TIBET, AND THE MCMAHON LINE

At the turn of the twentieth century, British officials eyed developments across their northern frontier in Tibet with trepidation and, for the many players engaged in the "Great Game," perhaps a certain level of anticipation and excitement. "Here, on the Roof of the World," British adventurer and author Peter Fleming wrote, "there was space for maneuver, scope for brilliance and boldness. . . . Only in Tibet, where neither side's pieces were as yet committed, might an adroit stroke thwart the adversary's plans before he could put them into effect."[4] With Chinese influence waning after China's defeat by Japanese forces during the First Sino-Japanese War in 1895 and Peking's preoccupation with the Dungan Revolt in the country's Northwest soon after, British officials saw Russian ambitions seeking to fill the void; one Russian count active in the region remarked that "there are not and there cannot be any frontiers for us in Asia." In 1898, British India's director of military intelligence surmised, "Unless we secure the reversion of Lhasa, we may find the Russians there before us."[5]

Following several unsuccessful attempts to open communications with the Dalai Lama and finalize a treaty with the Tibetan government, British Indian authorities finally authorized a military incursion into the isolated Himalayan state. In December 1903, an expedition led by famed British explorer Francis Younghusband departed for Lhasa. As the expedition marched north, it achieved a series of decisive military engagements against the poorly armed and outmatched Tibetan forces. By the following September, the British expedition reached the Tibetan capital, where Younghusband forced Tibetan authorities to sign a treaty pledging them to avoid any dealings or interactions of any kind with foreign powers without the consent of the British government.[6] This treaty extended the British sphere of influence over Tibet and opened its markets to British trade.

Following Younghusband's expedition, and amid local backlash to foreign intervention, British officials were increasingly aware of Chinese imperial ambitions to reassert China's influence and exert its control over Tibet, thereby reducing Tibet's position to a regularly administered province of the Chinese state and restricting British and Russian access to the region.[7] The strength of China's political claims within Tibet, which had risen and fallen over the preceding centuries, dated back to the twelfth century, when Tibetan authorities pledged allegiance to the Mongol conquerors of China. Under the government of the Dalai Lama, Tibet enjoyed internal autonomy through the nineteenth century. However, in pursuit of China's historic claims, Chinese troops invaded the eastern Kham region in 1905 and central Tibet in 1910, occupying Lhasa and forcing the thirteenth Dalai Lama to seek refuge in Darjeeling, in British India, where he remained in exile until 1913 (a foreshadowing of his successor's exodus to India in 1959). Chinese imperial forces moved through eastern and southern Tibet and established garrisons in several places. According to British intelligence reports, the Chinese advance into Tibet never reached across the Himalayas into the Indian side of the frontier, save for a brief foray into Walong, in the northeastern corner of present-day Arunachal Pradesh. Chinese troops left a handful of border markers, which were later found by a British survey party in the area, and promptly left.[8]

Chinese incursions into Tibet were noted for their brutality, with troops burning villages throughout the Tibetan frontier, prompting stiff local resistance. In the face of such resistance, Chinese troops were in retreat to Lhasa by January 1912, one month before the Xinhai Revolution led to the fall of the Qing dynasty's imperial rule.[9] With the end of China's imperial government, Chinese troops eventually withdrew from the region in early 1913. During the tumultuous years of the 1920s, 1930s, and 1940s, Chinese influence in Tibet waned once again, leaving the Tibetan government to enjoy de facto independence with financial backing from the British. The Republic of China, however, continued to claim sovereign rights over Tibetan territory.[10]

In the early twentieth century, British officials increasingly sought to protect Tibet's autonomy as a buffer region against foreign interference within British-controlled territory. While the British government recognized Chinese suzerainty over Tibet in a 1907 agreement with imperial Russia, it did so with a special interest in maintaining the prevailing political status quo and with assurances that China would not interfere with Tibet's autonomy.[11] Despite this recognition, local authorities in Assam pushed the colonial government for a swift response as Chinese troops moved into the region, as they were fearful of Chinese expansionism and its implications for the border region. In November 1910, with Chinese troops consolidating their positions in Tibet, a British official on the frontier wrote to the British viceroy, Lord Hardinge,

> Should the Chinese establish themselves in strength or obtain complete control up to our outer line, they could attack us whenever they pleased, and the defence would be extremely difficult. . . . It seems to me, in view of the possibility of the Chinese pushing forward, that it would be a mistake not to put ourselves in a position to take up suitable strategic points of defence . . . [, which] we could only do if we establish our suzerainty or could claim the consent of the hill people who are in occupation, as being under our protection.[12]

Yet, officials in Calcutta were initially wary of overextending their hand on the frontier to counter any Chinese movements across the border, which they thought carried little danger to British India given the difficulty of the mountainous terrain. In December 1910, Lord Hardinge initially rebuffed calls for offensive action and remarked that "any forward movement beyond the administrative frontier was strongly to be deprecated. Chinese aggression would . . . be met, not in the tribal territory bordering Assam, but by attack on the coast of China."[13]

By this time, British authorities had already long been debating the appropriate approach to handling unrest on the frontier, particularly to protest economic investments in the region's tea industry. A potential Chinese threat across the border became just one more point of consideration in their strategic calculus toward the Northeast. The British had originally annexed Assam following the First Anglo-Burmese War (1824–1826) and quickly set about exploiting the region's vast tea forests. The growth of the tea industry over the coming decades led to an influx of outside labor and the encroachment on and seizure of traditional tribal lands often used for *jhum* cultivation, or slash-and-burn agriculture, used by tribal communities within the region's hilly terrain.[14] While the tribes had a history of paying tribute to local Assamese rajas and periodically bearing the brunt of Burmese military expeditions, the drastic shifts in the region's economic base, demographics, and increased government presence led to violent clashes with both tea cultivators and British authorities.[15]

The first military engagement between the British and Naga tribes occurred in 1832 as a British military expedition was opening a road through the Assam frontier. Violent encounters persisted in the coming decades as the British extended their presence into the frontier. Tribal groups, often armed with spears and crossbows but increasingly with firearms, attacked British military convoys and posts intended to symbolize government control. They also raided tea estates and disrupted road work and communication lines throughout the region. Given the continued law-and-order difficulties, British authorities eventually shifted the focus of the region's tea production to Upper Assam's settled valleys and established a defensive line against the costly raiding of tea plantations.[16]

Up to this point, the British position toward the hill tribes had been fundamentally an adversarial one, with local authorities simply seeking to contain tribal raiding and not accepting the submission of any villages in the hill areas, promising any protection, or drawing revenue of any kind.[17] Yet, during the coming decades, British officials argued for a new approach to law and order in the hill areas. Political officers serving on the frontier and a select few officials in Calcutta, including the commander in chief of the Indian Army and the governor-general, felt that, even more than simply expanding the government's political presence, constructing practicable and navigable roads through the difficult terrain connecting the tribal areas with British territory would not only introduce "civilization" to the tribes but, more importantly, also help promote law and order within the region by extending access to the region for colonial administration and military presence.[18] In the early 1870s, as British authorities connected the frequent raids into British territory with internal feuding and overall "turbulence and disorganization across the border," colonial political officers serving in the region observed the importance of a more active frontier policy in order to remove the "great shield" of "these wild people"—that is, their isolation—and promote "permanent pacification of this frontier."[19]

On the other hand, some officials in Shillong and Calcutta bristled over the many logistical difficulties, the high costs, and ultimately the ineffectiveness of British dealings with the "warlike" Nagas and other tribal groups on the frontier, complaining that however much they pushed forward British control in these areas, tribal unrest continued just beyond their reach.[20] Instead, they called for internal feuding to be treated with indifference, even as local authorities warned that the security of the settled territory abutting the tribal areas was not possible unless the military occupation of the tribal areas was relied upon to contain any unrest on the frontier. Senior British leaders further recognized that the many challenges associated with working on a distant frontier, including poor lines of communication and colonial officials' frequent lack of understanding of the local political and social context, further undermined government planning. In 1892, the foreign secretary of British India, Henry Mortimer Durand, further complained that the government's intelligence gathering, and thus its general understanding of frontier conditions, was "too fragmentary to afford a clue to the easiest and most inexpensive method of maintaining peace and order among the hillmen."[21]

By the mid-1880s, British policy on the northeastern frontier had shifted to a general approach of "absolute non-interference with trans-frontier tribes and their feuds, so long as they leave their British subjects alone, and are careful not to raid across our border."[22] Nevertheless, the British government continued its effort to incrementally push the boundaries of political control deeper into the frontier well into the twentieth century, all while keeping an eye on ensuring such actions did not increase the cost of administration in the region.[23] While frontier officials broadly tried to abide by a policy of noninterference when possible, the British continued to extend their political influence in a piecemeal fashion and held fast to their willingness to deploy military expeditions on the frontier if they felt circumstances dictated such action. Bengal official Alexander Mackenzie surmised that the general policy of moderate disengagement "was too thoroughly English to be appreciated by ignorant Nagas," with many British officers believing violence served as the only effective check on the tribes' actions, such as British military operations in 1917–1918 against Kuki and Haka uprisings in Manipur and the Chin Hills.[24] The government introduced new regulations for various areas on the northeastern frontier that allowed for the blockade and collective punishment of tribal communities, in addition to preventive detention, to deal with any potential unrest spilling out of the region; these regulations were based on the Frontier Crimes Regulations that governed the Pashtun tribesmen within the tribal areas on British India's northwestern frontier abutting Afghanistan.[25]

With the sparse government presence and access to outsiders limited among the hill tribes, Christian missionaries often bore the primary responsibility of providing education, health care, and other services to the tribes as part of their proselytization in the region.[26] Permanent missions were established in the Naga Hills by the early 1870s, with missionaries winning the first Christian converts among the Ao Nagas in November 1872. Colonial officials came to see missionary work as a means of introducing "civilizing influences" on the northeastern tribal communities with the hope of reducing overall lawlessness without incurring costs to the government. In June 1930, the chief secretary for the Assam government, W. A. Cosgrave, wrote to the political secretary of the British Indian government that "it would seem foolish to reject the offer of a reliable missionary organization which offers these benefits free to the backward Hill tribes in the south west corner of Manipur. With the advance of civilization in this area, the Kukis should become as law-abiding as their neighbours the Lushais in the adjoining British district."[27] These proselytization efforts were wildly successful. For instance, in the 2011 Indian census, nearly 90 percent of Nagaland residents identified as Christian, while roughly the same percentage of Kukis identify as Christian today. Indeed, the Christian faith formed a key aspect of burgeoning nationalist movements in the border region during the early twentieth century as another marker of difference from the majority of the Indian population.

By 1911, with Assam officials continuing to press for an active policy to control unrest within the hill areas, Calcutta also acquiesced to a more proactive approach along the Tibetan border as a means of guarding against potential Chinese infiltration. As Chinese troops moved deeper into Tibetan territory, British authorities dispatched several survey parties (a key activity to make these regions "knowable" in support of the expansion of British control)[28] and military expeditions to bolster British claims on the frontier. In addition to the many challenges presented by the difficult terrain and weather, the survey parties soon ran into local resistance as they pushed into the unmapped and unadministered tribal territories. In March 1911, for instance, Abor tribesmen attacked a small exploration party in the Dhiang Valley, killing the group's political officer. The following October, a large force was assembled at Kobo, near Dibrugarh, to punish the culprits. However, it was not only for punitive reasons that the government dispatched this force; it was also "owing to China's move in Thibet [*sic*] and along its south-eastern borders [that] a real interest was at last being stirred in this long stretch of unknown border-lands," according to one British official serving on the frontier during the early twentieth century.[29]

Yet, many Tibetans viewed British penetration into the border region with suspicion. In 1913, Tibetan officials expressed their fears to a British survey party moving through the area that the latter's presence was a signal that the British government intended to annex Tibetan territory. They further pressed the British officers for their explanation of the sudden activities of the British Indian government along the frontier.[30] Among Tibetans in Lagung, there was further distrust over British intentions as a rumor circulated that British personnel were helping Chinese troops move into Tibet through Abor territory to take revenge for the previous massacre of Chinese forces at Pome in southeastern Tibet. However, some local officials dismissed such a rumor, and instead asked members of the survey party if the British viceroy would send troops from India to assist them against any future Chinese invasion. If that was unlikely, they asked if the British authorities in India could send a letter to the Chinese government requesting that it refrain from interfering in Tibetan affairs.[31]

To settle any misunderstandings that could potentially lead to conflict in the region, the British government extended invitations to the Chinese and Tibetan governments to participate in a conference to discuss the status of Tibet and define its border with British India.[32] In October 1913, British colonial authorities convened a conference at the Raj's summer capital, the hill station of Simla, in the Himalayan foothills. Following months of deliberation, British and Tibetan representatives agreed to an international border on July 3, 1914, despite opposition from the Chinese officials present, who declined to sign the final agreement (the Chinese government later fully repudiated it). The newly demarcated, 550-mile-long border followed the watershed of the Himalayan mountain chain from Bhutan to Burma and became known as the McMahon Line (named after British India's foreign secretary, Sir Henry McMahon, who served as the chief negotiator at the Simla Conference). The agreement, however, did not go so far as to recognize Tibetan independence from China, which the Tibetans had unilaterally declared the previous year with the fall of the Qing dynasty and the withdrawal of Chinese troops.

Following the 1914 agreement, the chief commissioner of Assam argued that the government should establish, at minimum, loose political control within the frontier tracts lying north of Assam and up to the border with Tibet and that roads should be opened as opportunities arose for the purpose of opening trade routes with the frontier area and Tibet. By November 1914, shortly after the United Kingdom declared war on Germany, British authorities made the decision to go slow on the frontier and to avoid any further action in regard to the chief commissioner's recommendations until the war in Europe had passed.[33] Following the end of World War I, however, New Delhi's attention to the problems of the northeastern frontier, now free from the pressure of Chinese expansion in Tibet (particularly after the Republican revolution in China), failed to materialize beyond the periodic dispatch of punitive military campaigns against raiding tribes.

Moreover, the proceedings and outcome of the Simla Conference were largely kept secret over the next two decades, with no maps publicly declaring the existence of the McMahon Line at the time. Only after the constitutional reforms of 1935 did the colonial government make a concerted effort to provide a more accurate assessment of conditions in the border region and to assert its sovereignty, particularly with Tibetan officials in the border area disregarding the earlier agreement and claiming territory on the Indian side of the border.[34] In April 1938, authorities dispatched two platoons of the Assam Rifles, a local paramilitary force, to the Buddhist-populated Tawang region, where Tibetan officials were still present and performing governmental duties. During the visit, the British officers pressed local Monpa leaders that, under the Simla Convention, they were British subjects and owed their allegiance to the British government. On their return, the officers advocated to New Delhi the need to assert administrative control in the region, including over the influential Tawang Monastery, a center of Buddhist learning and power in the region. Frontier officials also recommended the disbursement of funds to support various beneficial activities to undercut Tibetan influence.[35] Fearful of provoking protests from Chinese authorities, who still laid claim to the region, little was overtly done to follow up on these recommendations, leaving the administrative status of the region "to simmer for the time being."[36]

In the early 1940s, the Assam government once again pushed to assert administrative control in the border region, including with the appointment of a responsible official within the government to oversee these efforts.[37] Yet, British plans for expanding control within the Northeast were quickly overtaken by the outbreak of World War II, with the demands of the war putting constraints on the civil government's actions, particularly as Japanese forces advanced on British India's borders through Burma. On August 5, 1943, as the United Kingdom was preoccupied with fighting the Axis powers, the British government again recognized Chinese suzerainty in Tibet, with the Republic of China joining the fight against Japanese forces in Asia, which directly threatened Assam. This recognition was once again premised on the understanding that Tibet would remain autonomous. Within the so-called Eden Memorandum, Anthony Eden, then serving as the British foreign secretary, wrote to the Chinese foreign minister, T. V. Soong, declaring that "Neither the British Government nor the Government of India have any territorial ambitions in Tibet but they are interested in the maintenance of friendly relations with, and in the preservation of peaceful conditions in, an area which is coterminous with the North-East frontiers of India."[38] Officials in both New Delhi and Shillong were in agreement about the need to extend government administration up to the McMahon Line once the war came to an end, with local officials beginning to draw up postwar reconstruction plans in the region as a political and strategic necessity.[39] These plans never came to fruition as events were quickly overtaken by the British withdrawal from the subcontinent. In the run-up to Indian independence, the British government's position toward the border remained one of noninterference in the engagement between Tibet and China while stressing its commitment to maintaining the McMahon Line and its opposition to any incursions into Indian territory.[40]

At this time, there also was a growing sense of ethnic nationalism among the different groups inhabiting the northeastern frontier, including the Naga and Mizo. From the 1920s through the 1940s, several political organizations were formed among these distinct ethnic identities to oppose continued colonial rule and advocate for their political future. With the outbreak of World War II, many inhabitants in the region would fight with British forces to repel the Japanese invasion, and they were renowned for their bravery in key turning points of the war such as the Battles of Imphal and Kohima. Some saw the fighting as an opportunity for advancing Naga nationalism, with others swayed by Japanese promises of Naga independence in return for their support. For instance, leading Naga nationalist Angami Zapu Phizo had migrated to Burma before the war and from there later joined Subhas Chandra Bose's Japanese-backed Indian National Army during World War II in return for a promise of support for Naga independence should Japan emerge victorious. British authorities arrested him in Rangoon in May 1945 and jailed him for seven months. Returning to India at war's end, Phizo joined the newly established Naga National Council (NNC) in pursuit of his goal of an independent Nagaland.[41]

The experience of fighting Japanese forces in the border region not only brought greater attention from the colonial authorities; it also contributed to a growing sense of unity among these disparate groups on the northeastern frontier. After World War II, several local political organizations focused their work on postwar relief efforts, but they soon transitioned to advocating for political autonomy or even outright independence from New Delhi following the British withdrawal, given the unique social, cultural, and political identities of the Northeast.[42] In 1946, the NNC submitted a four-point memorandum to a British cabinet mission. The memorandum asserted the following:

- This Naga National Council stands for the solidarity of all Naga tribes, including those in the unadministered areas;
- This Council strongly protests against the grouping of Assam with Bengal;
- The Naga Hills should be constitutionally included in an autonomous Assam, in a free India, with local autonomy and due safeguards for the interests of the Nagas;
- The Naga tribes should have a separate electorate.[43]

Unsatisfied with the immediate response, the group's leaders submitted a request directly to British Viceroy Lord Mountbatten to establish an interim Naga government for a period of ten years, after which the Naga people would have the right to choose their own political status. While this request was ignored, the governor of Assam, Akbar Hydari, and the NNC, with representatives from ten Naga tribes, signed a nine-point agreement in Kohima in June 1947 ensuring that judicial, executive, and legislative arrangements within the state of Assam would respect Naga culture and customs and work with the NNC as a governing partner.[44] Some Nagas rejected this agreement for not providing a potential path to Naga independence and continuing to subject the Naga people to further Assamese domination from the plains. Undeterred by the framework of this new agreement, the NNC's Angami Zapu Phizo unilaterally declared Nagaland's independence on August 14, 1947, one day before the transfer of power from British to Indian hands. However, this was largely ignored by Indian political elites.

While British officials remained somewhat aloof to developments on the frontier, with local officials even advising frontier tribes that they should not worry themselves too much about their future relationship with an independent India given the unsettled nature of any future

Indian Union,[45] the position of the Indian National Congress toward the tribal communities, not only in the northeastern frontier but elsewhere in India, was clear. Congress leaders sought to open these areas up to mainstream political, economic, and social forces and further integrate them into a unified Indian nation, in stark contrast to the isolationism many of them experienced under British rule. In October 1943, one Congress member accused Verrier Elwin, the British-born anthropologist and noted champion of tribal India who famously advocated for a protectionist approach to tribal administration, of pushing India into further political and social divisions along communal lines and advocating for the creation of an "Aboriginalisthan" similar to the Muslim League's vision for Pakistan.[46] It was British imperial rule, another Indian scholar argued in response to Elwin's position in the 1940s, that lay the foundation for tribal discontent, with any Hindu exploitation a secondary phenomenon to its primary cause. Therefore, in his view, increasing contact between mainstream Hindu culture and tribal communities was a means of improving the latter's position within an independent India, alleviating tribal poverty, and generally improving their overall welfare.[47] As these debates were playing out, the newly independent India inherited a border region that largely lacked any administrative presence or governing institutions, even into the 1960s in some areas. With the threat of Chinese expansionism increasingly looming over the region, this quickly became a key point of concern for New Delhi.

A BURGEONING ADVERSARIAL RELATIONSHIP

One of Chairman Mao Zedong's first moves following the 1949 Communist Revolution was to secure China's near periphery, including Tibet and Xinjiang. This move was purportedly a means of pushing back against foreign influence and reclaiming territory seen as rightfully China's, including within India's Northeast, whose population was ethnically and culturally related to the Tibetans. In early October 1950, one year after the Communist Party seized control, forty thousand soldiers of the People's Liberation Army (PLA) crossed the Jinsha River into Tibet and quickly overwhelmed the ill-equipped and outnumbered Tibetan Army. In May of the following year, the Chinese Communist government forced the Tibetan government to sign a seventeen-point agreement on the "Peaceful Liberation of Tibet" that established Communist rule over the isolated Himalayan kingdom. The agreement included provisions for deploying the PLA into Tibet for "national defences" as well as assurances that Chinese authorities would not alter Tibet's existing political system or interfere with Tibetans' religious freedom.[48]

Jawaharlal Nehru, the Indian National Congress leader who served simultaneously as India's first prime minister and external affairs minister following the country's independence in August 1947, had been pursuing friendly relations with China since the Communist Party came to power. Yet, he was quick to criticize the Tibet invasion. He directed India's ambassador in Beijing, K. M. Panikkar, to communicate Indian protestations over the invasion to the Chinese foreign minister (India had established diplomatic ties with the People's Republic on April 1, 1950). "We tried our utmost to develop these friendly relations and to work for peace," Nehru later wrote. "It is [a] matter of great regret to us that [the] Chinese Government have suddenly taken this action, which appears to us to be contrary to assurances of peaceful settlement given to us."[49] While speaking in Parliament, Nehru argued that Chinese suzerainty did not translate to Chinese sovereignty and questioned the idea that Tibet was a threat to China requiring a military response. In private, he saw the Chinese as acting "foolishly" and pointed to "a strong feeling here [in India] of being let down by them."[50] Despite this discomfort with the annexation of its northern neighbor, India would come to recognize Chinese suzerainty over Tibet. Deputy Prime Minister and Home Minister Sardar Vallabhbhai Patel argued that, in exchange for this recognition, India should get definitive acknowledgment from China of the McMahon Line as the international border between the two countries, though ultimately this would not be forthcoming.[51]

In response to such protestations, the Chinese Foreign Ministry sent a cable to several embassies in Beijing arguing that Nehru's criticisms presaged India's intentions to interfere with China's incursions into

Tibet. The Communist government's efforts to "liberate" Tibet as "an inalienable part of China," the cable affirmed, was a purely domestic issue aimed at "safeguard[ing] the frontier of China" and for which "no foreign interference is allowed."[52]

Despite Chinese assurances, the invasion brought to mind many difficult questions for Nehru and other senior political leaders in New Delhi about India's future relationship with China. Foremost among them, as asked by Nehru in a November 17, 1950, letter to the country's chief ministers: With the two countries now sharing such an extensive frontier, and the Chinese government displaying "new-born strength and dynamism," would there be peace or conflict between China and India? And perhaps more worrisome, he wrote, the expansion of the Communist ideology added to the gravity of the situation as many Indians feared the "infiltration of Communist ideas even more than the attack of armed men." Nehru reiterated his view that the invasion of Tibet was "wrong and foolish" and a blow to India's "new-born attempts at friendship." With the growing Chinese military presence in Tibet, he further observed, "We have to become more frontier-conscious and to take all reasonable steps to guard the mountain passes, which lead to our country."[53]

However, the prime minister also felt that a large-scale Chinese invasion over the difficult terrain at India's northern border was exceedingly unlikely, and that taking excessive defensive precautions would be overly burdensome for the new government.[54] Nehru ruled out a major attack by Chinese forces from the north and felt that any undue preparations would cast "an intolerable burden on [India], financial and otherwise," not to mention weakening India's general defensive position as it faced military pressure from its new neighbor Pakistan over the disputed princely state of Jammu and Kashmir. "There are limits beyond which we cannot go at least for some years," he wrote, "and a spreading out of our army in distant frontiers would be bad from every military or strategic point of view."[55] He further argued that the idea that communism necessarily leads to expansionist policies that threatened India was "naïve." The real protection, he thought, was seeking "some kind of understanding of China."[56] In an April 1952 conversation with Lord

Reading, then serving as British undersecretary of state for foreign affairs, Nehru repeated his views on the matter and pointed to reports he had received that the Chinese government was having trouble maintaining a sizable occupation force in the border region due to supply difficulties. Therefore, he did not see China as an immediate military threat to India and its hold on the northeastern frontier.[57]

Nehru's views were not shared by all at the senior levels of government. On the other side of the debate within the Indian cabinet, Patel, who had earlier clashed with the prime minister over the handling of the princely states after the transfer of power in 1947, was vocal about the serious danger that Chinese expansionism posed for India's national security, especially when paired with what he viewed as the false sense of confidence that had settled among the Indian political elite after Ambassador Panikkar's cordial meeting with Mao in May 1950. In a lengthy letter to Nehru, Patel warned, "China is no longer divided. It is united and strong." India had, thus far, focused its defensive measures against Pakistan and the struggle over Jammu and Kashmir. With the Chinese invasion of Tibet, he argued that India would also have to deal with a Communist China along the northern and northeastern frontiers—"a Communist China which has definite ambitions and aims and which does not, in any way, seem friendly disposed towards us." With the Communist government refusing to recognize the McMahon Line as the international border and laying claim to Indian territory in the northeastern frontier, he further stated, "Recent and bitter history also tells us that communism is no shield against imperialism and that the Communists are as good or as bad imperialists as any other. Chinese ambitions in this respect not only cover the Himalayan slopes on our side but also include important parts of Assam."[58]

In particular, Patel highlighted India's northeastern tribal areas as weak spots in the face of Chinese aggression. During the early 1950s, New Delhi received a steady stream of reporting concerning the expansion of China's military presence in Tibet, alongside development efforts to secure Beijing's hold over the territory. On October 15, 1951, Indian diplomats in Gangtok, Sikkim, received intelligence reports that fresh groups of Chinese troops were arriving almost daily in Tibet, with estimates that at least ten thousand soldiers were now located in the region.[59] Three days later, the officer in charge of the Indian mission in Lhasa described seeing a "non-stop flow of soldiers in irregular formation."[60] By February 1952, he further reported that the Chinese military had moved heavy artillery, mountain guns, and three-inch mortars into the city, noting that there was no apparent necessity for the military deployments unless the Chinese government anticipated the prospect of international war on this front.[61]

On the Indian side of the McMahon Line, however, the defensive outposts positioned along the frontier were poorly manned by local security forces and only covered a small number of passes in the mountainous terrain; as such, they were quite unable to stop any offensive action by Chinese forces. Moreover, Patel continued to stress that these areas lacked historical contact with the rest of India given the administrative approach of the British colonial government, with the result that the tribal populations "have no established loyalty or devotion to India." And under the "cloak of ideology," argued Patel, Chinese expansionism would be ten times more dangerous than Western imperialism, concealing as it does racial, national, or historical claims that could dangerously exploit domestic divisions within India. "Side by side with these external dangers," Patel stressed that India faced serious internal problems, particularly pointing to Indian Communists' comparatively easy access to China as a factor amplifying the threat. He concluded,

> Instead of having to deal with isolated communist pockets in Telangana and Warangal we may have to deal with communist threats to our security along our northern and north-eastern frontiers where, for supplies of arms and ammunition, they can safely depend on communist arsenals in China. . . . It is also clear that the actions will have to be fairly comprehensive involving not only our defence strategy and state of preparations but also problems of internal security to deal with which we have not a moment to lose. We shall also have to deal with administrative and political problems in the weak spots along the frontier to which I have already referred.[62]

Patel urged the Prime Minister to be "alive to the new danger" and to bolster India's defenses by expanding internal security in the border areas, as well as strengthening the political and administrative position of the government within the northeastern frontier.[63] Just before his death in December 1950, Patel again wrote to Nehru on the looming Chinese threat. "It looks as though it is not a friend speaking in that language," he warned, "but a potential enemy."[64]

Despite Patel's warnings, Nehru hoped that promoting a policy of friendship and Asian solidarity with China would do more to maintain peaceful relations than any deterrence offered from a large military buildup along the border. During the 1950s, he was also pushing for India to become a leader in what would become the Non-Aligned Movement (whose foundation was laid at the April 1955 Asian-African Conference in Bandung, Indonesia), uniting postcolonial states in Asia and Africa that sought to avoid being formally aligned with any major power bloc during the Cold War. Nehru saw in China a country that had likewise struggled under the oppressive hand of European imperialism and thus was wary of pushing too hard against the government over the disputed border. He even advocated for the People's Republic of China to be admitted to the United Nations and take over China's seat as a permanent member of the UN Security Council, then held by Chiang Kai-shek's Republic of China, based on the island of Taiwan. Taking a pragmatic approach to engagement with China, he also argued that the United States should recognize the Communist government, feeling that such a large country could not simply be ignored forever. In an October 1952 press conference, he asserted that Communist control of the Chinese mainland was a reality that needed to be acknowledged, and that any refusal to recognize this fact would mean "endless complications, awkwardness and sham in negotiations." He felt that if it was inevitable that the Communist Party would be accepted as the de facto government of China, "why not go about recognising the regime in a way that will bring the greatest possible benefits in terms of Chinese goodwill?"[65]

In October 1954, Nehru traveled to Beijing to meet with senior Chinese leadership, including Mao himself. This was the first visit by the head of a non-Communist government since the Communist Party came to power. Even though Nehru had been advocating for goodwill and understanding as the bedrock of Indian and Chinese friendship, the prime minister and accompanying Indian officials found Chinese leaders they met with to be largely rigid and doctrinaire, which only served to reinforce their grave concerns about China's growing strength and unity potentially positioning India as the weaker partner within the bilateral relationship.[66] Despite these private apprehensions, however, Chinese and Indian political leaders signed an agreement outlining the Five Principles of Peaceful Coexistence, known as the *Panchsheel*, as foundational guidelines for China-India relations. The five principles were as follows:

(1) mutual respect for each other's territorial integrity and sovereignty,
(2) mutual non-aggression,
(3) mutual non-interference in each other's internal affairs,
(4) equality and mutual benefit, and
(5) peaceful co-existence.[67]

The following year, on the eve of the Bandung Conference, Nehru told Chinese Premier Zhou Enlai that he felt the first three of the five principles were the most important.[68] Publicly, Chinese officials championed the *Panchsheel* as the key to their relationship with India. Nehru saw some cause for optimism in China's public rhetoric and felt that he could at least trust Zhou, referring to him as an "honourable man."[69] He argued that a "definite feeling of friendliness towards India" existed among Chinese political leaders. "That is due partly to historical reasons," he surmised, "partly to an Asian outlook and partly no doubt to their appraisal of the world situation."[70] Throughout the 1950s, Indian society reciprocated this perceived bonhomie and sought to expand cultural, educational, and economic contacts with China.[71]

While cordial relations persisted between senior officials in Beijing and New Delhi, Indian diplomats outside of China's capital warned of the hypocrisy of Chinese officials seeking to strengthen relations with India. "It looks to me that they are itching for a fight, while protesting undying friendship for India," a political officer stationed in Lhasa observed in a report back to New Delhi. "One would have thought that these are matters which could suitably be dealt with by our Embassy at Peking, but as long as our diplomats there specialise in saying 'sweet nothingness' about the Chinese communists, we shall, I fear, have to take knocks from them."[72] In December 1951, Indian diplomats in Tibet also reported on local Chinese officials' growing hostility toward India and their efforts to sow this animosity among the Tibetans, writing back to New Delhi,

> There is one aspect of Chinese propaganda here which has ominous implications for India, and which we can only neglect at our own peril. This is the glib and insidious talk, never too loud nor too sober, which the Chinese officers and men in Lhasa are spreading from door to door, in the bazaar and the monasteries, making the whole town buzz with one refrain—that the Chinese will liberate Sikkim, Bhutan, portions of the Assam tribal areas, Kalimpong, and Darjeeling. It is hard to come by a Tibetan who has not heard of Chinese indignation and wrath over the fact that large areas of Tibet are under Indian control. [These areas], the Chinese say, must and will be liberated. The Tibetans are under constant pressure and incitement to eschew their passive way of life and to adopt an aggressive, war-like course to reassert their authority over the lost areas and to reclaim their strayed brethren living under the ignominy of foreign rule. . . . Indeed the present buzz seems to be inspired by Peking.[73]

Despite these assessments, Indian diplomats serving in the Himalayan region in the coming years remained generally reticent in their cables back to New Delhi to frame Chinese actions in Tibet as an overt and serious military threat. Nevertheless, they still warned of the dangers of Chinese actions for Indian control over the northeastern periphery. Their reporting portrayed China's reforms as potentially pulling northeastern communities into the Chinese orbit, as little headway was then being made on the Indian side of the border to match these efforts. Through the first half of the 1950s, Indian diplomats were even describing as purely altruistic the Chinese government's attempts to improve the lives of Tibetans through economic assistance, public health measures, and agricultural reform programs, which ultimately came to naught as crop failures led to widespread famine. For instance, in August 1955, Indian diplomats observed that the Chinese army was initiating various agricultural schemes and other development projects in the region. They reported back to New Delhi that the government had instructed Chinese troops to actively assist Tibetans in their farm work, and "it has been reported that in Yatung a few of the army personnel are deputed to serve water to the bazaar people!! All these acts of cooperation and kindness are bound to have some effect upon the Tibetan mind."[74]

Indian officials in New Delhi soon also grew concerned that, as India's chronically underdeveloped tribal communities heard such reports about the Chinese government working to develop Tibet, they would hope to benefit themselves, further encouraging separatism in the region.[75] In January 1952, in response to intelligence reports on Chinese development schemes in Tibet, the Home Ministry commented that the body administering the frontier tracts along the international border, the North-East Frontier Agency (NEFA), was doing the best it could with limited resources, but that the level of support NEFA received from New Delhi was "incommensurate with the vastness of the problem." The Home Ministry recommended to the cabinet that the local administration should be provided with adequate resources to launch similar large-scale development schemes on the Indian side of the border so that tribal communities in the region would not look to the Chinese government "for their salvation."[76]

To address these concerns, the Assam government expanded development plans and improved working conditions in the border areas. Nari Rustomji, the adviser for tribal affairs to the governor of Assam, advocated for improved working conditions for laborers and porters working in NEFA's Agency Service Corps. In 1953, he wrote to the joint secretary of the Ministry of External Affairs that the Chinese government appeared to be offering up "more liberal terms" to laborers on its side of the border. As a result, tribal members of the Agency Service Corps expressed their discontent with the existing terms of their own employment, arguing that they were at a comparative disadvantage from their counterparts across the border. "In the interests of Government and the security of the frontier," Rustomji argued, "such discontent must be nipped in the bud by fixing fair and reasonable terms of service for the Agency Service Corps personnel."[77] New benefits included free medical aid, especially valuable given the harsh conditions and susceptibility to disease that NEFA employees faced in the hill areas during their service; new provisions for holidays, casual leave, leave on private affairs, sick leave, and leave without pay; provisions for gratuity; access to regular savings accounts through the Post Office Savings Bank; and increased pay.[78]

While Nehru and other senior officials continued to believe there was little chance of a Chinese military invasion and made further public overtures for Indo-Chinese friendship, internal political pressure and warnings over China's intentions through diplomatic and intelligence channels continued to pile up in New Delhi. While some sections of the government provided assurances that Chinese actions in Tibet posed no immediate danger, Nehru personally received intelligence reports at the time that Chinese military movements in the border areas were a direct breach of Beijing's declared friendly intentions and presaged Chinese military action against India aimed at securing possession of the McMahon Line and the disputed territory surrounding it.[79] As a result, Indian leaders began to take several actions to address growing concerns about China's expanding presence along the McMahon Line.

Soon after the Chinese invasion of Tibet, the Defense Ministry appointed a special committee of five officers under the chairmanship of Brigadier Bikram Singh, the commander of the army's 181 Independent Brigade Group in Assam, to examine the possibility of Chinese troops occupying disputed territory on the Indian side of the border and the feasibility of advanced outposts of the Assam Rifles to forestall such incursions.[80] By November 1950, the committee had arrived at eight recommendations to counter any potential Chinese military action into Indian-claimed territory, as outlined in the following internal report for Defense Ministry leadership:

(1) The Assam Rifles outposts were to be pushed up further north and various centres up to which advance was considered feasible by the Assam Rifles representatives and the Governor's Adviser for the Frontier Areas, were fixed upon and are to be established by 15th December.

(2) The Committee studied the question of sending up supplies and maintaining them for these forward outposts and were emphatic that the only method of doing so was to have air-dropping operations in this winter season. The supplies are to last 10 months, as neither air-dropping nor foot-porterage would be possible during the rainy weather from March to October.

(3) The Committee decided that a Joint Intelligence Bureau should be set up at the Brigade Headquarters at Shillong in which should be absorbed the existing military Intelligence staff of Shillong and staff of the Central Intelligence Bureau of the Home Ministry working in Assam.

(4) It was also felt that the Sino-Tibetan branch of the Assam Section of the Central Intelligence Bureau should be immediately expanded.

(5) In view of dearth of topographical information of the area concerned, the Committee recommended air-photography of the main routes into India and that this air-photography should be completed before the weather conditions become again unfavourable.

(6) The military members of the Committee were of the view that the operational control of the Assam Rifles Battalions engaged on border protection duty on the north and north-east, should immediately pass into the hands of the Brigadier in charge of the Regular Troops in Assam.

(7) The Committee recommended the conversion of present foot-tracks into jeepable routes and suggested that the construction of this should be taken in hand by the Army.

(8) The Committee also recommended the construction of all-weather Dakota airstrips at Pasighat, Sadiya and North Lakhmipur in that order of priority, and also airstrips for smaller aircrafts at three centres in the hill areas where suitable open spaces were available.[81]

The committee, finally, highlighted the importance of Indian officers, who were outsiders to the region, relying on the Assam Rifles to support the planning for any future operations, given the paramilitary force's familiarity with the local terrain and population.[82]

The following month, the Assam governor reported that the Assam Rifles had taken steps to implement these recommendations by strengthening existing forward outposts and moving additional men into newly established border outposts. India's movement of troops to the border was intended to make clear that the government considered the McMahon Line the definitive frontier of an independent Indian Union.[83] That same month, Nehru made the decision to deploy three platoons of the Assam Rifles to push Tibetan officials, known as *dzongpen*, and their supporters out of the Tawang area and assert Indian authority up to the McMahon Line, in part to serve as a deterrent against any future moves by Chinese troops from Tibet.[84] As these units pushed deeper into the frontier, political officers accompanying the paramilitary forces informed lamas in the area that they no longer owed tribute to Lhasa.[85] Three years later, the Indian government installed a pro-India abbot at the influential Tawang Monastery, the second-largest monastery in the world after the Drepung Monastery in Lhasa, to reduce the region's ties to Tibet.[86]

In December 1950, the Indian government formed the North and North-Eastern Border Defence Committee, under the chairmanship of Major General Kumar Himmatsinhji, the deputy defense minister, to survey broader security threats along its lengthy international border, particularly Chinese actions in Tibet and continuing tensions with Pakistan. Its first report, released the following year, focused on the northeastern frontier. The Himmatsinhji Committee, as it was known, likewise stressed the urgent necessity of further integrating the region and securing government control right up to the border through expanded road construction, an extension of the civil administration, and an increase in the Assam Rifles and civil armed police deployed there.[87]

The Intelligence Bureau (IB), housed within the Home Ministry, echoed the committee's assessments and warned that the Chinese occupation of Tibet could pose new problems for India's internal security. IB officials pointed to the weak hold the central government had over the region's tribal population as ripe for exploitation. "Every method will be adopted to disrupt the integrity of India," they argued in one assessment for Patel and other senior officials, with the result that it

> will be more opportune and easy . . . to foster trouble in these frontier areas where India's administrative control is not strong and where her cultural influence is less. All these tribes living in the frontier regions will be directly encouraged to agitate for independence so that they can after be drawn into the Communist fold. . . . Communists will no doubt arm these tribals and make them the spearheads of their attacks on and forays into India.[88]

To protect the broader security of the nation, IB officials advised, "India must firmly retain her hold or influence in these areas because once India loses her control her entire belly will be opened up to direct attacks." They recommended the strengthening of local administration and police forces in place of customary tribal systems, making detailed economic surveys of the tribal areas to assess their needs, introducing public health schemes, opening schools with Hindi as the medium of instruction to gradually strengthen cultural links with the rest of India, and improving communication and transportation infrastructure in the region.[89]

Throughout the 1950s, Nehru maintained that a policy of friendship with China would be the most constructive means of protecting Indian strategic interests. However, he privately took heed of these military and intelligence warnings and stressed the need for vigilance on the domestic front. He saw the necessity of expanding the government's hold over the border region as an obstruction to any potential Chinese infiltration, while simultaneously putting forward a public hand of friendship to India's northern neighbor. Given the difficult terrain and climate in the mountainous border region and the logistic difficulties this presented to any invading army, Nehru reiterated his opinion that there was no reason to expect any overt Chinese aggression along the northeastern frontier. Yet, he recognized that gradual infiltration and influence across the border remained a concern, with the potential of Chinese-backed forces entering and taking possession of disputed territory if faced with no obstruction to such advances, and that the Indian government needed to take necessary precautions to prevent this.[90]

In an August 2, 1952, letter to the country's chief ministers, Nehru laid out the government's dual position regarding China:

> For us it became a vital matter to consider that we had this great power as our neighbor with 2000 miles of frontier between us. There were inherent dangers in that and we had to protect ourselves against them. These dangers were not because China was Communist but rather that a great power had grown and spread out to our frontiers. Our policy had to be adjusted to this fact. We wanted to be friendly to our neighbor, but, at the same time, we wanted to be firm about our own vital interests. Where these interests were not vital or important or were such that we could not define them, such as in Tibet, we were prepared to adjust ourselves to change. But in vital matters, there could be no compromise. It is for this reason that I declared in Parliament on several occasions that our frontier with Tibet, known as the McMahon line, was our fixed and definite border and we were not prepared to consider any change in it.[91]

India's basic policy was to promote and maintain a friendly relationship with China, "subject always to protecting our interests with firmness," with Nehru assuring his chief ministers that the government had "taken steps accordingly" to guard against Chinese influence and infiltration into the frontier.[92]

EXPANDING INDIAN ADMINISTRATION ON THE FRONTIER

While various groups in the Northeast advocated for greater political autonomy during the transition to independence, the Indian government reversed the fundamental approach of British colonial authorities toward frontier administration, the fundamental purpose of which had been to assert political control only to the extent necessary to prevent raiding into settled areas; beyond this, British political officers largely pursued a policy of noninterference within the internal affairs of the tribes. Following the transfer of power, this approach left the Indian government little actual presence or political influence within a region comprising approximately thirty-three thousand square miles and with a population of over half a million.[93] An April 1947 cabinet summary document referred to the northeastern frontier tracts as the "largest *terra incognita*" in India, an area whose climate and terrain deterred state penetration or the establishment of an effective administrative presence, leaving it a "virgin territory with no communication beyond very rough foot-paths and inhabited by tribesmen to whom the modern world is almost unknown."[94] Indian officials primarily viewed the northeastern frontier as essentially a victim of British colonial policy, which had forced the tribal communities to remain in primitive conditions absent the benefits of the modern state.

Nehru took the position that the tribal communities, no less than other parts of India, should benefit from the opportunities offered by independence, and thus supported the expansion of Indian administration into the lightly governed frontier. However, with the northeastern tribal communities cut off from the remainder of the country due to colonial policies, he recognized the need for gradual integration, accompanied by certain institutional protections, so as not to overwhelm tribal cultures, given that groups on the frontier were "sensitive and proud and jealous of such as they have" and "resent interference with it."[95] In 1951, Nehru wrote to the chief minister of Assam regarding the region's tribal population, in particular the Nagas:

> They are very different from the people of the old North West Frontier of India. But, to some extent, they offer the same problems. You will remember that the North West Frontier tribes, have for hundreds of years, given trouble to whatever Government controlled in India. The British, in spite of every effort, could not wholly suppress them and

> ultimately agreed to a more or less independent belt between what was called the British India and the Durand Line. . . . We have therefore to be rather careful in our dealings with these people, lest we produce a problem which may pursue us for long years later. I am sure that essentially our approach should be friendly and not coercive. The latter approach will not succeed easily and will be a tremendous burden to India and Assam.[96]

To support this gradual integration, the Indian government maintained the Inner Line Regulation for the tribal areas to ensure limited access to outsiders as a protective measure for tribal culture, but also to avoid potential points of conflict that could further alienate the periphery. In 1873, the British government established the Inner Line Regulation to cordon the tribal areas off from the remainder of Assam, with outsiders required to obtain an Inner Line Permit from the authorities to enter the region (though the boundary of the Inner Line was repeatedly altered according to varying economic and political interests or security demands of the day).[97] The Inner Line Regulation served to limit the tribes' contact with outsiders and worked as a control against undue interference in and external access to the hill areas. It was also intended as a check against actions that officials feared could incite the tribesmen to raid tea plantations and attack other symbols of British rule. Ultimately, this administrative division helped to keep the region isolated and underdeveloped. The Inner Line Regulation's original purpose was to protect the plantations and their workers, but it essentially established a boundary between the districts under government control and what was perceived as the "savage" and "backward" periphery.[98]

The Indian government also introduced plans for a new governance structure to buttress administrative control in the Northeast in a piecemeal fashion, which the British left as a patchwork of directly administered territories, unadministered frontier tracts, and princely states. On the eve of Indian independence, the Assam government expressed the need to extend government control within the tribal areas, in particular the Naga Hills, which had remained practically unadministered up to this point. While state officials recognized that the British government had attempted to introduce some level of administration in 1925 and again in 1927, they now lacked any definitive information on the current state and degree of actual administration present in the tribal villages on the frontier.[99] With the departure of the British, these issues were compounded by the resulting vacuum in the local administration; around two-thirds of the officials in the region had been British, and there was a dearth of suitably trained Indian officers available to fill their spots. A 1947 Indian cabinet note explained that the government's plan was for the gradual extension of "a light form of administration" into the frontier, "coupled with beneficent activities which, it is hoped, will enable the tribes inhabiting these Areas to develop along their own lines and gradually raise their status to something comparable to that in other parts of India, a natural and inevitable sequence to the establishment of factual control."[100]

The following year, the Indian government approved a five-year development plan to support the extension of an administrative presence in the region and demonstrate that the frontier was both a de facto and de jure part of India. This plan appropriated approximately 128 lakh rupees (1 lakh equals 100,000) over five years, with the recurring annual expenditure in the last of the five years (1951–1952) adding up to approximately 276 lakh rupees in all. These funds supported the expansion of administrative and engineering staff; the construction of permanent government buildings; the expansion of the road system, including an extension of 103 miles of the province's primary road, 60 miles of smaller roads, 631 miles of track, and 200 miles of bridal paths, which were intended to link administrative headquarters in the region with the subdivisional headquarters and to provide improved lines of communications; the construction of new medical facilities (a base hospital at Pasighat, two leper hospitals, and twenty-seven other hospitals); forest management staff; agriculture staff to support the expansion of terraced cultivation; the construction of fifty-five primary schools; and veterinary staff (three dispensaries and touring staff to deal with epidemics).[101]

The Assam government submitted to New Delhi a proposal for additional funds for expanding administrative control into the Naga Hills. This funding was intended to provide support for more administrative staff, additional deployments of the Assam Rifles, health-care facilities, and transportation infrastructure in the region. In June 1947, the External Affairs Ministry endorsed the plan for added expenditures, arguing that the extension of administrative control would improve the standard of living in the tribal areas, allow the tribes to realize the benefits of living under an independent Indian government, reduce the need for costly punitive expeditions, and boost economic opportunities by increasing access to the "virgin land" and its valuable natural resources such as timber. Above all, the External Affairs Ministry argued that the posting of Indian administrative personnel, supported by medical and public works facilities and units of the Assam Rifles, constituted "effective action towards the extension of administration. The presence of the administrative staff and of the Assam Rifles will itself be conducive to a decrease in lawless activity of every kind, and this after all is the first essential."[102] Given the security framework through which Indian officials viewed the region, former Assam Governor B. K. Nehru further stressed the important role that the Assam Rifles played in supporting the extension of the government's reach into previously unadministered tribal areas.[103]

These development plans soon met resistance from within the central government. Senior Finance Ministry officials questioned the necessity of the costs associated with this plan, pushed back on the additional funds requested, and asked for a clearer defense of the urgency of the proposed scheme. On October 30, 1947, the External Affairs Ministry stressed the international dynamics at play in the border region:

> The head of the Assam Government considers the extension of administration at least in some small measure to the Naga Hills tribal area a matter of such urgency as to justify his acting in anticipation of our sanction. . . . With the transfer of power, the question of securing our eastern Frontier where China has open designs and in which Burma is not disinterested, is a matter of considerable moment. We suggest that, in so far as the necessity of the proposed venture is concerned, we should be guided by the advice of H. E. the Governor who is, after all, the man on the spot and capable of judging the situation better than us.[104]

The following month, the Finance Ministry, focused as it was on an overall reduction in government spending, was unwilling to authorize the additional expenditures due to the considerable financial strain placed on the government by Partition and the myriad other problems associated with the influx of refugees from Pakistan. The ministry did, however, authorize the Assam government to pursue the proposed extension of the administration within the funds already sanctioned for the five-year development plan, which the governor agreed to do.[105]

Yet, with New Delhi's attention pulled elsewhere, early development plans for the border region largely failed to come to fruition.[106] In the immediate aftermath of Partition, New Delhi struggled with settling the mass of refugees from Pakistan, conflict in Kashmir, the drafting of a constitution, and the political drama of integrating the hundreds of princely states. With many officials arguing that the government's attention should focus on such pressing issues first, there was no consensus among the various government departments on the necessity of pursuing an expansion of administrative control on the northeastern frontier. The problems elsewhere were too many, and funds were too limited to justify such an initiative by the new government. Moreover, in respect to the areas along the international border with Tibet, New Delhi was content to leave this region as a "zone of neglect," in the words of international relations scholars Boaz Atzili and Min Jung Kim, to provide essentially an internal buffer region against regional rivals.[107] As one Assam government official noted, "There was also no great urgency, because Tibet was still free and acted as a buffer state between India and China."[108]

Thus, during the early years of independence, the northeastern frontier played little role in the broader security of the state and was largely left as an afterthought for the Indian political elite, who could be dismissive of the tribal communities and their locally driven problems. How could the needs of the sparsely populated tribal communities in an unknown and distant frontier, the thinking went, eclipse the many burdens of building a modern democratic nation on a continental scale? Describing his service in the Northeast, B. K. Nehru later wrote in his memoirs that "it was time for me to try and discover what on earth this strange country to which I had been sent was. . . . I had come from an environment . . . where the unit of account was the nation state and the problems, if they could possibly have been given a monetary value, were worth trillions of dollars. What I was faced with here was incredibly tiny groups of separate identities with problems so small that I could not grasp why they should be bothered about."[109] For the leading figures of the Indian National Congress, the expansion of Indian administration into the northeastern frontier was far from a national priority and could wait until more pressing problems had been resolved.

Yet, the Chinese invasion of Tibet and the growing presence of Chinese forces across the disputed border quickly led to a shift in New Delhi's perspective and approach to its northeastern periphery. After China's invasion, and amid increased Communist activity in the Northeast, Nari Rustomji traveled widely throughout the tribal areas to assess conditions on the ground and noted the importance of extending Indian administration throughout the frontier. With China consolidating control on the other side of the border, he observed the need for "a heavier physical presence of the bureaucracy and of the engines of law and order in the very centre of the hills, and not merely at their extreme southern periphery as in the past."[110] An official in the Assam government likewise wrote at the time, "So long as Assam was a safe and sheltered backwater all this ineptitude and inertia would have had no disastrous consequences." However, he continued, "Now Assam suddenly finds itself in the frontline, surrounded on all sides by unfriendly, if not hostile, States, tenuously linked to India by a narrow corridor and a precarious rail route. . . . Assam, which is today an exposed salient, must in its own interest, and of that of India as a whole, be converted into a strong bulwark."[111] However, the Indian government had to build off of a largely ad hoc approach to frontier governance developed under the British colonial government, leaving an absence of clear lines of administrative responsibility, with much of the tribal areas treated essentially as beyond the official borders of the colonial state.

With increased expenditures available for administrative expansion in the 1950s, and under orders to push the forward outposts as far as possible into the border region, the government undertook a number of new initiatives to extend its reach into frontier areas.[112] The Assam government worked to establish administrative centers throughout NEFA (officially formed in 1954 out of the frontier tracts abutting the McMahon Line) to consolidate control of the border area with the support of the Assam Rifles. Given the difficulty and high costs of roadbuilding in the region, these new posts were even established prior to the construction of road links, necessitating airdrops to provide the necessary supplies.[113] Indeed, the lack of motorable roads at the time required many officials visiting the area to travel by foot. These conditions undermined the government's ability to consolidate its control and reduced the local administration to a largely symbolic presence.[114] By the mid-1950s, the government also created a new cadre of Indian officers, the Indian Frontier Administrative Service (IFAS), to serve these new administrative structures in the frontier. Many of those chosen for this new service had a tribal background and had previously served in the military or police, with the assumption that these characteristics would increase their effectiveness. IFAS officers underwent extensive training for service in the difficult conditions of the frontier and to bestow them with a "frontier mind."[115] The expansion of administrative structures was matched with the expansion of health and education opportunities in addition to agricultural reforms, with the aim of enhancing the self-sufficiency of the region and removing its economic reliance on Tibet.[116]

In 1952, the Assam government introduced autonomous district councils in the six hill districts, with 75 percent of their members elected and the remainder appointed by the government to ensure equitable representation. These new institutions were endowed with wide-ranging legislative, executive, financial, and judicial responsibilities. However, the assent of Assam's governor was required for any laws passed by the councils. Their fundamental purpose was to introduce new political and administrative institutions without disturbing the tribes' customs in respect to land use, agricultural practices, and modes of settling disputes.[117] However, up until the late 1960s, there was very little institutionalized monitoring and evaluation of the councils' actions. As a result, many local leaders used them as a platform for consolidating their own political power rather than addressing the many development challenges within their jurisdictions.

The extension of government control was not always a smooth process as local tribes resisted what they saw as outside interference in their territory. On October 22, 1953, for instance, a group of Tagin tribesmen attacked an Assam Rifles platoon while it was at rest in the Achingmori area of NEFA's Siang Frontier Division, killing forty-seven troops and taking several more hostage.[118] With the massacre catching national attention, the government responded by deploying three columns of troops from both the Assam Rifles and army to the area, though it took them three weeks of marching through difficult terrain to reach Achingmori. Operation Mop, which effectively turned the area into a war zone, was backed by airpower to overawe and deter the tribesmen from future violence. Officials, however, hoped to avoid framing the operation as a punitive expedition reminiscent of those carried out by the colonial government. As a result, the Assam government directed the troops to avoid any unnecessary use of force and to show restraint in its engagement with the local population, in addition to prohibiting the practice of burning villages, so commonly deployed by colonial forces. The use of the military, however, further highlighted the limitations of the civil administration at the time in immediately responding to law-and-order problems.

In October 1952, Nehru himself conducted a week-long tour of NEFA and saw firsthand the necessity of balancing such firmness with an understanding of tribal conditions and needs. Just before his visit, the anthropologist Verrier Elwin, who had adopted Indian citizenship and continued his work among tribal communities in India, wrote to Nehru in the hope of procuring official government sanction to conduct a study of tribal art in Assam. Nehru soon wrote to Governor Jairamdas Daulatram to suggest that Elwin visit Assam not only to conduct his own research but also to write a report for the government on tribes that remained untouched by "Hindu influence" and were prone to resistance against the state. Elwin arrived in Assam in November 1952 to begin a study tour of the region.[119] When his final report reached Nehru's hands, the prime minister dispatched copies to the chief ministers of states with tribal populations, explaining that "if we try to impose our ways on [tribals], imagining that we are doing them good . . . we merely alienate them and, at the same time, probably injure them in many ways. They lose their artistic way of life and become drab imitations of something else."[120] A year later, Elwin was appointed tribal adviser to the NEFA administration based in Shillong, an appointment made with Nehru's endorsement.

Following an August 1955 visit to Shillong, and under the influence of Elwin's warnings about the dangers of rapid modernization for tribal culture, Nehru wrote to the NEFA administration urging caution in handling the tribal population as it extended its reach into the tribal areas and encouraging it not to uproot them from their way of life without providing them anything in return. He understood that such measures would only serve to further alienate the periphery and add to the government's numerous problems in the border region. Nehru had earlier warned against the tendency to view integration as simply merging tribal communities into the neighboring Assamese culture with the aim of establishing a homogenous society. "I think that this is not a desirable movement and instead of achieving its objective, will lead to conflicts and difficulties," he wrote. Instead, Nehru advised the following:

> The first problem we have to face there is to inspire them with confidence and to make them feel at one with India, and to realize that they are part of India and have an honoured place in it. This can only be done by allowing them to retain their own cultural traits and habits and leaving them to develop along their own lines without any compulsion from outside. . . . Any conception that India is ruling them and that they are ruled, or that the customs and habits with which they are unfamiliar are going to be imposed upon them, will alienate them and make our frontier problems more difficult.[121]

In his work within the NEFA administration, Elwin was sensitive to the changing political context of an independent India. He disavowed his earlier protectionist approach to India's tribal populations, wary as he was of appearing to promote communalism or separatism in the frontier, which he viewed as a politically dangerous position to hold. He now advocated for the integration of the tribes, while also recognizing the need to do so in such a way as not to destroy their culture, in line with Nehru's personal directives. Elwin directed the training of political officers on the frontier, advising them to live among the tribal communities and adapt to tribal life, despite its many hardships. He told them, "I don't want you to ever give tribals a feeling of inferiority. Integration can only take place on the basis of equality: moral and political equality."[122]

In his 1957 book *A Philosophy for NEFA*, which carried a foreword from Nehru, Elwin argued that such a middle way would help to foster "a spirit of love and loyalty for India, without a trace of suspicion that Government has come into tribal areas to colonize or exploit, a full integration of mind and heart with the great society of which the tribal people form a part, and to whose infinite variety they may make a unique contribution." The real challenge facing the government, he said, was "how to bring the blessings and advantages of modern medicine, agriculture and education to them, without destroying the rare and precious values of tribal life." Elwin saw the necessity of pursuing the political integration of the region at a slow pace and controlling the opening of its markets to outside traders carrying mass-produced commercial goods, so as not to overwhelm tribal culture and customs.[123]

Despite the interest in protecting tribal culture, even an idealized version of it, among the highest echelons of government, tensions between local officers pushing Indian administration into the frontier and local communities persisted. During a November 1955 tour of the Lohit Frontier Division, in the eastern section of NEFA, a member of the Mishmi population remarked to Elwin, "Remember that we are not by culture or even by race Indian. If you continue to send among us officers who look down on our culture and religion, and above all look down on us as human beings, then within a few years we will be against you."[124] Many development projects also clashed with various tribal customs, such as constructing modern schools whose students would be arrayed in rows before the teacher, which was in direct contrast to the tribal practice of sitting in a circle. Such construction practices drew a direct rebuke from Nehru, who saw the need for development to work hand in hand with tribal customs.[125] While traveling through the Tawang region in June 1956, Elwin noted the difficulties Indian officials continued to have in the region as the majority were still unfamiliar with local tribal culture and required interpreters to speak with the local population, despite their intensive training. Moreover, he reported on the persistent underdevelopment of the region and the resulting material influence coming across the border from China.[126]

Throughout the 1950s, competing international and domestic pressures succeeded in hastening the region's integration into India. The expansion of administrative control and market linkages with the rest of India continued at pace, with the government adopting a second five-year plan for the frontier in 1955. Leading Indian politicians, foremost among them the Socialist leader Ram Manohar Lohia, saw many of the border region's administrative structures, and particularly the Inner Line Regulation, as outdated relics of the colonial past that needed to be cast aside. In 1959, Lohia attempted to enter NEFA without an Inner Line Permit, his second such attempt, compelling local authorities to arrest him. He was quickly released, but the arrest helped to generate media attention on the issue. Moreover, local Assamese politicians pointed to historical links between the tribal population and the Assamese and were clamoring for NEFA to be fully integrated into the state of Assam, which would open the region to traders and workers from the neighboring plains. The Assam legislature even sent study teams into NEFA and pushed for the development of a common economic development plan for the whole northeastern region, the use of Assamese in place of Hindi as the language of administration and education, and the tribal tracts to be administratively joined to the state.[127] During debates in the Lok Sabha, a member of Parliament from Assam, Hem Barua, framed his argument for unifying the tribal areas with Assam in the context of the Chinese threat, asking, "Should we cut a frontier into piecemeal entities like this . . . [or] should we not have a consolidated entity in the frontier for the sake of our defense?"[128]

Amid India's growing tensions with China over the disputed border, officials in NEFA worried over the slow pace of development and the fact that the border area did not receive a level of attention from the central government they felt was needed given the prevailing circumstances on the frontier, despite communication problems and other difficulties. They further understood that, considering developments across the border within Tibet, it was necessary to provide the region's inhabitants new opportunities for economic development and social engagement with the rest of the country in order to bolster the region's integration into the country. In support of this goal, there was an increased effort to expand the use of Hindi as a medium of instruction in schools in the Northeast and to sponsor tours across India for students from NEFA to increase their sense of belonging within India.[129]

As the Indian government worked to bolster its administrative and military presence in the Northeast, such efforts often clashed with local political leaders clamoring for greater political autonomy and even independence from India. Among the Nagas, Phizo, the president of the NNC, continued to push for an independent Nagaland. In April 1950, he traveled to New Delhi to make his case directly to Nehru, who considered Phizo to be a "troublesome and obstinate person." Mindful of international political developments, the prime minister dismissed Phizo outright, stating, "In the present context of affairs both in India and the world, it is impossible to consider, even for a moment, such an absurd demand for independence for the Nagas. It is doubtful whether the Nagas realize the consequences of what they are asking for. For their present demand would lead them to ruin."[130] In a subsequent meeting with Nehru in New Delhi almost two years later, Phizo, accompanied by two other Naga leaders, continued to push for the cause of Naga independence. Nehru again stated that this was out of the question, though he conceded that greater autonomy could be discussed.

After being rebuffed by Nehru, Phizo organized a plebiscite in May 1951, in which seven thousand Nagas participated. When the voting rolls were taken, he claimed that 99.9 percent supported the NNC's bid for independence. Indian authorities ignored the results as a political stunt and pushed forward with holding democratic elections in the Naga Hills to help politically integrate the region into the Indian Union. The NNC boycotted the general election and launched a campaign of civil disobedience in which it called on Nagas to stop paying taxes or engaging with expanded government services in the region. In response, the government issued arrest warrants for the NNC leaders. In October 1952, tensions only increased when an assistant judge of the Angami Tribal Council Court was killed by police after they opened fire on a political demonstration in Kohima.[131]

In March 1953, as the situation in the Naga Hills further deteriorated, Nehru traveled there to attempt to defuse the situation, but he was not to receive a warm welcome. During a reception at the Kohima football grounds, a group of Naga elders walked out after being refused the opportunity to speak with the prime minister. The visit ultimately did little to help find a resolution to the political impasse. The following year, events took a turn for the worse as the NNC leadership went underground and committed themselves to armed struggle. The police and units from the Assam Rifles raided Angami villages in their search for the NNC leadership, which only served to further alienate Nagas in the area.[132] In early 1956, the NNC announced the formation of the Federal Government of Nagaland headed by Phizo and supported by a guerrilla army whose ranks had reportedly swelled to some five thousand troops.[133] With increasing clashes between Indian security forces and insurgents, Naga civilians were caught in the middle of the conflict; villages perceived to be loyal to the government were attacked by antistate insurgents, while villages perceived to be loyal to the insurgents were attacked by government forces.

With violent unrest on the frontier, Nehru wrote to his cabinet on the difficult problems facing the tribal areas. He saw that the Indian government had so far failed in winning over the tribal communities. "In fact," he argued, "they have been drifting away. In the Naga Hills district, they have non-cooperated for the last three and a half years and done so with discipline and success."[134] While Nehru stated that any armed insurgency must be met with military force, he conceded that "our whole past and present outlook is based on force by itself being no remedy. We have repeated this in regard to the greater problems of the world. Much more must we remember this when dealing with our own countrymen who have to be won over and not merely suppressed."[135] Indian officials also worried about the broader impact of an insurgency that could spread in a strategic border region. Aware of the looming threats across the border, Nehru remarked, "We are living in difficult times with international situations always on the verge of crisis and the possibility of wars etc. Border areas and border tribes have always to be remembered in this connection."[136]

In 1956, the government declared the entirety of the Naga Hills a disturbed area, with responsibility for law and order handed over to the army. Nearly two army divisions and thirty-five battalions of the Assam Rifles eventually deployed in counterinsurgency operations in the area to exert maximum pressure on the insurgents.[137] Instead of quelling the insurgency, the military response proved counterproductive. In particular, the violence perpetrated against civilians stoked resentment against the state and increased recruitment for the insurgency.[138] In July 1956, for instance, a group of soldiers in Kohima killed a well-known and elderly allopathic doctor after he refused to get off the road when he was out after curfew. Such incidents increasingly harmed the image of the growing Indian military presence in the region and turned more Nagas against the government.[139] A Naga doctor explained at the time, "As I see it, 0.5% of the Nagas are with Phizo; 1% are more moderate, and want to break away from Assam and come under Delhi, and 98.5% just want to be left alone. . . . Of course the way the army has behaved and is behaving means that now voluntary co-operation between the Nagas and any Government is beyond hope."[140] In a parliamentary debate, Rishang Keishing, a Thangkul Naga from Manipur, stated, "The Army men have shown an utter disregard for the sentiments of the local Nagas, for, they have tried to terrify them by carrying the naked corpses of the Nagas killed by them."[141]

In April 1956, with the insurgency only gaining in strength, the government shifted its counterinsurgency strategy and sought to increase control over the population to break the link between insurgents and local communities, upon whom the former relied for food, shelter, and intelligence on military movements.[142] Security forces increasingly relied on the concentration of Naga civilians into what were known as Regrouped Villages (RGVs) to control their movements and inhibit contact with insurgents. Each RGV was surrounded by three-meter-high double walls of thick logs with pointed tops and *punjis*, or sharpened sticks, in between them, and only possessed two gates to control the movement of the villagers in and out. Indian soldiers, who frequently did not speak the local language, conducted checks on the villagers as they passed through the gates and escorted them to work their fields during the day. After Naga civilians had been moved into the RGVs, their original villages were often burned down to keep them from returning to them. The concentration of the population led to many hardships, including inhibiting local food production, which in turn resulted in starvation among local communities. Moreover, this tactic required large numbers of soldiers to implement without demonstrating any substantial progress in halting the violence. According to the head of the Indian IB, Bhola Nath Mullik, there was almost one Indian soldier for every adult male in the Naga Hills–Tuensang Area. Yet, even with this concentration of troops in the region, Mullik felt that there was "never a time when it could be claimed that the Naga guerrillas had been broken into submission."[143]

By the beginning of 1957, Naga militants were increasingly active in neighboring districts of the Assamese plains, firing on passenger trains and police outposts, harassing security forces, burning houses, disrupting rail services, and damaging telephone connections. As a result of these activities, districts adjoining the Naga Hills were likewise declared disturbed areas in January 1957.[144] The following month, Naga militants began kidnapping pro-government *gaonburas* (village elders) in Sangratsu and Longsamtam villages and engaging in criminal activities in the plains districts as they ran short on foodstuffs and cash.[145] Through the spring and summer, Naga militants continued to snipe at government posts and convoys, abduct pro-government elders, and make attempts to thwart government plans to regroup villages. According to intelligence reports, Naga militants were trying to control local villages and boost the morale of their inhabitants to encourage them to continue fighting Indian security forces until they could attain Naga independence through "bluff and false propaganda about foreign help," including spreading rumors that Phizo would shortly be sending arms and ammunition from the United States.[146]

On September 11, 1958, the Indian Parliament enacted the Armed Forces (Special Powers) Act (AFSPA), based on the colonial-era Armed

Forces (Special Powers) Ordinance, to expand the powers of security forces to battle the insurgents. The law authorized any member of the security forces to use deadly force "if he is of [the] opinion it is necessary so to do for the maintenance of public order," in addition to granting the ability to search any premise or arrest individuals without a warrant. It also provided legal protection from prosecution for any actions taken by members of the security forces authorized under the law.[147] The AFSPA was originally intended to be in effect for only one year to assist with counterinsurgency operations within Naga-populated disturbed areas. Yet, with the government facing continued problems with insurgents, and with violence emerging in other parts of the northeastern frontier, the government kept the law in place and expanded its jurisdiction to apply to any disturbed area in the broader region.[148]

Indian historian Ananya Vajpeyi has argued that the undemocratic AFSPA effectively created "an entirely separate space within India, a sort of second and shadow nation" where local communities were denied due process by the government and security forces were able to act without any check on their behavior.[149] Senior Indian officials frequently justified the widespread violence perpetrated against the Naga people under the auspices of the AFSPA as necessary for protecting India's broader security, simply dismissing any adverse effects on Naga civilians. While serving as the Assam governor in the late 1960s and early 1970s, B. K. Nehru once remarked, "The Nagas are about five hundred thousand only. India has a population of five hundred million people. If five hundred thousand Nagas are killed . . . it will not hurt India."[150] However, from the perspective of New Delhi, the conflict in this distant periphery took on an outsized status among Indian strategic concerns given fears over conflict contagion that would weaken India's strategic position against its regional rivals. In the mid-1960s, an Indian politician explained to a journalist,

> Suppose we agree to give the Nagas independence. It might not be a great loss to us. You could cut off Nagaland from India without creating any geographical anomaly. But then what are you going to do about the Lushais, who, as it happens, look like Europeans? Maybe we could

> let them make a separate nation out of the Mizo Hills; this would mean only cutting off the tail of Assam. But then how are you going to stop other tribes—other regional and linguistic groups—from seceding? Ultimately, everything is going to depend on our ability to deal with the guerillas in Nagaland and the Mizo Hills.[151]

As the Indian government expanded its military operations to address the threat of Naga separatism, Phizo attempted to internationalize the Naga cause. In August 1956 he traveled to East Pakistan, which insurgents used as a base of operations with Pakistani support, before reaching Zurich in 1959 and then London the following year. During the early 1960s, he held periodic press conferences from London highlighting atrocities committed against Naga civilians by the Indian security forces, whom he alleged caused the deaths of at least 75,000 Nagas. On February 11, 1962, Phizo submitted a request to the International Commission of Jurists, an international human rights NGO based in Geneva, Switzerland, to appoint a commission of inquiry to investigate charges that the Indian government had committed acts of genocide against the Nagas, just as it had investigated Chinese actions in Tibet. Pushing back against Phizo's figures, the Ministry of External Affairs labeled his claims "completely untrue or, at any rate, grossly exaggerated" and estimated that only 1,595 individuals were killed in this period, along with 306 members of the security forces and another 692 wounded.[152]

In 1962, while Phizo championed the Naga cause in Europe, British journalist Desmond Doig published a series of articles in *The Statesmen* providing an on-the-ground account of security conditions in the Naga Hills. His articles described the difficulties the army faced in operating in the "impossibly bad" mountainous terrain covered in thick jungle. "The entire Indian Army," he wrote, "could be deployed in Nagaland, a considerable force already is there and still the hostiles would be active. . . . Hostiles could sit four yards from an advancing column and not be seen." Doig continued: "The General Officer commanding the army in Nagaland related how impossible it is to discover hostile hideouts even with spotter aircraft. From the air, the dense jungles are an unending knobbly green with only an occasional glimpse of the earth below the trees. Even when hideouts are discovered, it takes army units days of toil to reach them. Hostile intelligence is good so that the camps are usually deserted when the troops move in."[153]

Doig took particular note of the damaging effects of the military presence on the Naga population. "A whole generation is growing up knowing only military occupation, dusk to dawn curfew, interrupted study, political argument, the sinister influence of informers, and the fear of hostile Nagas and Indian troops both," he wrote.[154] One Naga leader said to Doig, "Let me assure you from the outset that I want to be an Indian. That of course means I want to be treated like an Indian, not like a traitorous alien."[155] One senior army officer, however, explained "that the only course open to him is to order the complete 'liquidation' (his word) of the hostiles." Doig went on to highlight the contrast between military officers in their treatment of the Nagas: One army brigadier distributed sweets and cigarettes to every Naga he met, referring to them as "Jolly good chaps," while another high-ranking army officer argued that the army should be set free to destroy the Nagas, "a lot of dacoits." Doig asked, "Where, between these two gentlemen, both with the considerable power to do good or bad in the name of the Indian Union, is the official line?"[156]

Even as the government expanded military operations in the Northeast, it also responded to the demands of more moderate Nagas in an attempt to undercut potential support for the insurgents. However, there were several lines of division among the Naga political leaders on how to peacefully engage with the government to resolve the situation. In August 1957, the moderate Naga People's Convention, which opposed the violence perpetrated by Naga insurgents, was formed in Kohima with several Ao Naga among its leadership.[157] The group sought a negotiated resolution to the problems between New Delhi and the northeastern periphery and advocated for the Naga Hills District and Tuensang Frontier Division within NEFA to be formed into a single administrative unit; and indeed, in December 1957, the government formed the Naga Hills–Tuensang Area (NHTA). The following year, the group, along with the Baptist Mission Council, began advocating for the creation of a separate state of Nagaland as a solution to the continued violence.[158] Other Naga leaders were open to negotiating for peace with the government but remained committed to pursuing full independence. Amid these political debates, Naga insurgents continued sniping at administrative and military outposts in a demonstration of their continued opposition to the government presence and to the Kohima resolution.[159]

Indian officials were looking for a political solution to the violence, including Nehru and Mullik, who saw the potential benefits of administratively separating the Naga Hills as a means of directing and controlling Naga nationalism in favor of inclusion in the Indian Union.[160] Nehru also saw the need to acquiesce to demands for greater political autonomy given that the conflict was becoming increasingly internationalized, though he received criticism from the right-wing opposition in Parliament that he was bowing to terrorism by pursuing a political resolution.[161] In July 1960, Indian authorities met with the Naga People's Convention and reached an agreement by which Naga leaders would constitute a state of Nagaland with the intention of isolating any hostile elements among the Naga population.[162] On August 1, 1960, Nehru announced the government's decision to support the creation of the new state in the Lok Sabha.

Under sustained pressure from Nehru, the cabinet approved statehood for Nagaland, and the new state was inaugurated on December 1, 1963. In the months before the state's creation, the Indian government announced a general amnesty for Naga insurgents as part of a ceasefire agreement. New Delhi hoped this would give village leaders an opportunity to persuade members of the insurgency to give up their fight, surrender, and take advantage of various rehabilitation facilities and support offered as part of the government amnesty.[163] In a period of two months, however, only 164 Naga insurgents surrendered under the agreement, with many more reportedly rejecting the offer of amnesty.[164] Despite the continued violence, the first elections in Nagaland were held in January 1964, with the electoral turnout reaching 77 percent.[165] Shilu Ao, an Ao Naga leader, became the state's first chief minister. Even with the granting of statehood to Nagaland, the insurgency persisted, while the new state became almost entirely reliant on financial support from the central government.

Shortly after the 1960 agreement on statehood was reached, the government continued its plans for the development of the frontier areas as part of its effort to increase its influence within the region by improving lines of communication, agricultural production, and access to water, health, and educational facilities, seeing the lack of development as a leading problem in the Naga Hills.[166] In the late 1950s, the central government constructed some 300 miles of new roads and 45 new bridges, with 1,000 miles of road widened and improved, at a total cost of over 1 crore rupees (1 crore equals 10 million). The government spent 8 lakh rupees to increase badly needed water access in 135 villages, out of 718 total villages in the NHTA. Regarding health facilities, the government added 42 new dispensaries, a 50-bed tuberculosis hospital, and a leprosy colony at a combined cost of 32.1 lakh rupees, even though insurgents targeted dispensaries and medical workers in an attempt to prevent people from accessing the expanded government services. With the expansion of the road network, this also permitted mobile dispensaries to visit remote villages. The government also approved expenditures of 4.3 lakh rupees for agricultural improvements and 21 lakh rupees for the electrification of 7 towns.[167] The central government worked to expand access to education in the Naga Hills, though many schools were forced to close due to violence.

As India's political leaders struggled to find a resolution to the worsening violence on the northeastern frontier through the late 1950s and early 1960s, relations with China were growing more and more strained. Chinese and Indian troops increasingly clashed over the disputed border amid China's broader military crackdown against political unrest in Tibet. This would culminate in the Chinese military invasion into northeastern India in October 1962. Following the resulting border war, debates in New Delhi were no longer focused on whether China's Communist government posed a threat to India, but rather how best to counter Beijing's claims over Indian territory, which it had proved willing to back with military force. Adding to these concerns, the Chinese government would soon begin providing support to the increasing number of insurgent groups operating in the northeastern frontier. Through the 1960s, India now faced dual and intersecting threats, amplifying the imperative for New Delhi to assert government control within the border region.

3

THE CHINA-INDIA WAR AND THE NORTHEASTERN INSURGENCIES

In October 1962, Indian fears of Chinese aggression came to fruition as thousands of PLA soldiers poured across the border, overwhelming India's defenses. In terms of the immediate outcome, the 1962 border war was limited in scope, with Chinese forces withdrawing unilaterally after only a single month of combat. However, the invasion underlined China's willingness to use force to back its territorial claims. Beyond the immediate border dispute, the invasion also served as a key catalyst for intensifying efforts to consolidate Indian government control over the northeastern periphery. Given the increasing hostilities between China and India through the 1960s, the region's antistate insurgencies quickly saw the opportunities offered by the international rivalry and found common cause with the Chinese government, drawing some level of support for their struggle against the Indian government into the 1970s.

In the years leading up to the border war, relations between India and China deteriorated amid the emergence of a Tibetan rebellion and the PLA's subsequent military crackdown. In 1955 and 1956, Chinese officials grew concerned with what they saw as a growing sense of "independence and self-help" among Tibetans. To counter this trend, the Communist government moved away from a relatively lighter touch in the region and introduced new reforms to assert its political control, such as establishing an administrative hierarchy staffed primarily by Chinese officials and a wide range of economic and social development projects, including several "democratic reforms," a euphemism covering land redistribution, abolition of feudalism and other local customs, and general measures intended to strengthen the hold of Communist ideology among Tibetans.[1] As part of these efforts, the government also drastically expanded the road system throughout Tibet, which was vital to opening the mountainous terrain to Chinese military forces. In October 1955, for instance, the 103-mile road connecting Lhasa with the southern Tibetan towns of Gyantse and Phari, near the McMahon Line, was completed in only sixty days. Following its completion, the road was used primarily by military and other government vehicles, as public transport was prohibited.[2]

The expansion of Communist activities within Tibet, especially the so-called democratic reforms, provoked local rebellions in late 1955 and early 1956 among the Khampas in Kham near Li-Tang, Teko, and the Golok areas of Tsinghai. With rebellion spreading in Tibet, India's intelligence chief at the time, B. N. Mullik, later asserted that Nehru gave him permission to cultivate Tibetan fighters even while the Indian prime minister was attempting to foster Indo-Chinese friendship.[3] This clandestine support for the Tibetan resistance reportedly overlapped with support provided by the US Central Intelligence Agency (CIA). A retired Indian intelligence officer claimed that a working relationship between the Intelligence Bureau and CIA dated to as early as 1952. That year, claimed the retired officer, CIA operatives contacted the remnants of the Kuomintang military forces that had fled into northern Burma to organize operations across the border into China's Yunnan Province. These operations were intended to divert Chinese attention away from the Korean War. By mid-1957, there were reports that the Tibetan resistance had grown to over twenty thousand fighters, with the CIA providing training, supplies, and intelligence to support their cause (support that would dry up as the United States opened diplomatic relations with China in 1972).[4]

The Chinese government responded with an expanded military presence in Tibet to quell the unrest, fearing the broader ramifications of any antistate violence.[5] In the summer of 1956, as the Chinese were scaling up military operations against Tibetan rebels, an Indian political officer serving in Gangtok reported on the stationing of fresh Chinese troops just across the border from Tawang, bringing the total number of troops in the border area to around sixty thousand. In addition to the expanding troop presence, he reported that along the border with NEFA, the Chinese government was making significant strides in constructing local roads; he also forwarded eyewitness accounts of members of the majority Han community in China being settled in these areas. He warned,

> India of course has to watch these developments in Tibet carefully because of its immediate and lasting effect on the border areas of Sikkim, Bhutan, Nepal and further to the west and east. If the peoples living within our borders were not of the same Indo-Mongoloid stock and had no contacts with Tibet either historical, social, religious or economic then we could certainly have watched only with detached academic interest the happenings in Tibet. In more ways than one however all these things are going to affect deeply the lives of the peoples residing in our border areas.[6]

In early 1958, the number of Chinese troops dramatically increased as part of an escalation in fighting.[7] This culminated in the March 1959 Lhasa revolt and the resulting military crackdown that forced the Dalai Lama to escape into India, where a Tibetan government-in-exile was established in the northern Indian city of Dharamshala, where it remains to this day.

Chinese officials quickly connected India's offer of political asylum for the Dalai Lama with what they perceived as its role in supporting antistate activities within Tibet, along with concern about the expanding Indian presence on the northeastern frontier. In May 1959, the Chinese ambassador in New Delhi told the Indian foreign secretary, "No matter what the subjective intentions of the Indian Government may be, their statements and actions have played an objective role in encouraging Tibetans." A June 23, 1959, note from the Chinese government further accused the Indian military of colluding with "Tibetan counter-revolutionaries."[8] In early October of that year, during a conversation with Soviet Premier Nikita Khrushchev, Mao blamed Nehru for the disturbances in Tibet and the flight of the Dalai Lama. He told the Soviet leader that the Chinese government generally supported Nehru, "but in the question of Tibet we should crush him."[9] A Chinese intelligence report that same month outlined what it saw as Nehru's six main objectives:

> (1) To force China to accept the "McMahon Line." . . . It has gradually intensified its military presence in the region and repeatedly urged us to demonstrate our attitude.
> (2) Internal contradictions among moderates. . . . In order to alleviate such internal conflicts, Nehru has capitalized on the Sino-Indian border disputes to stimulate patriotism and unite the country in a foreign battle.
> (3) To reverse the disadvantages of interfering in the Tibet dispute.
> (4) To strike the Indian Communist Party.
> (5) To flatter the US for aid.
> (6) To create a Himalayan Union.[10]

Chinese intelligence officials surmised that the Indian government, in its "second anti-China wave," was trying to "kill six birds with one stone."[11] Zhou Enlai further argued that "Nehru's ideology is the British ideology," and that the Indian prime minister had betrayed his stated commitments to a neutral, nonaligned position in order to seek a closer relationship with the West.[12] The phrase coined by Nehru in the early 1950s to represent Indo-Chinese friendship, *Hindi-Chini Bhai Bhai* (India and China are brothers), so a popular joke at the time went, was becoming *Hindi-Chini Bye Bye*.

In the late 1950s, Nehru and Zhou Enlai exchanged letters laying out their main points of contention and seemingly irreconcilable positions over the disputed border. In September 1959, the Chinese premier wrote to Nehru accusing the Indian government of allowing Tibetans to use its territory for anti-Chinese activities and insisted that Chinese troops in the border area were present only to prevent rebel activities against the Chinese government. This, he asserted, did not constitute a threat to India. Nehru brusquely replied, "India's repudiation of imperialist policies was clearly manifested in its voluntary repudiation of extraterritorial privileges by the British in Tibet. No anti-Chinese campaigns originated in India, but I am distressed and surprised over Chinese claims to about 40,000 square miles of what in our view is indisputably Indian territory."[13]

Indian political leadership was growing ever more suspicious of Chinese intentions as PLA troops amassed in Tibet near the border, even as some within the government argued that such actions posed no threat to India, including Defense Minister V. K. Krishna Menon, who believed, "erroneously, that no Communist country can have bad relations with any Non-Aligned country like ours," according to Nehru's assessment of his key Congress ally. In a 1958 conversation with the Indian ambassador-designate to Beijing, Nehru reiterated, "I don't trust the Chinese one bit. They are a deceitful, opinionated, arrogant and hegemonistic lot. Eternal vigilance should be our watchword."[14] While Nehru had himself been a bit two-faced with China throughout the 1950s—publicly advocating for friendly relations while privately expressing his apprehension about Chinese movements in Tibet and increasing defensive measures along the northeastern frontier—this remark was a far cry from the views he had expressed, both publicly and privately, only four years earlier, when he perceived a definite feeling of friendliness among the Chinese toward India. It was a sign of just how far the relationship had soured.

In the spring of 1960, Nehru and a group of senior Indian officials visited Beijing to further engage on key points of contention between the two governments. Early in the visit, Chinese officials were pushing their position with several members of the Indian delegation. Zhou Enlai stressed in an April 21 conversation with Indian Vice President Sarvepalli Radhakrishnan that "neither the present nor the previous Central Governments of China had recognised the so-called McMahon Line" and that, in the eastern sector, India had only "advanced control in this area since her Independence." China, he stressed, "could not give up territory here or there without reason or justification." However, the Chinese premier also made sure to highlight that, even though China did not accept the validity or legality of the McMahon Line, given that Beijing did not recognize Tibet's sovereign right to sign the original agreement, it had never violated it, and the Chinese government "advocated the maintenance of the *status quo* and had not raised any territorial claims south of the MacMahon [*sic*] Line."[15] The following day, Marshall Chen Yi stated to cabinet minister Swaran Singh, "On behalf of China, we can say that we have no intention to take away large chunks of Indian territory. It is definite that the Indian friends also did not want to take Chinese territory. But it is also definite that we cannot give up any Chinese territory."[16]

The focus of the visit was a series of direct talks between Nehru and his Chinese counterpart, Zhou Enlai. On the first day of their talks, Nehru discussed the Indian government's relationship with its northeastern periphery, explaining,

> That part which you call the tribal part where rather primitive tribes live, has always been under the direct political control of whatever government had existed in India. Actual administration varied greatly. Britain was not interested in the progress of the tribes. They were only interested in exercising influence over them and they also had some treaties with them. . . . But after independence we could not treat any of our population differently. Therefore, we brought them under our administrative apparatus (like opening of schools, hospitals, etc.).[17]

Nehru then questioned Zhou over the purpose of Chinese troops being sent to the border and reports concerning the building of airfields, which provoked a strong negative reaction in India. Chou countered by pointing out that India had more aerodromes on its side of the border, with only one in Tibet. Nehru emphasized the importance of the Himalayas to India and the imperative to defend them but stressed that he hoped to maintain a peaceful border rather than a militarized one.[18]

Over the next two days, they continued a lengthy discussion and debate over many of the historical details underlying each country's claim to the border area. Reflecting China's preferred strategy for dealing with territorial disputes with other countries, such as Pakistan, Zhou pushed for a trade-off—Indian recognition of Chinese claims to Aksai Chin in return for Chinese recognition of Indian sovereignty in the northeastern frontier up to the "Line of Actual Control," a term of art first used by Zhou Enlai in a November 1959 letter to Nehru outlining a proposal for each country to withdraw its forces twenty kilometers from the "line up to which each side exercises actual control."[19] In a discussion over the Aksai Chin area, on the eastern edge of Kashmir's Ladakh region, according to a top-secret record of the talks, Zhou Enlai justified Chinese control over the area by referring to the presence of Chinese roads, administrative personnel, and patrols dating back two hundred years. He also referenced Chinese surveys conducted in the territory, one in 1891 and another in 1941, and its importance as a thoroughfare between Xinjiang and Tibet, where a highway was constructed in the late 1950s to facilitate movement through the mountainous and sparsely populated area. Zhou further stated, "The case is precisely the same as the eastern sector where India regards the line of actual control as her international boundary. As to when patrol parties of either country reached the line is an internal matter since the patrols were sent according to need and we may send them earlier or later as the need arises."[20] Zhou drew comparisons with the administrative reality of the northeastern border region:

> In the eastern sector we acknowledge that what India considers its border has been reached by India's actual administration. But, similarly, we think that India should accept that China's administrative personnel has reached the line which it considers to be her border in the Western sector. On our part, we have not exceeded the line; but on the other hand, India has not only exceeded the line but has even stationed troops at some places.[21]

Nehru spurned Zhou's proposition. He countered that neither Tibet nor China had exercised any kind of control in eastern Ladakh, a fact that was "in entire opposition to what your Excellency has said. What I meant was—the question is not only of dates [or] of visits by patrol parties, but, that for generations there has been no sign of Chinese or Tibetans in the eastern and southern parts of Ladakh." Moreover, Nehru distinguished between a country's jurisdiction and the establishment of administration. "A country may have jurisdiction," he explained, "and yet may not have full administration because of the area being uninhabited or being mountainous." Within the northeastern frontier, he continued, "We have fully and cent per cent exercised our jurisdiction in the eastern sector for a long time but we spread our administration slowly because we were dealing with primitive tribes and they had to be given training for it. Establishment of military check posts is easy, but that is not administration."[22] Ultimately, the talks yielded little in terms of resolving the border dispute and only served as an opportunity for both countries' leaders to reiterate their firm positions.

At the time, the Indian embassy in Beijing was reporting on the escalation of rhetoric and propaganda in China vilifying India. Chinese political leaders and state-controlled media outlets highlighted any "unsavoury news" out of India that painted the country in a negative light, personally attacked Nehru and other Indian leaders, denounced Indian claims about China occupying Indian territory, and gave the overall impression that India was building up its military strength along the border in preparation for offensive action into China.[23] In particular, according to Indian diplomatic reporting, Chinese officials were of the view that India had interfered in China's internal affairs by granting the Dalai Lama political asylum, allowing him to establish a government-in-exile within India, and continuing to act as the aggressor along the border as Indian troops attacked Chinese military posts.[24] Zhou Enlai explained to Nehru during his visit to Beijing, "We have no objection to the Indian Government granting political asylum to the Dalai Lama. All countries have a right to do so. But the Dalai Lama is today carrying out anti-Chinese activities and encouraging the movement for an independent Tibet. This is beyond the definition of political asylum."[25] While Indian leaders grew frustrated with what they perceived as Chinese intransigence, Chinese leaders were of a similar mind. In January 1962, the Chinese embassy in New Delhi reported in a cable back to

Beijing that Nehru and his ministers had no interest in resolving border tensions and sought instead to continue to cultivate long-term hostility with China as a means of procuring additional aid from the United States, which "has become the lifeblood with which they maintain reactionary rule."[26]

THE ROAD TO WAR

In the years leading up to 1962, China had been expanding its military capacity within Tibet and improving its ability to move troops along a network of roads right up to the border with Tawang in NEFA.[27] Despite resulting in longer supply lines than India, the expanded infrastructure gave the Chinese military greater ground access to the border area. Additionally, the nearest airfield in Tibet to NEFA was at Tang-hsiung, around two hundred miles north of the Tawang area, and could accommodate jet fighters and light bombers.[28] By May 1962, China had an estimated 110,000 troops in Tibet, double the number stationed there prior to the 1959 uprising, with around 40,000 located in eastern Tibet.[29]

Paired with troop movements within Tibet and the expansion of local military infrastructure, New Delhi received reports from officials within the region concerning Chinese intentions vis-à-vis India's northeastern frontier. In 1960, the political officer in Gangtok offered two explanations for the buildup of military forces along the border in Tibet: either this was part of a plan to militarize the entire frontier for potential action against India, or the Chinese government expected an onslaught from a "very large horde of well armed nomads," with the official strongly implying in his reporting back to New Delhi that the former was the more likely aim.[30] He further reported how local Chinese authorities in Yatung continued to sow anti-Indian prejudice in Tibet, including by ordering Tibetans to address Indian merchants as "dogs." The report also stated, "There have been again reports about Chinese telling in their secret meetings to the locals that there was no use for the locals to escape to India, specially to bordering areas as they would be taking these over shortly and then deal with these people. The Chinese 'brag' that they can take Nepal in one day and India in 4 days."[31] Later that year, the same officer submitted another report to New Delhi stating that "The Chinese have persistently been telling those who are actively co-operating with them that their aim is to bring about a revolution in the border areas of NEFA, Bhutan, Sikkim, Nepal, Ladakh and to liberate them. Thus whatever 'pacts' or 'arrangements' may have been entered into with the border countries are only temporary expedients to serve their own ends."[32] Two years earlier, *China Pictorial*, an official Chinese government magazine, had already printed a map showing the Chinese border extending over large swaths of both NEFA and Ladakh.[33]

The Indian government now boosted its plans to expand communication infrastructure and road access, including establishing the Border Roads Organization in May 1960 to work with the military to construct roads, porter tracks, and airfields in the border region.[34] However, along the McMahon Line, these endeavors were hampered by mountainous terrain and heavy rainfall. By the time of the Chinese invasion in 1962, besides a single road up to the Tawang area, motorable roads extended only thirty or forty miles into the frontier region, requiring border posts to be supplied by mule or airdrops.[35] In the broader northeastern frontier, there were growing concerns among locals that security was becoming entangled with development efforts as the region was placed on a war footing. Prominent local officials, such as Verrier Elwin, expressed opposition to the military playing a role in development activities, a key point of contention as the local population was largely barred from joining the military, with the result that the latter remained essentially a foreign presence in the area.[36] To lessen any negative impacts, the government attempted to implement a self-contained military presence on the frontier, limiting troops' interaction with local communities and the local economy in a bid to minimize disruption. Rustomji observed, "We just cannot afford . . . a situation where our tribes would resent our presence amongst them and decide to resist us."[37]

Yet, the Indian military continued to expand the troop presence along the border. Military planners received intelligence assessments that, while China was unlikely to invade India, a line of actual control would be defined by the troop presence on either side of the McMahon Line.[38] With increasing numbers of armed young men facing off across the border from one another, the combination of incessant boredom, itchy trigger fingers, and patriotic sentiment, not to mention periodic orders coming down from above to probe forward into the border region, was bound to lead to local clashes. The first encounter between Chinese and Indian troops at the border took place as early as 1954, and border skirmishes between the two sides persisted throughout the decade. While large swaths of the northeastern region became essentially militarized zones during the late 1950s and early 1960s, Indian military units in the region were largely occupied with counterinsurgency operations, leaving the paramilitary Assam Rifles with primary responsibility for patrolling the border and guarding against any encroachment of Chinese troops.

Beginning in the late 1950s, these border skirmishes increased in frequency. In August 1959, Chinese and Indian troops exchanged fire at Longju. Two months later, Chinese troops attacked an Indian patrol at Kongka Pass in Ladakh, with nine soldiers killed. In November of the same year, New Delhi responded to Chinese actions along the border with a swift expansion of its military reinforcements at the northeastern border, even with a consequent reduction in military strength along the West Pakistani border. Despite these movements, Nehru emphasized the importance of finding a peaceful solution to the border dispute, but he would not rule out the use of military force to recover Chinese-held Indian territory.[39] In September 1960, India's intelligence chief warned of widespread Chinese activities along the lengthy frontier and numerous instances of intrusions across the border. Yet, he also assessed that it remained unlikely that Chinese forces would react to the establishment of new posts on the Indian side of the border or use force against Indian military positions, even if Chinese forces were in a tactical position to act.[40]

In November 1961, Nehru implemented a new forward policy expanding India's military presence along the Line of Actual Control (LAC), leading to increased incidents of skirmishes along the border. Both sides continued to accuse the other of committing territorial violations and escalating tensions. The following April, the Chinese Foreign Ministry sent a diplomatic note accusing Indian troops of crossing into Chinese territory and violating the precarious status quo in the border region. The note added, "The Chinese government has reason to believe that the abovementioned invasive activities in Chinese territory signal India's intent to destroy the status quo along this part of the border. The Chinese government again sternly demands that the Indian government put an immediate halt to these kinds of activities, which may lead to serious consequences."[41] The tit-for-tat expansion of military outposts along the border continued through the summer and autumn of 1962. In June, the Assam Rifles established a post in Dhola as part of India's forward policy.[42] On September 8, China established a post of its own at Thag La overlooking Dhola, resulting in skirmishes over control of the Dhola–Thag La ridge in the valley of the Namka Chu River sixty miles west of Tawang. In early October, Lieutenant General B. M. Kaul replaced Umrao Singh as the military commander in NEFA and quickly moved two battalions up from the Assamese plains to dislodge the Chinese from Thag La.

Yet, Indian officials were aware of the supply difficulties their forces faced in the region. In an October 18, 1962, meeting with US Ambassador to India John Kenneth Galbraith, Nehru complained that Chinese troops, enjoying easier access to their supply lines, came into the region with better cold-weather clothing and equipment; their road head was only six miles away from their positions. The Indians, on the other hand, faced great difficulties in supplying their troops as they were forced to rely on lengthier overland supply routes through difficult terrain following equipment losses sustained during several airdrops, highlighting the Indian government's precarious hold over the border territory. A week later, the US embassy in New Delhi reported that some Indian troops were even fighting with old rifles left over from World War I. In speaking with the US ambassador on the eve of the Chinese invasion, Nehru further expressed his alarm about the prospect of war in the area. He outlined the determined decision of Indian leadership to keep steady pressure on the Chinese with ground forces who would drive the

Chinese out of the region, "whether it takes a year, five years or ten."[43] Yet, Nehru still felt that large-scale war between India and China was not likely. In an October 1, 1962, letter, Nehru wrote,

> This tension that has arisen between India and China is, of course, of great concern to us. That does not mean that we should get alarmed in the present or fear any serious consequences. I do not think any such development is likely in the foreseeable future. But the basic fact remains that India and China have fallen out and, even though relative peace may continue at the frontier, it is some kind of an armed peace, and the future appears to be one of continuing tension.[44]

Only three weeks later, events would prove Nehru's prediction disastrously wrong.

On the evening of October 19, China's military launched an artillery bombardment against Indian military positions, followed by tens of thousands of Chinese troops crossing the contested border. The advancing troops quickly overran the poorly defended Indian border posts. The Indian military faced several difficulties in challenging the Chinese advance, including poor communication and supply lines in the region, which required the Indians to use unreliable airdrops to rush supplies like ammunition and clothing to Indian forces, and the need to rush additional troops from other parts of India into battle against the Chinese military without their being properly acclimatized to the drastic altitude change.[45] Five days after entering Indian territory, Chinese forces halted their advance. With the road network that had been built up in Tibet, it was estimated that the Chinese military could move 1,440 tons of supplies daily to sustain approximately 170,000 troops in frontline combat units. Yet, it was reported that these roads were only being used at 20 percent of their capacity during combat operations, and, when Chinese troops passed through the Tawang Valley, they had moved beyond their serviceable supply lines and had to rely on animal transport and porters.[46]

The Chinese invasion stunned the Indian political elite, many of whom took almost as an article of faith that China would not pursue a military assault against India across the Himalayas. In a November 1962 conversation with US diplomats, Nehru now surmised that Chinese actions "obviously required long preparation."[47] On November 8, Nehru announced in Parliament that China had exposed itself as "an expansionist, imperious-minded country," echoing Patel's warning twelve years prior.[48] After the first Chinese advance, Nehru and Zhou Enlai exchanged letters seeking a solution. Zhou hoped to resolve the conflict while keeping China's territorial gains. Nehru, on the other hand, argued for the necessity of China fully withdrawing back across the McMahon Line and reverting to positions held as of November 7, 1959.[49]

Instead, on November 15, 1962, Chinese military forces launch a second offensive, attacking a five-hundred-mile front in NEFA. However, they enacted a unilateral ceasefire six days later, effectively ending the conflict. The Chinese army pulled back north of the LAC, with the Chinese government telling India to remain twenty kilometers from the border. India rejected this proposal. Nehru affirmed that India would not negotiate unless China recognized the LAC as it existed before September 8, 1962. He explained, "Events since 8 September 1962 have completely shattered any hope that anyone would have entertained about settling the India-China differences peacefully in accordance with normal principles observed by all civilized governments. India would never submit, whatever the consequences, and however long and hard the struggle may be." Chinese officials responded that such an arrangement would leave six thousand square kilometers of Chinese land in the hands of India. Despite Nehru's refusal to negotiate, he ordered Indian troops not to take any provocative or aggressive actions.[50]

In early December, six Non-Aligned nations (Ceylon, the United Arab Republic, Ghana, Indonesia, Burma, and Cambodia) gathered in Colombo to mediate talks to end the border conflict. The resulting Colombo Proposals called for Chinese forces to withdraw twenty kilometers from the LAC, creating a demilitarized zone to be administered by civilian authorities, while India would be permitted to maintain its existing military positions. Following several changes to the proposal regarding the positioning of Indian civilian posts within the demilitarized zone, India's Parliament approved it on January 25, 1963. However, while China had indicated its acceptance of the original proposal, it would not agree to the updated version approved by India. In the absence of total acceptance, New Delhi interpreted China's position as a rejection of the proposal.[51] Despite this effort failing to resolve the dispute, neither county resumed hostilities, allowing the status quo to persist. Yet, issues at the border remained. In August 1963, the China Division of the External Affairs Ministry reported to the Lok Sabha that, despite the Chinese withdrawal to the other side of the McMahon Line, Chinese civilian posts constructed in the area of withdrawal were in fact within Indian territory, and thus were a clear violation of the agreement.[52]

After the war's conclusion, the Indian government remained wary of Chinese propaganda claiming parts of northeastern India as Chinese territory, with Beijing continuing to refer to the McMahon Line as an outdated relic and illegal imposition on the part of British colonial authorities.[53] During parliamentary debates, Indian opposition parties were strongly critical of the prime minister's previous acceptance of the Colombo Proposals and used the Indian defeat as an opportunity to challenge the Congress-controlled government. The leader of the Swatantra Party, for example, condemned the government and argued that even with China opting for a unilateral ceasefire, "There was no necessity for India to sit down at the conference table, when she had been so effectively humiliated militarily, politically and in terms of propaganda."[54]

THE FALLOUT FROM INDIA'S DEFEAT

The 1962 war drastically altered New Delhi's perception of China, with a newfound "unity of purpose" setting in among India's political elite as they began to recognize the long-term danger of Chinese aggression.[55] Indian hopes of friendly relations between these Asian neighbors, encouraged by Chinese political leaders' past rhetoric, was tossed aside as the Chinese threat became all too palpable. Every political decision, troop movement, or even development scheme across India's northern border became clouded by China's 1962 invasion; Indian officials now interpreted each move through the lens of potential hostile actions from China.

Following the war, Indian diplomats in Beijing reported back to New Delhi that, even if the boundary question was resolved, China had grown strong enough that Indian friendship would do little to stop China's grand designs within the region, unlike in the 1950s. They warned that India must confront the reality that it would henceforth "have to live with a hostile neighbour watching and under cutting [*sic*] our influence and dampening our progress."[56] In a July 1964 dispatch, the Indian embassy in Beijing further expounded on the "Continuing Threat of Aggression from China" and outlined the perceived motivations of long-term Chinese actions against India. In its aim to challenge the political dominance of the United States and the Soviet Union, the dispatch argued, China sought

> to demonstrate that the other great rival, India, was only a secondary power in the Afro-Asian world. . . . Therefore, in terms of both ideology and power-politics the progress and prestige of India had to be struck a blow if Chinese ambitions were to be realized. China chose India's weakest spot—the military field—for a dramatic show-down. This was combined and followed by an integrated propaganda campaign characterizing India as a bourgeois capitalist state and a stooge of the imperialists propounding bogus policies of socialism and non-alignment.[57]

Following the 1962 conflict, China's continued military and infrastructure buildup in Tibet, coupled with its intensifying efforts to further develop the border region and implementing political indoctrination programs for the local tribes, played into these fears. Indian diplomats in China warned that another invasion of India was only a matter of "if and when a political decision to that effect is taken by the rulers of Peking." As a result, the increased civil and military presence in Tibet "should be taken as [evidence of a] palpable and ever present menace to our freedom and security."[58] Embassy staff concluded that the best means of countering Chinese pressure and stymieing future attacks was "to preserve our political stability, to expedite our economic progress and to build up our military strength. India cannot relax her vigilance on the basis of some excellent hypothesis that due to internal and international factors it may be inconvenient or unwise for China to commit fresh aggression on our territory."[59]

Subsequent actions by the Chinese government would help to convince Indian officials in New Delhi that diplomats' assessments were in no way hyperbolic, but rather pointed to a continued threat that required significant action on the part of India. By early 1964, China was continuing its military buildup in Tibet and working to consolidate Chinese control over 14,500 square miles of Indian-claimed territory in Ladakh. These measures included establishing six posts within the 20-kilometer demilitarized zone along the border and setting up stone cairns along the LAC in the Western Sector, which Indian officials argued was in violation of the Colombo Proposals.[60]

In a series of letters, the two governments continued to accuse one another of violating the Colombo Proposals and committing territorial intrusions across the LAC, including clashes between troops at the border leading to the deaths of three Indian soldiers. The Indian embassy in Beijing warned on March 21, 1964, that even though China had been calling for negotiations and claimed the situation on the border had relaxed, Chinese officials were, in fact, "stepping up tension and flouting the spirit as well as the letter of the Colombo proposals."[61] In September 1965, as fighting was renewed between India and Pakistan in the Sialkot area of the Punjab, the Chinese government pushed its claims along the disputed border, especially to territory within the Indian protectorate of Sikkim, to increase pressure on India. Chinese officials told Indian authorities to dismantle all military installations along the border with Tibet within three days or face serious consequences.[62] China effectively threatened military action against Sikkim and the potential occupation of the Siliguri Corridor, which would cut off northeastern India from the rest of the country.

Military tensions at the border remained high—so much so, indeed, that in September 1965 the CIA recommended U-2 coverage over NEFA, operating out of a base in Ban Takhli, Thailand, given the fact that China could on very short notice initiate renewed hostilities with India.[63] Over the next year, Chinese and Indian troops faced off along the border and even exchanged fire as India expanded its patrols of the border and Chinese troops continued to probe the LAC.[64] On September 11, 1966, Chinese troops at Nathu La opened fire on Indian troops constructing barbed wire fencing along the border, with the Indians returning fire and killing at least thirty-six PLA soldiers. The following day, the Chinese Foreign Affairs Ministry sent a protest note to the Indian embassy, stating, "Do not misjudge the situation and repeat your mistake of 1962. . . . The Chinese People's Liberation Army will certainly deal a crushing blow at any enemy who dares to invade us."[65] In August 1967, the chief of staff of India's Eastern Command, Major General N. S. Nair, told US officials in Calcutta that he doubted Chinese military patrols along the border were operating on their own without orders or would engage in widespread and provocative firing, including with artillery support, without the specific approval of higher authorities, "presumably from Peking."[66] Over the next month, Nathu La was the site of several clashes between Chinese and Indian troops as the Chinese military bolstered its presence in the area and probed across the border. Following exchanges of fire, both sides accused the other of acting as the aggressor.[67]

By this point, India had undertaken significant reforms to overhaul its defense industries and drastically strengthen its overall military position with assistance from the Soviet Union, including earnestly pursuing a nuclear weapon, as well as improving its military defenses on the northeastern frontier. By the beginning of 1970, for instance, the Indian Air Force had expanded the Hasimara Airfield to be the longest runway in the border area. Before the extension, the 2,713-meter airfield was already capable of supporting jet aircraft; with its expansion it could now safely support heavily loaded bombers. At the same time, the air force also improved the Tezpur Airfield, located 140 nautical miles to the east. The Indian Army strengthened its defenses at Nathu La and Bomdilla Pass near the Chinese border, including the construction of a fence marking the Indian-recognized border within the Nathu La area along the Tibet-Sikkim border.[68] In turn, China continued to expand its own border defenses, which had the dual purpose of preventing Tibetans from fleeing across the border.[69]

In international engagements at the time, in particular those with the United States, foreign officials pressed senior Indian officials to pull back from the country's military expansion, fearing a runaway arms race between India and Pakistan. Indian diplomats rebuffed these arguments by citing the dual threat from Beijing and Rawalpindi. During a June 14, 1965, meeting with Secretary of State Dean Rusk, for instance, the Indian ambassador to the United States explained that his government's focus was "inescapably Chinese oriented." He further explained that there was "evident collusion between Pakistan and China to bring pressure on India and to disrupt Indian plans of development as effectively as possible."[70]

On June 6, 1966, the Indian ambassador met again with senior State Department officials in Washington, DC, to further discuss this point. US officials pressed their Indian counterparts on the need to reverse the emerging arms race between India and Pakistan, adding that the US government had exercised considerable pressure on Pakistan to limit its arms spending and that it now wanted India to give some thought to this matter as well. It was in India's own interest, they argued, to come to terms with Pakistan on this subject. According to a Ministry of External Affairs note on the meeting, the ambassador responded that "it was essential that the two countries should be treated as separate entities and the irrational habit of equating them against all realities of the situation, should be ended once for all." He explained that India faced "a substantial military threat from China which had to be met by substantial response by India." Regarding Pakistan, the ambassador remarked, "India's defence requirements were only governed by the need for matching Pakistan's forces which are solely intended to be used against India." While India faced a two-front threat, "Pakistan by her own admission was neither threatened by the Soviet Union nor by China nor by any of its other neighbour[s]. She was suffering from a self-imposed threat from India and therefore all her accumulation of military hardware and military preparations, whether assisted by China or by her West Asian allies were directed against India. Therefore, if Pakistan was willing to reduce her armaments, India would also consider the reduction in her component of armament[s] meant for defence against Pakistan." The ambassador concluded with a refusal to consider the American proposal, stating that "there could be no hope if Pakistan wanted to bring about a reduction of Indian forces against China."[71]

In the aftermath of the 1962 war, Indian diplomats in Beijing further warned of China's broader long-term goal of undermining the Indian state from both without and within, a far cry from the Five Principles agreed to in 1954 espousing noninterference, nonaggression, and respect of one another's sovereignty. In their reporting back to New Delhi, they described the ways in which the Chinese government's propaganda and military efforts were laying the groundwork for "a pro-Peking revolution within India." The humiliation of India's military defeat, combined with the political stalemate at the border, would help to keep India "in a perpetual state of tension," they argued, a problem that would only be exacerbated by the country's economic difficulties and popular opposition to the government. "The combination of territorial claims with larger political objectives," Indian diplomats warned, "has made the Chinese threat to India a fundamental and long-term one. The border dispute itself seems to be a vehicle for the larger political aims of the Chinese."[72]

Beginning in 1949, Indian leaders were already thinking about potential Chinese influence on Communist activities within India and expressed concerns about attempts on Beijing's part to bolster internal subversion against the Indian government. Indian officials feared the Chinese invasion of Tibet, combined with Chinese propaganda, could further embolden Communist revolutionaries active in areas such as Telangana, West Bengal, and Tripura, and further stoke separatism within the northeastern frontier. A senior Indian general at the time argued that the Communist movement within India's borders was quickly becoming the government's primary enemy. With the Chinese Communist Party's growing influence in the region, he stated that there was considerable Communist infiltration into Manipur and that the recent political troubles in Assam and Sikkim provided a fertile ground for Communist exploitation.[73] In October 1950, on the first anniversary of the Communist takeover in China, Mao directly fed these fears by recognizing the greetings of the general secretary of the Communist Party of India, B. T. Ranadive, stating, "Under the leadership of the [Communist Party], a free India, like a free China, will emerge."[74]

With an increase in Communist activity in the northeastern region and the Communist Party expanding its political control within China at this time, the chief minister of Assam, Gopinath Bordoloi, pushed for improved frontier administration with competent officials—the proverbial men on the spot—to fill its ranks. In defense of his position, he asserted that the Naga National Council was being "instigated by the Communists" to pursue independence in order to undermine the integrity of the Indian state.[75] As the perceived Communist threat persisted, Bordoloi wrote to Sardar Patel warning that if the region's tribes are granted the autonomy to act as they like, this could potentially undermine Indian strategic interests.[76] In September 1948, three months before his untimely death from a stroke, Assam Governor Akbar Hydari similarly expressed his concerns with three recent disturbances among Mao Nagas in Manipur to India's newly appointed governor-general, Chakravarti Rajagopalachari. It was the connection between international politics and domestic disturbances that turned these incidents into a serious threat to India. "To my mind," he argued, "these are not just outbreaks of lawlessness which come natural to a warlike and excitable people. As such there would have been nothing to worry about, but it may be that they are engineered by some agency or agencies across our borders and as such should be treated with respect and preparation."[77]

Communist groups active in the region were able to take advantage of the absence of effective lines of communications and the inability of the administration to easily reach into the area—ideal conditions that allowed guerrillas to operate outside of government control in hilly and inaccessible terrain. Therefore, officials in Shillong continued to push for the extension of Indian administration, the increased presence of Indian security forces for anti-Communist operations, and expanded development for the tribal communities, arguing that this was vital to the security of the border region and a means of countering Communist influence. In his 1949–1950 budget speech, Assam's finance minister, Bishnuram Medhi, justified expenditures allocated for expanding administrative control through a security framework, pointing to the fact that within the frontier areas abutting the international border, local groups and interests were susceptible to being misled by propaganda and that "the disparity in the level of social and administrative standards constitute a serious threat to the integrity of India."[78]

In June 1950, Assam Governor Jairamdas Daulatram wrote to the Indian president with confidential reports he had been receiving about Communist activity in the northeastern region and pushed for an expansion of government-led development to counter it. "Communists seem to be planning to create a number of fronts for their action in Assam," he argued. "Manipur, Tripura, the Naga Hills and the Garo Hills have claimed their special attention. All these areas have considerable mountainous territory. There are hardly any communications linking the plains with these potentially invulnerable strongholds of the Communists. They are exploiting every possible grievance to secure the backing of the hill population with a view to make these mountainous areas both bases for operations into the plains as well as safe shelters in time of danger." Therefore, the Assam government requested the assistance of the central government to address the law-and-order situation given poor transportation infrastructure, limited resources, and lack of communications throughout the frontier. He pressed, "Unless Assam is very substantially assisted in a programme of rapid development of communications, the internal situation may not be effectively controlled."[79] While traveling through Assam and Manipur to assess conditions in the hill areas, H. V. R. Iengar of the Indian Civil Service further surmised that the current situation within the frontier was becoming "aggravated by the fact that the Communists are now trying to fish in the troubled waters of the north eastern hills. They are not trying to preach the Marxist doctrine to the hill tribes because they know that this would not achieve any useful result. On the other hand, they are preaching nationalism to these people which undoubtedly has an appeal on racial and ethnical ground[s]."[80]

Facing the perceived twin threat of a future Chinese invasion and China's support for separatism within the northeastern frontier, India increased its efforts to expand administrative control within the border region. Even before Chinese troops marched across the border in 1962, Major Sita Ram Johri, a retired Indian Army officer, wrote a book on NEFA, *Where India, China, and Burma Meet*, in which he criticized the NEFA administration and its officials for keeping the region in isolation, "an inaccessible Shangrila," to protect their privileges within the existing status quo. He pushed for the need to increase the frontier region's contact with rest of the nation rather than keeping the tribal communities "within their own narrow circle."[81] The chief secretary of the Assam government later warned that in the case of another invasion, the Indian government may not be able to rely on the loyalty of the tribes within NEFA and Assam given a perceived disinterest on the part of the government in expanding development within the region and a degree of scornfulness on the part of the local population stemming from the Indian Army's initial collapse. A Buddhist monk in the border region later recalled to an Indian journalist, "You can raise Indian flags, and call us Indian. But people do not forget that the Indian Army deserted us. [The] Chinese occupied parts of this land and [these] people. We lived under occupation."[82] Assam's chief secretary argued that if New Delhi did not take measures to address their concerns, the periphery's inhabitants may be inclined to side with the Chinese government in the future.[83]

After the Chinese invasion in 1962, these arguments were quickly grasped by India's political elite, who blamed the region's administrative isolation for abetting the invasion and India's military failure. India made a much more concerted effort to reverse the policy advocated by the likes of Rustomji and Elwin and accelerate the opening up of NEFA, including by increasing government funding for road construction and various development schemes in the region aimed at improving its defensive position (though the Defense Ministry banned the construction of roads directly along the McMahon Line fearing that they could aid a future Chinese invasion).[84] The Indian government also proactively recruited local tribesmen to join the civil administration and the army to more closely align the region with India. Some politicians in Delhi even floated the idea of settling 100,000 Punjabi farmers in NEFA to hasten the assimilation of the tribal population and dissuade any future Chinese advances, submitting proposals to the Home Ministry for such an effort over the next two years.[85]

With India's improved military position, the possibility for another Chinese military invasion was further diminished. However, hostilities between the two countries remained. Beginning in the mid-1960s, the Chinese government now pursued a new strategy of subversion focused on extending assistance to antistate insurgents within the northeastern periphery as proxies against India. While Chinese support was not the cause of the northeastern insurgencies, officials in Beijing saw an opportunity in backing them as Indian military forces would potentially be bogged down in fighting antistate guerrillas. A secret Indian Defense Ministry white paper from 1972 noted China's "hostile moods and designs in fomenting and sustaining tribal insurgency in north eastern India with the intention of disintegrating and weakening India."[86]

CHINA'S PROXY WAR IN NORTHEASTERN INDIA

As security conditions on the northeastern frontier worsened in the coming years and the Naga insurgency swiftly became the preeminent focus of the Indian government, New Delhi's fears of Chinese influence over and assistance to antistate militants deepened. Such fears would soon come to fruition as the Chinese government provided low levels of assistance to the Nagas and other insurgencies operating in the region. This internal conflict became enmeshed in the broader regional politics of South Asia with India's rivals—both China and Pakistan—seeing this as an opportunity to target India through support of domestic proxies that could further weaken the country on another front.

During the 1950s and 1960s, the Naga insurgents quietly received assistance from Pakistan, largely by access to training camps and the use of its territory in East Pakistan to evade Indian authorities. In a June 1958 press conference, Nehru remarked, "I believe some Pakistan authorities have encouraged the Nagas—to what extent I cannot say—Pakistan's policy appears to be based solely on hatred of India, and wherever they find anybody opposing India they line up with them."[87] In the face of the expanding military presence in the Northeast, the Naga insurgents were only too happy to receive any assistance they could find from external supporters.

Yet, by the early 1960s, the Nagas' attitude toward China had become more ambiguous, with different Naga factions pushing conflicting positions. Following the Chinese invasion in October 1962, the leadership of both the more moderate and the openly hostile wings of the Naga nationalist movement made calls to resist the Chinese advance and cooperate with Indian forces in the defense of northeastern India. Even with such public calls, there were reports that insurgent activity increased following the redeployment of Indian forces from the Naga areas to the northern border to repel the Chinese invasion.[88] However, in June of that year, the Naga military leader Mowu Gwizan stopped off in Karachi on his way to London to meet Phizo, where he was reportedly introduced to his Pakistani hosts' "Chinese friend," who promised Chinese aid and military assistance to the Naga struggle.[89] On May 29, 1963, the *ato kilonser* (prime minister) of the self-proclaimed Federal Government of Nagaland also wrote to Zhou Enlai requesting that China recognize the sovereignty and territorial rights of Nagaland and promised to "honour and follow their principles of safeguarding and upholding the cause of any suppressed nation of Mongoloid stock." Copies of the letter were sent to the prime ministers of Britain and India.[90] Alongside Phizo's efforts to win foreign backing in Europe, the Nagas hoped to internationalize their struggle by reaching out to China, despite some within the largely Christian movement being opposed to the idea of receiving aid from the officially atheist Communist government.

While Nagaland's chief minister, Shilu Ao, negotiated a 1964 ceasefire with the Naga rebels that saw the Indian Army suspend operations in the region, the peace process with the Nagas quickly broke down, and a fresh wave of attacks against civilian targets beginning in 1966, which included train bombings and derailments, the kidnapping of civilians, and attacks on private vehicles, necessitated a military response.[91] Yet, with the renewed violence, Nagas could no longer rely on the same level of Pakistani assistance. Following the Tashkent Declaration of January 1966, which brought the Indo-Pakistani war of 1965 to a resolution, Pakistani President General Ayub Khan gave specific instructions that no aid was to be extended to any Naga or Mizo insurgents that crossed the border into East Pakistan.[92] While the insurgents' ability to exploit Pakistani territory and unofficially receive some small arms from Pakistani sources did not completely dry up, they increasingly looked to China for military aid in their fight against the Indian government. In early 1965, members of the Naga insurgency confided to Sir Charles Pawsey, a former British administrator on the northeastern frontier who was then on an Indian government–sponsored tour through Nagaland, that they had already been in contact with Chinese representatives in Chittagong, East Pakistan.[93] One Indian general remarked that the largely Christian Nagas turned to the Chinese government as a last resort.[94]

The first Naga fighters arrived in China in November 1966, when a group of over 130 Nagas led by Thinouselie, a key military leader of the Naga rebels, made their way overland through the jungles of Burma and across the border into China. They had contacted the Chinese military through guides provided by the Kachin Independence Army, a militant group in Burma that had already been receiving Chinese support. China set up a military camp in western Yunnan Province near the Burmese border and provided the Naga fighters with training, additional funding, and equipment, including rifles, machines guns, pistols, ammunition, mortars, hand grenades, mines, wireless radio sets, and rocket launchers. Two of the Naga leaders even traveled to Beijing to meet with high-ranking Foreign Ministry officials and held four rounds of talks with officers of the PLA. Chinese officials gave them a tour of historic sites such as the Great Wall and had them participate in mass meetings in Tiananmen Square. One of the leaders, Thuingaleng Muivah, stated during a meeting, "We have our rights too, even if we used to be half-naked savages. Tell us if we have the right to fight against India. If we don't, we can stop. Right now." A Chinese official reportedly answered, "Continue your fight. We'll support you to the end. Our help is selfless and there are no strings attached."[95]

Despite arriving amid the Cultural Revolution, Naga fighters, who were largely Christian, continued to practice their faith in the camp with the approval of Chinese authorities; indeed, the Chinese were careful to avoid any mention of religion altogether. Following interrogations of captured Naga insurgents, Indian military authorities even expressed their admiration for China's subtle indoctrination of the Naga fighters. Rather than openly pushing Chinese propaganda and ideology, Chinese officials instead relied on indoctrination by example. They highlighted aspects of communism that aligned with Naga society, such as the shared ownership of land and other possessions within a tribe or village and various social practices including communal agriculture organized in an almost military manner. The Nagas later reported their admiration for the "austerity and discipline of life in China," which they found "not at all strange."[96] In November 1967, many Naga fighters made the two-month return journey to India through the northern Burma highlands armed with Chinese weaponry. Muivah would stay in Beijing until 1972, becoming the official Naga representative to Chinese authorities.[97]

Upon hearing word of the warm reception their comrades had enjoyed in China, another group of around 300 Nagas made the trip in December 1967, led by Mowu Gwizan and Isak Chishi Swu. They also were provided with military training. Between 1965 and 1968, Indian intelligence estimated that approximately 1,650 Naga insurgents traveled to China for training and returned with arms and ammunition, in addition to literature on guerrilla warfare and Mao's writings. In March 1970, during another Naga visit to China, there were reports that Chinese officials promised enough military equipment to outfit 10,000 Naga soldiers in their fight against the Indian government.[98] In the early 1970s, Indian intelligence reported that Chinese officials also offered to increase their military presence on the LAC so as to occupy Indian security forces and relieve the pressure on insurgents in Nagaland.[99]

Government concerns about the continued insurgent violence in the Northeast were compounded by such assistance. In June 1968, over a thousand Indian troops engaged Naga forces in battle near the village of Jotsoma, on the outskirts of the state capital of Kohima. Armed with Chinese machine guns and rocket launchers, the Naga rebels were able to inflict heavy casualties on the Indian troops. Indian authorities recovered Chinese equipment, including machine guns, mortars, and medical supplies, at the scene of the battle. Photos of the Chinese weapons and other Chinese materials accompanied articles in numerous Indian media outlets on Chinese support to the Naga insurgents, including extracts from recovered diaries that outlined detailed instructions on the use of Chinese-made weapons and general knowledge about Communist ideology. Indian officials announced that the discovery of the Chinese-supplied weapons added a new dimension to the conflict with the Naga insurgents.[100]

Throughout the late 1960s, the Indian government sent a series of protest notes to the Chinese embassy in New Delhi demanding that the Chinese government cease all assistance to the "mis-guided tribal elements" in the northeastern frontier.[101] On June 19, 1968, for instance, the Ministry of External Affairs submitted a long note to the Chinese embassy outlining the Indian government's outrage at the clear evidence of Beijing's support for the Naga insurgents. The note explained that the Indian government had uncovered "concrete and irrefutable proof" that Chinese-provided arms and ammunition had been smuggled into India "with the clear purpose of aiding some subversive elements in Nagaland. . . . It is obvious the material could not have found its way into India without assistance and encouragement of the Chinese government." The ministry's note asserted that "there is conclusive evidence of the Chinese government's masterminding this covert scheme in order to stir lawlessness against the legally constituted authority in India." The note further warned that

> the Government of India [would] take a very serious view of such interference which is in flagrant violation of all canons of international behaviour and an affront to India's sovereignty. The Government of India, therefore, strongly protest[s] against the conduct of the Chinese government and would like to make it clear that they will not tolerate

> interference of any kind in India's internal affairs. The Chinese government are warned that they will be entirely responsible for the consequences of their interference in the internal affairs of India. . . . Needless to say that the authorities of the Government of India responsible for law and order will deal with all such subversive activities in a firm and resolute manner.[102]

China offered no response to India's protests.

The following month, the Indian government officially terminated the four-year-old ceasefire with the Naga insurgents. On July 24, 1968, Indian Prime Minister Indira Gandhi, Nehru's daughter, who rose to the position of prime minister two years after her father's death, stated in the Lok Sabha that her government had no intention of resuming peace negotiations due to the repeated violations of the ceasefire agreement by the Nagas.[103] At this time, there were around fifty thousand troops in the Northeast fighting the Naga insurgency.[104] The Indian government also stepped up its efforts at this time to seal the India-Burma border to prevent northeastern insurgents from making contact with Chinese authorities; yet, the director of military intelligence admitted to a military adviser at the British High Commission that there was no possibility of cordoning off this porous frontier.[105] Burmese authorities, whose own antistate insurgencies were receiving Chinese support, helped to stoke Indian fears. In March 1968, Burmese Prime Minister Ne Win had warned Prime Minister Gandhi that the immediate threat from China no longer stemmed from direct military aggression, but rather from Beijing's support for subversive activities within their countries, including offering support to insurgent groups in both India and Burma.[106] Other voices in the Indian bureaucracy surmised that such support from the Chinese government was only temporary and not something that would permanently shape relations between Delhi and Beijing. An official serving on the Indian Ministry of External Affairs' China desk communicated his view that Chinese assistance to the insurgent groups would only continue for the duration of the Cultural Revolution; once the ideological fervor surrounding it ended and China's domestic affairs settled down, he felt that this assistance would likely dry up.[107]

China's material aid was matched by moral support through various types of propaganda, including radio broadcasts in Naga dialects. Through the 1960s, Chinese media frequently reported on any clashes between the Naga insurgents and Indian government forces; the stories were always biased toward the insurgents to show that they fought "under the banner of Mao's Thought."[108] Indian authorities also increasingly recovered large amounts of Chinese propaganda and Maoist literature translated into the Naga language, with local officials expressing concern with the extent of China's ideological penetration into Naga areas.[109] The Home and External Affairs Ministries saw this propaganda as evidence of flagrant interference in India's internal politics and an effort to undermine the integrity of the Indian state by inciting a small number of "subversive elements" to undertake an armed struggle against the state.[110] To counter Chinese support, the Indian government launched an anti-China propaganda campaign in Nagaland. In May 1968, for example, the Nagaland state government produced and disseminated a poster showing a Chinese soldier threatening a Naga woman with a bayonet. The accompanying text read,

> If Chinese Communists come from the other side of the mountain, our Naga way of life will be destroyed. Every plot of our land will be confiscated and we will be deprived of the harvest by the Chinese. As a result, we will have to line up in front of our ration shops for the meager daily rations provided by the Chinese. Thus we will all be forced to work as coolies in our own land, feeding the Chinese. Then they will take away our beloved children, who will be sent to Peking for Communist indoctrination.[111]

Even in the absence of direct assistance, officials in the External Affairs Ministry warned that China's political pressure on India alone could have an adverse effect on northeastern tribal communities, causing them to become increasingly audacious in their demands of the state.[112] This was made all the more urgent as the Indian government debated the impact of China's first nuclear weapons test at Lop Nor, Xinjiang, in October 1964 and how India should respond. Following the nuclear explosion, the Indian chiefs of staff made a preliminary evaluation that the most immediate threat from China remained its conventional arms.[113] Despite the absence of an immediate military threat, the director of the External Affairs Ministry's China Division, K. R. Narayanan, stressed the importance of the political and psychological effects of China's nuclear test, alongside the military implications. "Coming after the traumatic experience of the 1962 military defeat and in the context of continuing conflict with China," he wrote, "the Lop Nor explosion is likely to exert a demoralising influence on the mass mind of India unless we can produce some kind of a counterblast to the Chinese bomb." China's nuclear explosion, Narayanan further argued, could also "expedite the process of polarization in the domestic politics of India. . . . The Chinese leaders want to tear asunder this veil of artificial unity so that fissiparous and revolutionary developments may come to the fore. An alliance with the West would profoundly split Indian politics into Right and Left. A polarization of this kind would open the sluice-gates of revolutionary forces in India, and the Communists alone stand to gain from it."[114]

Adding to officials' worries, the Indian government continued to claim that Chinese and Pakistani officials were colluding to support the northeastern insurgencies. Pakistan had served as a facilitator and intermediary connecting militants in India with the Chinese, especially in East Pakistan prior to 1971, which Naga and Mizo insurgents had used as a safe haven with the support of Pakistani intelligence. The Indian government received reports of Chinese personnel in East Pakistan training insurgents at a camp in the Chittagong area, in addition to the training provided to the Pakistanis (though, in the late 1960s, British intelligence questioned the presence of Chinese trainers on Pakistani territory).[115] Yet, the Indian Defense Ministry concluded that the Chinese and Pakistani governments often made common cause in stoking and supporting the tribal insurgencies in the northeastern periphery with the intention of weakening India's internal cohesion. India's Intelligence Bureau likewise determined that the support and assistance that Pakistan and China provided to tribal insurgents in northeastern India were closely linked, with Pakistan playing a complementary role by channeling Chinese arms, aid, financial assistance, and other support to insurgents.[116] In December 1972, Deputy Home Secretary K. S. Puri added,

> There is irrefutable evidence of Pakistan and China fomenting unrest among the tribals of North-Eastern India as also aiding, abetting and supporting them in blatant violation of all codes and international conduct. It is mainly due to their support and assistance that the Nagas as also the Mizo rebels could sustain their adventurist violent movements. The main object of Pakistan and China has been to encourage the misguided sections of these tribals to demand secession from India, and to use them to organize sabotage and subversion within India with the hope of weakening India and thereby gain[ing] political and military advantage.[117]

Indian officials feared this was part of a broader campaign of collusion between the two countries against India. In July 1967, the Indian embassy in Beijing reported on the visit of the Pakistani defense minister to China, during which it was strongly suspected that the Chinese officials he met with encouraged Pakistan to reopen a military front with India and guaranteed a corresponding move by China. The embassy staff noted the necessity of watching the border region with renewed vigilance. They warned that the Chinese government would be less inhibited than it had been in the past and would be willing to exploit any opportunities that emerged due to tensions between India and Pakistan, especially regarding the dispute over the former princely state of Jammu and Kashmir. "Should there be any dramatic deterioration particularly in relation to Pakistan and West Bengal," the Embassy warned, "Chinese military moves against us will almost be a certainty."[118]

On September 1, 1972, the Indian government declared the Naga National Council and its affiliates, including the Federal Government of Nagaland and the Naga Army, unlawful organizations under the Unlawful Activities (Prevention) Act of 1967. The trove of documents used as evidence in support of the determination to outlaw these groups included a number of financial reports that government officials argued definitively proved Naga insurgents had received financial assistance from China; documents detailing the names and movements of Naga insurgents into and out of China for military training; and evidence of attempts to negotiate a "friendship treaty with China" or a "joint defence pact" for the purpose of "expelling Indian aggression once for all."[119] With this 1972 declaration, the Home Ministry produced further evidence of Naga insurgents continuing to fight for Naga independence, challenging the sovereignty of India, and illegally and violently undermining the territorial integrity of the country. The Home Ministry noted as well that Naga insurgents still retained links with foreign powers and continued to pursue Chinese military assistance.[120] Indian authorities later came into possession of a 1974 letter from the president of the Federal Government of Nagaland to China's prime minister introducing a new Naga delegation to China led by Muivah. The delegation's purpose in China, as laid out in the letter, was to seek all-out support from China, to make appeals to the Chinese government to undertake immediate steps to "rescue Naga people from the aggressive wanton hands of India," and to approach other countries friendly to China to garner their support for the Naga cause. The Naga president further expressed "how deeply grateful we feel for the help extended to us in our time of need" and his hope that additional Chinese aid would "help us to tread the path to win final victory." He concluded, "Long live People's Republic of China! Long live Sino-Naga fraternal relationship!"[121]

Yet, sustained military pressure by Indian security forces eventually led to the surrender of many Naga rebels, undermining the movement's ability to continue its fight, even with limited Chinese assistance. A peace agreement, known as the Shillong Accord, was signed on November 11, 1975, in Shillong in which the NNC laid down their arms, renounced their calls for independence, and accepted the Indian Constitution.[122] In the 1980s, there was a resurgence in Naga militancy under the leadership of Muivah, who had stayed for four years in China's Yunnan Province and was trained by the PLA. He set up the National Socialist Council of Nagaland (an NNC splinter group that opposed the peace agreement), blending evangelical Christianity with revolutionary socialism. However, by that point, Chinese aid was no longer forthcoming. On February 19,

1982, the insurgents attacked an army convoy on the Imphal–Ukhrul road, killing twenty-two soldiers. In response, the army conducted a retributive campaign throughout the area, searching villages and attacking anyone seen to sympathize with the insurgents. A civil liberties research team who visited the area found that even though only a handful of people in the region supported the underground Naga movement, the army was suspicious of all Nagas.[123]

Following the eruption of the Naga insurgency, political unrest and opposition to the Indian government continued to spread in other parts of the northeastern periphery. This manifested in a growing number of insurgent groups fighting for independence for the varying ethnic communities in the region, many of whom would likewise look to China for international assistance. Problems between the Mizo people and the Indian government date to a devastating famine that struck the region in the late 1950s. The outbreak of the famine was originally sparked by an invasion of rats that decimated the bamboo crop and community food stores, a cyclical occurrence that had long plagued the region; in 1881, for instance, a famine caused by a rat infestation killed fifteen thousand people. On October 29, 1958, the Mizo Hills District Council released a statement calling for increased government support in the face of the looming disaster:

> With the flowering of bamboos in the Mizo District, the rat population has phenomenally increased and it is feared that in the next year the whole district would be affected. As a precautionary measure against the imminence of famine, following the flowering of bamboos, the District Council feels that the Government [should] be moved to sanction to the Mizo District Council a sum of Rs. Fifteen lakhs, to be expended on a test relief measure for the whole of Mizo district including the Pawi-Lakher region.[124]

However, the Assam government did not take the famine seriously at first. This was especially true of Chief Minister Bimala Prasad Chaliha, who treated with mockery the notion that a growing infestation of rats might be connected with the outbreak of famine, initially dismissing such concerns as mere tribal beliefs without any basis in fact. The secretary of the Mizo Hills District Council at the time, H. K. Bawichuaka, explained, "The Assam Government initially shrugged off our warnings. When famine stared the district in the face like an angry demon, they tried to drop rice from the air. . . . The population had already started living on roots and wild vegetables from the jungle. The Government tried relief work but that did little to restore the morale of the people."[125] The effects of the famine were exacerbated by the economic hardship sparked by Partition, as the political division of the subcontinent cut off the Mizo Hills from the nearest port and railhead—Chittagong, which was now in East Pakistan—meaning outside access to the region came only through a long, winding road built in 1942. This single roadway was far from adequate to move sufficient aid effectively and quickly into the region to help mitigate the famine.

In 1959, a group of Mizos organized the Mizo National Famine Front (MNFF) to distribute relief supplies in remote and inaccessible villages. Though the Assam government provided some assistance, many Mizos saw its response as insufficient to address the famine, and the MNFF subsequently became a focal point for Mizo rights advocacy. The famine also saw the rise of the Mizo leader Laldenga, a veteran of the Indian Army turned civil servant in Aizawl who took the reigns as president of the MNFF. On October 12, 1962, only eight days before the Chinese invasion, the MNFF dropped the word "famine" from its name to become the Mizo National Front (MNF) and began to advocate for Mizo independence. As the chief minister of the union territory of Mizoram later explained, "The impact of the famine and the ineptitude of the Assamese Government made even the least conscious of Mizos receptive to Laldenga's gospel of independence. History often provides such people with the charge of driving home the most impractical of ideas. The Great Depression in the 1930s produced and sustained Hitler in Germany. Laldenga was the product of the Great Mautam [rat] famine, the MNF was the child born in its womb."[126]

The MNF initially pursued a political path, winning 2 seats in the Assam Legislative Assembly and 145 seats in the Village Council in the Mizo Hills District in 1963, though failing to win control of the council against the Mizo Union's 228 seats. The Mizo Union opposed Laldenga's calls for secession, with its leadership arguing that such a move would be impossible given the region's small population and limited economy.[127] Despite such concerns about the region's ability to sustain an independent polity, Laldenga remained undeterred. On October 30, 1965, the MNF submitted a memorandum to Prime Minister Lal Bahadur Shastri, Nehru's successor following his death in May 1964, explaining the rationale for Mizo independence:

> The Mizos from time immemorial lived in complete independence without foreign interference. Chiefs of different clans ruled over the separate hills and Valleys with supreme authority and their administration was very much like the Greek city-states of the past. . . . Scattered as they are divided, the Mizo people are inseparably knitted together by their strong bond of tradition, custom, language, social life and religion wherever they are. The Mizos stood [as] a separate nation, even before the advent of the British Government, having a nationality distinct and separate from India. In a nutshell, they are a distinct nation, created, moulded and nurtured by God and nature.[128]

With the Mizo population even smaller than the Nagas, few in New Delhi at the time took this argument seriously.

In the late evening of February 28, 1966, the MNF launched Operation Jericho, a simultaneous attack in the Mizo Hills targeting the region's three main Assam Rifles posts in Aizawl, Champhai, and Lunglei, as well as the nine smaller outposts. Local security forces were quickly overrun by the well-organized show of force. General Sam Manekshaw, the commander of the Indian Army's Eastern Command, remarked that Indian security forces in the region "were caught with our pants down."[129] The MNF followed this operation with a declaration of independence for the Mizo Hills. The military response was prompt and overwhelming. Two days after the attack, the Mizo Hills were declared a disturbed area, and an army division subsequently moved in. On March 5, 1966, the Indian Air Force bombed rebel forces besieging units of the Assam Rifles in Aizawl. The next day, fighter jets strafed Aizawl, machine-gunning the area and dropping incendiary bombs. This was the first and only instance of the Indian military conducting bombing raids on its own civilians. Almost the entire population of the area was displaced to remote villages in the surrounding hills. The government, now under the leadership of Indira Gandhi, quickly launched a massive counterinsurgency operation throughout the Mizo Hills, with military leaders focused on the insurgents' ability to exploit the region's long and porous border with East Pakistan to evade security forces.

Echoing its treatment of the Nagas, the Indian Army's strategy was to concentrate the Mizo population into strategic hamlets, known as "Protected and Progressive Villages," as part of a resettlement program, essentially treating the entire population as potentially hostile to the Indian state. In the first two months of 1967, 45,107 people from 109 villages were relocated to group centers along the main road.[130] From 1967 to 1969, the region's rural population, which comprised roughly 80 percent of the total Mizo population, was uprooted and placed into such villages, often miles away from their homes, according to the former chief secretary of Assam, Vijendra Singh Jafa. While the army argued this approach was necessary for a successful counterinsurgency campaign among the Mizo population, Jafa stated, "The general humiliation, loss of freedom and of property, and, very often, injury and death involved in this process of so-called 'grouping of villages' . . . was tantamount to annihilation of reason and sensibility and certainly not the best policy to follow against our own ethnic minorities."[131] When villagers resisted relocation, the army resorted to the use of force and burning of villages. Ultimately, this program did little to halt the rebellion. By the summer of 1968, the Mizo insurgency occupied almost 20,000 Indian troops and showed little sign of letting up.[132]

Following Operation Jericho, China began to show interest in offering support to the MNF. Aware that the Nagas received help from abroad, Laldenga, who had maintained his headquarters within East Pakistan, met with Chinese officials for the first time at the country's consulate in Dhaka in 1968. The Chinese government soon provided his group with wireless transmitters, medicines, and 400,000 yuan. That same year, he made his first trip to China, though by air through East Pakistan rather than trekking across Burma as members of the Naga insurgency had done. He was accompanied by fellow Mizo leader Lalthangliana, who stayed in China until February 1969. Lalthangliana met with Zhou Enlai during his visit and was promised enough supplies to equip a standing army of three thousand men and financial aid adding up to 500,000 yuan. He also met with a number of Nagas who were training in China at the time, as their Chinese hosts were encouraging the different insurgent groups to collaborate with one another "for the purpose of dismembering India," according to Indian intelligence reports.[133] On February 15, 1969, the Indian government claimed that a meeting was held in the Chittagong Hill Tracts of East Pakistan with representatives from Pakistan and China to discuss collaboration between Mizo and Naga rebels and further establish East Pakistan as a center of intertribal coordination with Chinese support.[134]

In October 1970, Laldenga and his secretary, Zoramthanga, traveled again to Beijing and attended the Chinese National Day celebrations.[135] There, they met with Zhou Enlai, who promised that China would supply additional arms and economic assistance to Mizo insurgents.[136] Around this time, Pakistani officials were growing suspicious of the links between the Mizos and Chinese, recognizing as they did that assistance from Beijing was made in the name of Greater Mizoram, which included parts of East Pakistan.[137] After the 1971 war leading to Bangladeshi independence, however, the MNF lost their safe havens in erstwhile East Pakistan and came increasingly to rely on Chinese support. In 1972, they sent their first group of soldiers for training with the Chinese, thirty-eight fighters who reached China after traveling through northern Burma in early 1973. They were quickly followed by a second group of MNF fighters. In 1976, these fighters returned to India loaded with Chinese weaponry.

On January 21, 1972, the Mizo Hills District was redesignated the union territory of Mizoram as part of the North-Eastern Areas (Reorganisation) Act. The government also announced an amnesty for Mizo rebel fighters aimed at boosting support for a political solution to the violence. The insurgency gradually faded out during the 1970s, with the MNF unable to generate continued foreign support following the independence of Bangladesh and the gradual shift in Chinese foreign policy after Mao's death in 1976. On June 30, 1986, Laldenga signed a peace agreement with the Indian government. The following year, Mizoram was elevated to the status of a state, with Laldenga appointed as the head of the interim government and later becoming the state's first chief minister.

Within the former princely state of Manipur, armed groups similarly emerged in the 1960s to push for Manipuri independence. Following Manipur's accession and integration into the Indian Union following Partition, the territory was administered by the central government, becoming a union territory in 1956 and governed by a centrally appointed chief commissioner. The United National Liberation Front (UNLF) was formed in November 1964 under the leadership of Arambam Samarendra Singh with the goal of establishing an independent, socialist Manipur to liberate it from "Indian colonial occupation."[138] However, the group experienced considerable infighting, with a breakaway faction, the Revolutionary Government of Manipur (RGM), forming in December 1968 under the leadership of Oinam Sudhir Kumar. The UNLF was based in Sylhet, East Pakistan, and Pakistani authorities provided early support for the group, though this ended with the 1971 Bangladesh Liberation War. Several Manipuri militants were captured by the Indian Army when it took Dhaka in December 1971.

In December 1966, ex-Communists under the leadership of W. Tomba Singh formed another group in Manipur, the Meitei State Committee, which sought greater cooperation with the Nagas and the Chinese government. In January 1968, Naga insurgents planned to take a group of Meiteis, the dominant ethnic group in Manipur, to China for training and to receive Chinese arms. However, this plan was foiled in September 1968 when all the leaders of the committee were arrested, along with seventy volunteers, leading to its dissolution in February 1969. Following this, some Meitei leaders made an effort to create a unifying movement among the various anti-Indian insurgent groups in Manipur, Nagaland, Assam, and Tripura on the basis of common ethnic origin and shared objectives.[139] The Home Ministry argued that the strategy of coordinating the various insurgencies on the northeastern frontier, embracing the Meiteis, the Communist Naxalites within Assam, and various other tribal groups in rebellion, had been "outlined by China and endorsed by Pakistan."[140] In the late 1960s, according to a Home Ministry note, Phizo was also pushing the Nagas, along with the Meiteis, Mizos, Kukis, and insurgents in Tripura, to increase their violent activities as he felt such an intensification was necessary to assure the Chinese and Pakistani governments of the insurgents' ability to launch effective campaigns of resistance against the Indian government.[141]

The loss of East Pakistan as a base of support pushed the UNLF, like the MNF, to look to China for further assistance. Even before losing their Pakistani support, Singh and the Meitei State Committee had contacted the Chinese consulate in Dhaka. After Manipur was made a state in 1972 under the North-Eastern Areas (Reorganisation) Act and a general amnesty declared for fighters, the UNLF reestablished contact with China. In 1976, Nameirakpam Bisheswar Singh led a group of Manipuris who had fought with the RGM to Tibet through Nepal. One of them recalled,

> There were sixteen of us when we set out from Manipur in April 1976. Another three comrades followed a few months later. We stayed in Tibet for two years. The Chinese were quite strict during the first six months, but after a while we could move about more freely by bicycle and sometimes by car. We received political as well as military training, and the Chinese offered us weapons. But Bisheswar declined the offer. He gave me 6 rupees and 50 paise, saying: "This is the price of a big dagger. You must use that and capture arms from the Indians."[142]

They returned to India in 1978 and formed the People's Liberation Army, expressing their commitment to Maoism and opposition to the Communist Party of India and the Soviet Union. On their return, the new group began attacking both Indian security personnel and those they considered traitors in Manipur's Imphal Valley. The slogan "Outsiders, Leave Manipur" began popping up on walls.[143] They also formed a political arm in February 1979, the Revolutionary People's Front.

The fighting was bloody, all the more so because of its factional nature. In September 1980, the entirety of Manipur was declared a disturbed area under the Armed Forces (Special Powers) Act. Yet, by this time, with Deng Xiaoping transitioning China to a trade-based foreign policy and laying the foundations for his Good Neighbor Policy, Singh's People's Liberation Army in Manipur had difficulty generating Chinese support and instead fostered a relationship with the Kachin Independence Army in Burma, given the ethnic and linguistic links between communities in Manipur and the Kachin people. A number of Manipuris, armed with Chinese weapons, began training in camps in Burma near the Chinese border. Though China no longer offered direct support for insurgent groups in the Northeast, the groups were able to purchase weapons from Chinese intermediaries.[144]

Beginning in the 1970s, some within the Indian government were beginning to reassess the nature of the Chinese threat amid changes in Beijing's foreign policy. Despite the continued Chinese hostility toward India—a state of deadlock still prevailed along the disputed McMahon Line and China continued to provide low levels of assistance to antistate insurgencies in the Northeast—by 1970 the External Affairs Ministry saw the potential emergence of a new attitude among Chinese leaders toward India, citing improved personal relations between members of the Chinese Foreign Ministry and their Indian counterparts. Mao himself even informally suggested that "India and China should be friends again," with the Indian External Affairs Ministry deciding "to make a general friendly response to this friendly gesture of Mao." Under these guidelines, New Delhi authorized its embassy in Beijing to inform Chinese authorities that the Indian government was prepared to initiate a dialogue with the aim of "removing the state of tension and hostility overhanging the relations between the two countries."[145]

Nevertheless, China continued, at least symbolically, to assert its claims over territory within northeastern India. In October 1975, for example, the Indian delegation to the International Telecommunication Union's Administrative Radio Conference on LF/MF Broadcasting, held in Geneva, noted Chinese opposition to Indian requests for radio frequencies within Arunachal Pradesh, with China pushing back against Indian claims of sovereignty over the territory. The Indian representative at the conference observed, "My assessment is that China has raised [this] matter to enter its reservations on the record. Since we have stated to ITU that we require radio frequencies for such places as Tawang, Bomdila, Pasighat, etc. obviously China cannot allow international action without at least reserving its position on the territorial question."[146]

By 1975, officials in the External Affairs Ministry recognized that China's refusal to consider any overt steps to improve relations between the two countries or resolve the border dispute was connected to China's hostility to the Soviet Union, with whom India enjoyed warm relations. They believed that so long as Beijing's territorial and ideological dispute with the Soviet Union persisted, so, too, would tensions with India, and they communicated that this was an essentially irreconcilable problem with which India would have to live. Nevertheless, Indian officials did harbor some optimism on the prospects of at least maintaining a broadly peaceful status quo at the border. "There is no substitute for vigilance," a 1975 External Affairs Ministry note read, "but it would not be undue optimism to hope that the comparative tranquility of the last eight years would be the normal state on our northern border even though we should always be prepared for sudden incidents like the October ambush."[147] Recognizing that a precarious status quo, a cold peace, was settling in at the border, India continued its diplomatic efforts to normalize relations with China. The Chinese response to these Indian overtures for normalization, however, was "slow and lukewarm." Even though China had refrained from disrupting the status quo along the border through the mid-1970s, the Indian government warned that China had been active in "sowing distrust and dissention among the border states and people," with the Chinese government viewing interactions with India as a part of a power struggle with the Soviet Union.[148]

Despite China's general position remaining unchanged, the altered international political landscape at the time, including India's growing alliance with the Soviet Union, diminished the likelihood of Chinese military action across India's northern border. Therefore, the policy planning staff of India's External Affairs Ministry recognized their ability to act slowly on rapprochement and other sensitive matters such as Tibet. They also highlighted that it was possible to speed up efforts to consolidate Indian control in Arunachel Pradesh, Nagaland, and Mizo areas.[149] In 1972, the Lok Sabha passed the North-Eastern Areas (Reorganisation) Act, which expanded the political autonomy of the northeastern region in order to undercut support for insurgent groups and bolster negotiations for a political resolution to the insurgencies. This act created the states of Manipur, Tripura, and Meghalaya and established Mizoram and NEFA as union territories. In February 1987, NEFA was reconstituted as the state of Arunachal Pradesh (meaning "Land of the Rising Sun" in Sanskrit), covering approximately 83,000 square kilometers and with a population of 1.3 million people. The Chinese, however, continued to refer to the new Indian state as "southern Tibet."

Even with some improvements, the Indian embassy in Beijing noted continued obstacles to the establishment of normal relations, the most important of which was the lingering border dispute. Embassy officials also pointed to other points of tension that hampered India's efforts at normalization, included China's continued support for rebel elements in Nagaland and Mizoram throughout the 1970s.[150] In February 1979, Indian External Affairs Minister Atal Bihari Vajpayee of the Janata Party government (which had defeated Indira Gandhi in the elections of 1977, at the conclusion of her Emergency, the nearly two-year period when, citing internal and external threats, she had invoked emergency powers and suspended many of the country's democratic rights) visited China. Among the issues he intended to raise with Chinese officials in Beijing was the ample evidence of Chinese-supplied arms and training for insurgents in Nagaland, Mizoram, and Manipur. From the Indian perspective, this was irrefutable proof of Beijing's interference in India's internal affairs, which contrasted with India's "scrupulous policy in Tibet."[151] During the visit, according to an External Affairs secret memorandum, the external affairs minister stressed that, while there had been no recent instances of such support, the Indian government was "keen to bring home to the Chinese leaders that this sort of interference in our affairs would undermine the prospects of improvement of our relations." Chinese officials, for their part, assured the external affairs minister that "their connections with the Nagas etc., which arose out of certain historical reasons, were a thing of the past."[152] During a later conversation with a US diplomat, Chinese Foreign Ministry officials interpreted Indian diplomats' reactions to their assurances as relatively positive.[153] Even with such assurances that China no longer provided any direct aid to insurgents in northeastern India, Chinese arms continued to find their way into insurgent hands through the black market as insecurity within the northeastern periphery persisted in the coming decades.[154]

With China's shift toward economic modernization in the 1980s, followed by the end of the Cold War, the broader political pressures that strained the relationship between India and China subsided. After the collapse of the Soviet Union, Chinese concerns about being encircled by a Soviet-Indian military alliance were rendered moot. Indian Prime Minister Rajiv Gandhi's visit to Beijing in 1988 was a major step forward in improving Indian relations with China. Yet, following the visit of the Chinese foreign minister to India in March 1990, the External Affairs Ministry's joint secretary for East Asia, Vijay K. Nambiar, reported that there had been no discussions about formalizing peace along the border. While he acknowledged that both sides had reduced their military presence in the region, he denied that this was a signal of peaceful intentions on China's part, pointing to an improved road system within Tibet that allowed for more efficient troop movements, thus giving China the ability to reduce its overall troop presence at the border.[155] During the Indian foreign secretary's visit to Beijing in late October 1992, almost a year after the dissolution of the Soviet Union, India and China agreed in principle on actions to reduce border tensions at the local level, including mutual troop reductions, regular contact between local commanders, and advanced notice of large-scale military exercise or troop movements.[156] The following year, both countries signed the Agreement on the Maintenance of Peace and Tranquility along the LAC as a framework for resolving the border dispute and to formally reduce troop numbers at the border. Subsequently, China and India worked to find other areas in which they could improve their relationship, such as strengthening trade as both countries pursued economic liberalization and expansion. By 2002, trade between India and China had increased to $5 billion, up from essentially zero a decade prior.[157]

Despite attempts to prevent armed clashes and improve overall bilateral relations, underlying tensions remained, however, resulting in periodic skirmishes between soldiers stationed along the border. China continued to oppose the Indian government's expansion of its military and administrative presence along the LAC and pushed, at least rhetorically, its claims within the northeastern region. In October 2009, China conveyed its concerns that Indian Prime Minister Manmohan Singh's visit to Arunachal Pradesh, which they argued was a "disputed region," would trigger a disturbance.[158] China also expressed disapproval of the Indian government's decision to revoke Jammu and Kashmir's political autonomy in 2019 by abrogating article 370 of the Indian Constitution and creating two union territories, those of Jammu and Kashmir and Ladakh, under the direct administrative control of New Delhi. Beijing claimed that sections of Chinese-controlled territory were included in the new political units. A Chinese Foreign Ministry spokesperson stated, "China deplores and firmly opposed that. India unilaterally changes its domestic law and administrative divisions, challenging China's sovereignty and interests. This is awful and void, and this is not effective in any way and will not change the fact that the area is under China's actual control." The Indian External Affairs Ministry responded, "We do not expect other countries, including China, to comment on the matters which are internal to India, just as India refrains from commenting on internal issues of other countries."[159] Yet, despite these more recent tensions, through the 2000s and 2010s, Chinese and Indian troops in the region generally maintained the status quo and patrolled up to their claimed borders through common agreement.[160]

India and China have engaged in a two-faced geopolitical rivalry; on one side, both countries have struggled to assert their political and economic weight within the region, while on the other they have adapted to find an increasing number of areas of cooperation and economic engagement. While tensions and skirmishes persist over the disputed border, leaving it a flashpoint for broader political competition, the two governments continue to expand their economic relationship. In 2020, China surpassed the United States as India's largest trading partner, with bilateral trade between China and India reaching $77.7 billion. Chinese imports, particularly Chinese-made heavy machinery, telecom equipment, and home appliances, constituted $58.7 billion of the total trade between the two countries; the value of Chinese imports surpassed that of the United States and the United Arab Emirates (India's second- and third-largest trading partners, respectively) combined.[161] With the rise of China as a global power over the past twenty years, a number of countries are now competing for influence across Asia; in addition to China and India, this includes the United States and Russia, among others. The India-China relationship has thus evolved away from outright hostility and war to something else, especially as both countries become increasingly economically connected. Nevertheless, tensions have only increased in the wake of the June 2020 clashes along the disputed border, with Indian External Affairs Minister Subrahmanyam Jaishankar stressing in September 2021 that the withdrawal of troops from the border region was a necessary precursor to improving bilateral relations between Beijing and New Delhi.[162] "What seems likely" going forward, wrote former Indian National Security Advisor Shivshankar Menon in December 2020, "is antagonistic cooperation in a fragmented world."[163]

II

THE ALLY

4

"ALL-WEATHER ALLIES"

Pakistan and China

In recent years, the expression "all-weather allies" has frequently been used to describe the Pakistan-China relationship by those inside and outside of Pakistan to point to the close relationship the two countries have shared since the early months of Communist rule in China. On January 5, 1950, only two months after the Communist Party seized control in Beijing, Pakistan was one of the first states, and the first Muslim-majority state, to officially recognize the People's Republic of China. This relationship would only grow in the coming decades, while relations between India and China deteriorated. China, seeing Pakistan as an additional bulwark against India, has consistently been a primary source of military assistance for its South Asian ally, while Pakistan sought Chinese support as a security guarantee against the larger Indian military.

However, the interactions between the two countries have not always been as friendly as the moniker "all-weather allies" implies, with political watchers during the 1950s far from certain where the relationship would land. At the time, while India was publicly courting Chinese friendship, China's relationship with Pakistan was on rockier footing. As India and Pakistan jockeyed for territorial control in Kashmir, Pakistan simultaneously faced a territorial dispute with China, which claimed 3,400 square miles of territory from the former princely state of Hunza, which had been under the suzerainty of Jammu and Kashmir. The ruler of Hunza, known as the *mir*, who claimed descent from Alexander the Great, had traditionally recognized Chinese suzerainty up to the British annexation of the territory in 1891, prompting the *mir* at the time to flee to China.[1] In November 1947, Hunza's ruler signed the instrument of accession to join Pakistan. But tensions remained with China over the demarcation of the border, with General Ayub Khan declaring in 1959 that any intrusions into Pakistani territory by Chinese forces "would be repelled by Pakistan with all the force at her command."[2]

During the 1950s and 1960s, as Pakistan faced a severe military imbalance with India, the government sought increased support from abroad as a counterbalance to Indian military strength. At Partition, the division of the assets of the British Indian Army between India and Pakistan was based on the relative size of each country. Pakistan, the less populous of the two, received 8 artillery regiments against India's 40 and 8 infantry regiments against India's 21. With the division of the naval forces, Pakistan received 16 ships, while India received 32.[3] Further complicating this division of military assets, most of the British Indian military stores and ordnance factories were located within what was now Indian territory. By March 1948, Pakistan had received only 3 percent of its allotted military supplies. To address this imbalance, military spending and national defense comprised approximately 75 percent of the national budget in 1948, and would continue to comprise a majority of state spending in the coming years.[4] In the early 1950s, the US ambassador in Karachi observed that the necessity of procuring military assistance was so prominent in Pakistani leaders' minds that it was the "exclusive subject of intimate discussions in all quarters."[5]

Sensitive to their military disadvantage and the corresponding need for international assistance, Pakistani officials often played a rhetorical balancing act with their current interlocutor in mind. On May 17, 1956, for example, the Chinese embassy in Karachi reported that the Pakistani president had made "a very foolish statement" when he told reporters "that nothing in Pakistan's stance and actions with regard to Communist China implies a lessening of its friendship with the United States, or a move toward neutrality in international affairs," and that "the Pakistani prime minister, on his upcoming visit to China on 2 June, will not reduce [Pakistan's] obligations toward the United States or other Western countries."[6] However, the following month, the Chinese embassy also reported that all Pakistani officials who recently visited China spoke at length about their wonderful impressions there and the strength of Sino-Pakistani friendship. Pakistani political leaders, as the Chinese embassy observed, "all emphasize when [we] meet that China's progress is amazing, that it is the strongest nation in Asia, and that Chinese and Pakistanis should be friendlier."[7] In the late 1960s, the British High Commission in Islamabad noted that Pakistani officials in the Ministry of Foreign Affairs tended to downplay the importance of Chinese military and economic assistance in conversations with Western diplomats in order to allay the latter's fears.[8] Some Pakistani military officials were even outright dismissive of the Chinese military and their technical prowess in conversations with Western interlocutors. Talking with the British air adviser in March 1967, one senior officer in the Pakistan Air Force remarked that they had "hung so much more on these machines than the people we got them from ever thought of," in reference to the delivery of Chinese MiG-19 aircraft.[9] And yet, Pakistani officials frequently expressed admiration for China's social and economic development, especially in the agricultural sector, and hoped to learn technical lessons from China's experience.[10]

During these early years, Chinese officials likewise had hesitations about Pakistan's position on their southwestern flank, and especially the country's participation in US-led defense alliances, a cornerstone of the US containment strategy. During a January 5, 1956, conversation with Pakistani Prime Minister Chaudhry Muhammad Ali, Zhou Enlai expressed his apprehension with Pakistan joining the US-led Southeast Asia Treaty Organization in 1954 and signing the 1955 Baghdad Pact with the United States, reminding his Pakistani counterpart that China had sent two previous diplomatic notes expressing such disapproval. Zhou not only saw the agreement as opening Pakistan to American influence; it was also, to his mind, part of a US plan to surround China's borders and use Pakistan as a military base for potential military action against China. Prime Minister Ali assured the Chinese premier that the purpose of the assistance was to defend against India, and that, if the United States decided to launch a war of invasion against China, Pakistan would not participate, nor would it supply the United States with a military base. The Pakistani ambassador in Beijing, who was also present at the meeting, added that Pakistan pays close and frequent attention so as to protect itself from undue American influence.[11] In 1964, General Ayub Khan likewise told a Muslim League gathering that the Pakistani government would never accede to any US demands that might be viewed by China with hostility.[12] By the 1960s, this "all-weather" alliance appeared to be finding stronger footing.

PAKISTAN'S "ALL-WEATHER ALLY"

With the Indian and Chinese relationship devolving into open warfare in the early 1960s, Pakistan, under the urging of then–Foreign Minister Zulfiqar Ali Bhutto, used this as an opportunity to push for a rapprochement with China over their disputed territory and an expansion of their strategic relationship. In March 1963, Pakistani and Chinese officials met in Beijing to sign an agreement according to which China would cede around 1,942 square kilometers of territory to Pakistan and Pakistan would recognize Chinese claims to territory in northern Kashmir and Ladakh (thus infuriating India).[13] In August 1963, Pakistan and China also signed a civil air agreement, which came into force in June 1964, marking China's first significant breakthrough in the realm of international civil aviation since the Communist Party came to power. This gave China direct air access to South Asia, with some speculation by State Department officials at the time that the Chinese government would use Pakistan as a thoroughfare to extend its reach into Africa.[14]

Three years later, China and Pakistan began construction on the Karakoram Highway, with the section including the Khunjerab Pass lying astride their mountainous border and providing a passable land link between the two countries. Given the difficulty of the terrain, the Pakistan Army's Frontier Works Organization held responsibility for its construction with support from Chinese engineers. The road would come at the cost of hundreds of workers' lives lost in the mountainous terrain. Once opened in 1979, it was periodically closed due to winter weather and landslides. While Pakistani and Chinese officials recognized the trade potential for an overland route, the Karakoram Highway's economic value was questionable. Ultimately, the road's value was primarily strategic in nature, running as it did through Pakistani-controlled Kashmir, and serving as an early example of the two countries' willingness to support infrastructure development as a political tool. "President [Ayub Khan] was pleased to remark that in order of priority the first urgency of the highway was strategic and one of the immediate significance," a 1966 Pakistan government memo read. "The second objective was economic and commercial importance of the highway, i.e. the opening up of an inaccessible region and the establishment of a land route to the adjourning country. The second was a long-term objective, as of necessity, the full utilization would be over a period of time."[15]

Chinese officials at the time primarily viewed their relationship with Pakistan through the lens of the latter's rivalry with India, though they were quick to stress that the relationship had deeper foundations, previewing the public rhetoric that would define their interactions in later years. In February 1964, Chinese Foreign Minister Chen Yi told Bhutto, "by uniting to obstruct it, China and Pakistan can stop Indian expansion. Our friendship is not a measure of expedience. Just now you said, even if the Kashmir issue were to be resolved, our friendship would not be abandoned—I very much admire this. We are the same: even if the Taiwan issue were to be resolved, and if relations with India and the US were to be improved, and if we were to enter the United Nations, we could never forget about Pakistan."[16] Pakistani officials factored such support into their war planning as they prepared for Operation Gibraltar, Pakistan's military action against the Indian position in Kashmir in August 1965, with Chinese leaders even signaling that they would open up another front in the Himalayas to maintain pressure on India.[17] Ayub Khan's foreign policy adviser, Aziz Ahmed, remarked that "the most powerful factor in Pakistan's favour was its growing friendship with

China which would stop India from invading Pakistan even if it was driven out of Kashmir."[18]

Despite China's promises of support, the 1965 war with India resulted in Pakistan's swift military defeat after Indian armored divisions opened a second front in the broad plains of the Punjab around Lahore, a move that caught Pakistan by surprise and resulted in some of the largest tank battles since World War II. In December 1965, General Ayub visited Washington, DC, to discuss with President Lyndon Johnson how to move forward in resolving the tense situation in South Asia. During his visit, the US president flatly told General Ayub that the Pakistani government could not have a close relationship with China if it expected to have a close relationship with the United States. At the time, General Ayub stressed to Johnson that Pakistan remain committed to its alliance with the United States and the government had not entered any security arrangements with China.[19]

However, Pakistan emerged from the 1965 war in desperate need of international assistance to help rebuild its military forces. Its battlefield loses resulted in a reduced tank force, a loss of 10–15 percent of its aircraft, crippling shortages of spare parts, and overall shortages of ammunition and other needed equipment. Adding to Pakistan's challenges, the war resulted in a 20 percent deficit in Pakistan's national budget for the year.[20] As the Pakistani government worked to rearm its military, General Ayub told the US ambassador to Pakistan that he would take weapons "even from the devil himself."[21] Pakistan's chief of general staff, Major General Yaqub Khan, repeated this sentiment at a June 1968 dinner party with several European diplomats, bluntly stating that he would "sup with the Devil with a long spoon" if it led to the procurement of more armaments for the military.[22] The US government had suspended arms shipments to both India and Pakistan because of the 1965 conflict over fears of feeding an arms race in South Asia. Forced to look elsewhere as a result, Pakistan, rather than turning to the devil, approached China. Shortly after the 1965 Indo-Pakistani war, General Ayub hurriedly undertook a secret trip to Beijing to secure the support of the Chinese government, the first such visit by a Pakistani president.[23] In the late 1960s and 1970s, Chinese military and economic aid, largely in the form of low- or zero-interest loans, was increasingly directed toward non-Communist nations as pragmatic considerations for promoting Chinese influence abroad gradually replaced an ideologically informed foreign policy. The military aid provided to Pakistan would be the first such aid provided by China to a non-Communist country.

China soon stepped in to become Pakistan's primary supplier of military hardware, with Chinese arm shipments beginning to arrive in-country in February 1966. By August of that year, the Chinese government had shipped to Pakistan around a dozen IL-28 jet light bombers, 50 MiG-19 jet fighters, and approximately 100 T-34 and T-54 tanks, as well as artillery, small arms, and ammunition, with more deliveries still to be made.[24] By 1972, China's military assistance to Pakistan had grown to an estimated $200 million worth of equipment, with reports that the Chinese officials were not too worried about repayments from their South Asian ally. This included 165 MiG-19 jet fighters, 750 medium tanks, about 700 artillery pieces and antiaircraft guns, over 50,000 small arms, ammunition, communications and other support equipment, and spare parts—all of which accounted for around half of Pakistan's military strength.[25] At the time, the CIA warned that Pakistan's procurement of Chinese hardware would establish the country's long-term reliance on China as a source for replacement and spare parts; however, by the early 1980s, US diplomats in Islamabad doubted China's ability to provide more sophisticated military equipment and support.[26] In the 1960s, the State Department also recognized that, besides military aid, Chinese collaboration with Pakistan on a nuclear weapons program was a possibility, but US officials remained "unconvinced by the evidence thus far obtained."[27]

At a time of heightened tensions with India, senior Chinese officials hoped that military assistance to Pakistan would foster tensions between the two South Asian nations and force the Indian government to split its forces between two fronts. Chinese officials frequently parroted Pakistan's position toward the dispute over Jammu and Kashmir and Pakistani fears that India's aim was to dismember and reabsorb Pakistan, necessitating international support for Pakistan's position.[28] Pakistani officials, in turn, adopted some Chinese rhetoric in foreign policy discussions, such as reiterating the view that Taiwan was an inalienable part of the People's Republic of China.[29] Pakistan's enthusiasm for Chinese support was on full display during Chinese President Liu Shaoqi's visit to Lahore in February 1966, when he was greeted by throngs of cheering Pakistanis. The US consul general in Lahore reportedly remarked at the time, "Pakistan is lost."[30]

Many Pakistanis ultimately felt betrayed by the US government's suspension of military assistance at a time when they desperately needed it, a point that would be raised repeatedly with American interlocutors in the coming decades. Bhutto told the US ambassador, who delivered the news that military aid would no longer be forthcoming, that Pakistan, "cornered, deserted . . . had no alternative but [to] interpret US action as a punitive one assisting India, a non-aligned and treacherous country aggressing against [a] US ally."[31] On the other hand, China's continuing support through a very difficult decade helped to solidify its position as an all-weather ally in the minds of the Pakistani elite. Ahead of a March 1966 state visit to Pakistan by Chinese President Liu Shaoqi, Ayub tersely responded to the US ambassador's criticism of the visit by saying, "After all, [the Chinese] came to our aid with unconditional offers of assistance when our national existence was at stake. That our people cannot forget."[32]

Following India's military intervention in East Pakistan in 1971, China once again offered support to Pakistan, accusing the Indian government of launching a "large-scale war of aggression" with the backing of the Soviet Union for the purpose of dismembering Pakistan. Beijing promised to "firmly support the Pakistan government and people in their struggle against aggression, division and subversion: we not only are doing this politically, but will continue to give them material assistance."[33] However, China's offers of political and military support did not commit it to anything beyond the assistance it was already providing to Pakistan, even with Pakistani authorities previously requesting China to conduct large-scale military maneuvers along the Sino-Indian border to divide the attention of India's military. Further, China's offer was announced at around the same time as the surrender of Dhaka, exposing its reticence to take any further actions that would lead to military confrontations with India and risk an escalation of the war on its southern flank.[34] Nevertheless, such rhetoric helped to entrench in the minds of the Pakistani elite China's status as an "all-weather ally." Ambassador Ali Sarwar Naqvi, the executive director of the Center for International Strategic Studies in Islamabad, who represented Pakistan in several senior diplomatic postings, further explained, "The Chinese have been good friends because they have always extended us assistance and help and they never, never attempted to impose communism on Pakistan. I mean, they were friends in the fifties and sixties, when communism was at its height, but they accepted us, they accepted our system as it was. They did not want to meddle in our internal matters. And that we value immensely."[35]

In return for military assistance, Pakistan offered China access to US military hardware in its possession, even if doing so violated the terms of its acceptance. In July 1968, the CIA reported that Chinese technicians were granted access to a US-supplied F-104 aircraft at Pakistan's Sargodha Air Base. The Pakistanis also permitted the Chinese to collect F-104 spare parts, material samples, and even a complete jet engine, and bring them back to China for analysis.[36] In November 1982, after the United States restarted military aid following the Soviet invasion of Afghanistan, the departure of the first squadron of F-16s for delivery in Pakistan was delayed over the Department of Defense's concern that the Pakistani government would pass the fighter jets' ALR-69 radar technology to China. Pakistani President General Muhammad Zia-ul-Haqq, who had come to power in a 1977 military coup, maintained a firm position that he would not purchase the fighter aircraft without radar. On November 18, 1982, Secretary of State George Shultz asked Defense Secretary Caspar Weinberger to reconsider the Defense Department's opposition to this sale over concerns that this position could seriously damage the overall US-Pakistan relationship and cooperation across a wide range of issues.[37] The problem was resolved after General Zia signed a General Security of Military Information Agreement with the United States concerning the unauthorized transfer of US weapons and technology, paving the way for the delivery of the F-16s from Texas. However, the CIA assessed that there remained a risk that China would eventually gain access to any US arms provided to Pakistan, given the intimacy of Pakistan's military engagement with China.[38]

Besides military assistance, China and Pakistan expanded their trade links, including drastically increasing Pakistani raw exports to China. Pakistani exports to China grew from 10,482,000 rupees of trade goods in 1961–1962 to 180,658,000 in 1964–1965; Pakistani imports increased from 16,544,000 rupees to 96,810,000 rupees during the same period, with imports partly financed with a $60 million interest-free loan from the Chinese government. A regular shipping link was also opened by the two countries in April 1965.[39] Through the 1960s and 1970s, however, China primarily focused its assistance on bolstering Pakistan's military position through both military equipment and expanding its industrial base, as well as road construction. This included a $100 million credit for military assistance with $35 million allocated for expanding and modernizing military industrial facilities, such as an F-6 rebuild facility, a foundry-forge facility, a heavy machinery complex near Rawalpindi, a cement plant in Taxila, and an ordnance factory at Joydebpur in East Pakistan.[40] With India's first nuclear test in 1974, Bhutto, now serving as prime minister, scrambled to find increased conventional military assistance and expanded his efforts to procure nuclear technology, approaching not only China but also the United States, the United Kingdom, France, and the Soviet Union.[41] In June 1976, Pakistan reached an agreement with the Chinese government for support on developing nuclear fuel processing capabilities to aid its quest for a nuclear bomb.[42]

Despite their support for the Pakistani military, Chinese officials sent mixed messages regarding Pakistan's nuclear program. During the late 1970s, China denied having any involvement in Pakistan's nuclear weapons program on several occasions, with Chinese diplomats in South Asia informing their US counterparts that they disapproved of the project and had counseled Pakistan against pursuing it. In a January 1980 conversation in Beijing with US Secretary of Defense Harold Brown, Vice Premier Deng Xiaoping stated, "Pakistan has its own reasons for developing a nuclear program. We ourselves oppose this because we believe it meaningless to spend money on such a program." He also informed Secretary Brown that China welcomed the US decision to restart military and economic aid, which he hoped would satisfy Pakistan's perceived national defense needs.[43] In May 1979, however, a Chinese diplomat in Islamabad strongly defended Pakistan's right to produce a nuclear weapon. Following the Communist coup in Afghanistan, Chinese officials stated that they would not pressure Pakistan to give up its nuclear weapons program, and even encouraged the United States to overlook this and renew military aid. Vice Foreign Minister Zhang Wenjin and Vice Premier Deng expressed sympathy toward Pakistan's nuclear program in various conversations with American officials.[44] There was an understanding among Chinese officials that a Pakistani bomb would be primarily defensive in nature and a check on Indian hegemony in South Asia.[45] By the mid-1980s, US intelligence agencies assessed that China had provided technical support to Pakistan's nuclear program. It expanded from operational support of the KANUPP power reactor at Karachi to supporting fissile material production and nuclear device design with on-site Chinese technical assistance. These efforts would eventually culminate in Pakistan's first nuclear explosion in late May 1998 in Balochistan, a response to India's second nuclear test two weeks earlier.[46]

Yet, following Deng Xiaoping's economic reforms beginning in the 1980s, the Chinese government soon shifted away from its past role as a patron and model for global revolution toward more pragmatic moves both domestically and abroad to establish a more peaceful international environment in Asia to support rapid economic growth. At this time, Beijing set a goal of quadrupling its GDP by the year 2000, which necessitated a drastic expansion of the country's energy production.[47] China also worked to normalize relations with neighboring countries within Asia as a counter to what it saw as aggressive Soviet expansionism at the time, including strengthening relations with Japan, increasing contacts with South Korea, improving relations with India, diminishing fears among ASEAN countries of aggressive Chinese expansionism, and continuing its close relations with Pakistan.[48] In the October 1984 meeting of the Communist Party's Twelfth Central Committee, party leadership loosened controls on the economy and introduced price reforms that led to greater profits from international trade. At this time, the Chinese government pushed forward with its Open-Door policy to attract foreign investment, including by allowing additional port cities to engage in business with foreign investors and granting these cities more autonomy in decision-making. Through the 1990s, as the Chinese economy was liberalizing and Beijing was pushing for expanded economic integration into the regional and international economy, Pakistan's leaders, seeking international investors to help its stagnant economy, soon turned to their long-time ally and the opportunities offered by its dramatic economic shift.

GWADAR PORT AND THE CHINA-PAKISTAN ECONOMIC CORRIDOR

Throughout the 1990s, Pakistan faced increasing economic problems, which were further exacerbated by US sanctions introduced in October 1990 under the Pressler Amendment in response to Pakistan's continued pursuit of a nuclear weapons program, with the result that most US military and economic assistance to the country was suspended. Poverty levels in the country increased, especially in rural areas, with as many as one-third of the population classified as poor by the end of the decade. At the same time, the Pakistani government struggled with social service delivery. Education and public health indicators fell far below those of countries at comparable income levels. The percentage of Pakistan's population with access to sanitation at the time was 23 percent lower than peer countries, in addition to 42 percent lower health spending per capita and 24 percent higher illiteracy rates.[49] The restrictions on public service delivery and the lagging social indicators were connected to broader fiscal limitations. The government faced increasing debt service burdens from high rates of external borrowing during the 1980s and persistently high defense expenditures combined with an overall reduction in government revenue during the 1990s, with revenues falling from 17 percent of GDP in 1991 to 16 percent in

1998.[50] By 2000, Pakistan's fiscal deficit remained high at 5 percent of GDP, which the government financed with loans.[51]

Senior Pakistani officials understood that they needed to seek increased foreign support to foster economic growth and improve the government's fiscal health, especially by taking advantage of Pakistan's energy and natural resource reserves. Pakistani President Farooq Leghari noted in an April 9, 1994, meeting in Islamabad with US Deputy Secretary of State Strobe Talbott that Pakistan needed more foreign investment, particularly in the energy sector, and expressed his desire for the US private sector to take advantage of economic opportunities in Pakistan. Leghari added that in the areas of education, women's development, and health, Pakistan's social development was "very, very bad," and that many within Pakistan wanted to make increased strides in these areas. He also pressed for the United States to reverse its decision to block funding for a private power initiative and an agricultural survey. Talbot, however, demurred and claimed that financial cuts, not only for Pakistan but also for other US allies like Egypt and the Philippines, were necessary due to financial pressure resulting from the January 1994 earthquake in Northridge, California, which caused more than $60 billion in damages and economic losses—the costliest earthquake disaster in US history.[52] Two years later, it was China that provided $500 million in balance-of-payment support when the Pakistani government was on the verge of default.[53]

On October 12, 1999, General Pervez Musharraf, the Pakistan Army chief of staff, led a military coup overthrowing the civilian government and arresting Prime Minister Nawaz Sharif. Five days after taking power, Musharraf addressed the nation to explain his actions. He lamented that the country had descended to a point "where our economy has crumbled; our credibility is lost; state institutions lie demolished; provincial disharmony has caused cracks in the federation; and people who were once brothers are now at each other's throat." His actions, he said, were intended to save "the body—that is the nation—at the cost of losing a limb," and he assured the country that he did not intend to impose martial law as much as take what he called "another path towards democracy." To address these problems, Musharraf outlined a seven-point agenda for his military government:

- Rebuild national confidence and morale
- Strengthen federation, remove inter-provincial disharmony and restore national cohesion
- Revive economy and restore investor confidence
- Ensure law and order and dispense speedy justice
- Depoliticise state institutions
- Devolution of power to the grass-roots level; and lastly,
- Ensure swift and across the board accountability.[54]

Promising that his priority after seizing political power was the revival of Pakistan's "sick economy,"[55] Musharraf also sought to increase local and overseas investment in the Pakistan economy by doing the following:

- Rebuilding of investors' confidence through stability and consistency in economic policies, and economic security. The objective is to encourage local investors, overseas Pakistanis and foreign investors.
- Increase domestic savings
- Carry out pragmatic tax reforms
- Turn around the state enterprises towards profitability
- Boost agriculture and revive industry
- Strict austerity measures

Musharraf understood the importance of constructive foreign relations in turning around the economy. He thus promised, "We will maintain and further reinforce our traditional and time-tested friendship and co-operation with China." But, the new president added, "We attach the highest importance to our friendly relations with all major powers, especially the United States."[56]

On June 23, 2000, President Musharraf gave an address at the Pakistan Institute of International Relations in Karachi in which he further outlined five key factors of Pakistani foreign policy under his new government. These were the security interests of Pakistan ("priority one"); the economic interests of Pakistan ("gas—the resource of the twenty-first century"); taking into account the concerns of international power centers; safeguarding Pakistan's ideological interests (including by "preserving our Islamic identity"); and upholding the country's principles (i.e., continuing to stand up to India over the disputed territory of Kashmir). He further argued that the government's foreign policy actions should be guided by the desire to make Pakistan an economic hub for the region to drive economic growth, requiring a drastic expansion of the country's transportation and energy infrastructure. "God has given us a strategic location," he stated, arguing that regional countries like Qatar, Iran, and the Central Asian republics hoping to export their gas and oil to the markets of India and further east should use Pakistan as an economic trade route. "Inshallah," Musharraf stated, "Pakistan will also be a market someday." He then discussed the importance of nurturing Pakistan's major trade relations with the United States, the European Union, Japan, and Malaysia, and exploring new opportunities in Southeast Asia and Africa. Of course, he also highlighted the importance of Pakistan's relationship with China, particularly for defense production.[57]

At the time, the Pakistani public largely put their trust in China. Survey data showed that only 1 percent of Pakistanis viewed the United States as Pakistan's "best friend," with many feeling the sting of additional US sanctions following Pakistan's first nuclear weapons test in May 1998. On the other hand, 67 percent of surveyed individuals in 2001 and 74 percent in 2002 applied this moniker to China, the same result found in earlier polling. Similarly, 87 percent of Pakistanis in a 2001 survey felt confident that China could be trusted "to deal responsibly with problems in our region." Only 11 percent felt the same way about the United States—a notable change from the 25 percent of respondents who described a feeling of trust toward the United States in a similar poll conducted in 1998.[58]

Three months after seizing power in Islamabad, Musharraf traveled to China, his first visit to a non-Islamic country as Pakistan's ruler, to meet with Chinese Premier Zhu Rongji and strengthen the economic ties between the two countries. Upon arriving in Beijing, Musharraf declared China to be Pakistan's "most reliable and trusted friend." During his visit, he signed an agreement with the Chinese government to expand economic and technological cooperation between the two countries.[59] The Pakistanis perceived several advantages in approaching the Chinese for financial support. One senior Pakistani diplomat explained, "There was a willingness to do things for the sake of political relations—giving loans, we don't have to stand in line; expeditious processing, approvals, facilitation and so on. We could take advantage of the political relationship but then the commercial side has to work."[60] With plans for large "megaprojects" spurring economic growth a key pillar of Pakistan's economic strategy, an early effort of the Musharraf government was to attract Chinese support to develop the Gwadar Port in Balochistan, which would eventually become the centerpiece of the China–Pakistan Economic Corridor (CPEC).[61] He envisioned transforming the barren coastal area into a new Dubai that could foster broader economic growth in the country and regional connectivity for Pakistan.

Gwadar (meaning "door of wind" in Balochi) is a hammerhead-shaped peninsula strategically located on the western edge of Balochistan's Arabian coast, sitting only 72 kilometers from Iran and 180 nautical miles from the Strait of Hormuz, through which 40 percent of the global oil trade passes. Gwadar was originally within the former princely state of Kalat, whose ruler had signed the instrument of accession to join Pakistan in March 1948 after an unsuccessful bid to assert Kalat's independence after the British transfer of power in August 1947. In 1784, the khan of Kalat transferred the coastal area to the sultan of Muscat. By the early 1900s, the Gwadar region had a population of some five thousand people, with fishing the primary occupation of most residents. Yet, the hot and "sandy strip of flat country" remained isolated and inhospitable to outsiders. At the turn of the twentieth century, European telegraph officials "found the place so unhealthy that it had to be abandoned."[62]

In 1958, following unrest in the port city, Pakistan purchased Gwadar from the Sultanate of Muscat and Oman for 3 million pounds, as

Pakistani officials had already eyed its potential as a transportation hub that could rival Karachi. Even though the area was of strategic interest—not only to Pakistan but also to competing nations in the region—the Pakistani government experienced several false starts attempting to develop isolated Gwadar as a deepwater port. During a visit to the coastal Makran region of Balochistan in September 1973, amid ongoing conflicts with several Baloch political figures, Prime Minister Bhutto asserted that the region's warm coastal waters had been Pakistan's "since time immemorial and no one would be allowed to pawn them away for personal advantage."[63] Yet, he failed to secure American support for developing the port, with US officials fearing that such a project would antagonize Pakistan's neighbors, while adding little to US strategic interests.[64] At the time, the British Foreign Office recognized that the development of a deepwater port for a naval base at Gwadar would require a massive investment and therefore seemed unlikely to make meaningful headway anytime soon.[65]

Successive governments in Islamabad maintained their interest in developing a strategic port at Gwadar. In 1993, the Pakistani government introduced plans for a British consortium to transform the coastal village into a commercial center, seeking to take advantage of economic opportunities that sprang up with the fall of the Soviet Union. These plans never got off the ground, however, due to political and financial difficulties.[66] Despite these continued efforts, Gwadar and the surrounding region remained severely underdeveloped with limited infrastructure throughout this period. By the 1980s, the region, comprising some 470 miles of coastline, had only 5 miles of paved roads, connecting the commissioner's house to a small airport.[67] A February 1980 *Washington Post* article referred to Gwadar as "a barren patch of earth and sand" that "does not have much to offer visitors."[68]

It was Chinese technical assistance and financing that finally put shovel to dirt. In 2001, China agreed to provide $198 million of the $248 million required to construct the port. The Chinese government at first saw Gwadar as a marginal project, with Chinese officials expressing their skepticism that Musharraf's ambitious plans for the port city would in the end prove tenable.[69] Despite this skepticism, China Harbour

Engineering Company took responsibility for the first phase of construction: three multipurpose ship berths, a service berth, dredging a deepwater channel, and several port facilities along with connecting roads. In addition, the Pakistani military's Frontier Works Organization, originally established to construct the Karakoram Highway, built a road link with Karachi, the Makran Coastal Highway, at a cost of $200 million.[70] The first phase of the Gwadar Port was completed in 2006.

The second phase of construction was contracted to the Port of Singapore Authority (PSA), with a total estimated cost of between $600 million and $1 billion. This phase consisted of the management and expansion of the port's facilities and operations, including constructing four container berths, a bulk cargo terminal, two oil terminals, a roll-on/roll-off terminal, and a grain terminal, as well as road links with Quetta and Sindh. The development of the second phase for the Gwadar Port slowed after Musharraf's resignation in 2008, and few of the original plans for that stage of construction ultimately materialized. The upshot of failing to finish the necessary connecting infrastructure to the port was that Gwadar was left standing "virtually isolated."[71] Blame aplenty was spread around; some held the Pakistan Navy accountable for refusing to hand over 584 acres of land to port operations, while others pointed at the PSA. In February 2013, after the PSA pulled out of the contract following a lengthy court battle, the China Overseas Port Holdings Company took over management of the port, and, two years later, the Chinese company took control of Gwadar's free trade zone. Even Pakistani businesses wishing to establish a presence in Gwadar were required to approach a Chinese manager to do so.[72]

The development of the Gwadar Port laid the foundation for broader economic cooperation between China and Pakistan in the coming years. In late April 2006, President Musharraf addressed a group of Chinese leaders from both the private and public sectors at the Pakistan-China Energy Forum in Islamabad and called for greater economic cooperation between the two countries. "When Karakoram Highway was built, the world called it the eighth wonder," Musharraf announced. "We can create the ninth and tenth wonders by establishing energy pipelines and railway linkages between the two fast growing economies." He continued, "Pakistan offers an ideal environment for Chinese investors as our economy is on the path of high economic growth. We particularly look forward to materialising cooperation in the energy sector where establishment of oil refineries, oil storage facilities and gas pipelines stand out. . . . Similarly, the Chinese investors can expand their business by establishing their export-oriented concerns in Pakistan as we are located at the heart of South Asia, Central Asia, the Gulf and China." Moreover, he promised Pakistani government support to facilitate Chinese investment in Pakistan's various industrial sectors.[73] Shortly after his July 2013 visit to Beijing and just before the Belt and Road Initiative (BRI) was unveiled in Kazakhstan, Pakistani Prime Minister Nawaz Sharif, elected to office again in June 2013, announced he was setting up a China cell within the Prime Minister's Office to oversee all Chinese-backed infrastructure projects within Pakistan and expedite their development.[74]

Even after Musharraf departed the political scene in 2008, the longstanding dominant role of the military in Pakistan's domestic politics and its influence over the civilian government, along with perceptions that China's support remained steady when other countries had wavered, has helped instill a broad-based consensus in favor of strengthening relations with China, especially under the umbrella of CPEC.[75] A senior Pakistani official remarked, "Pakistan-China relations is above personalities. All the major political parties in Pakistan have repeatedly expressed their consensus to increasingly develop and enhance Pak-China ties."[76] As a result, Pakistani leaders have consistently looked to China for financial support. In 2008, with Pakistan facing the possibility of defaulting on oil and food payments as currency reserves dwindled, Musharraf's successor as president, Asif Ali Zardari, traveled to Beijing seeking a cash infusion of between $3 and $4 billion to shore up Pakistan's economy before turning to the International Monetary Fund, which would require spending cuts and tax increases in return for financial assistance. However, Zardari faced a chilly reception in China, where his hosts were displeased that his first trip abroad had not been to Beijing and suspicious of the close Western ties of his late wife,

Benazir Bhutto, who had served as the country's first female prime minister in the 1990s and had been assassinated in 2007. With Chinese leaders aghast at the exorbitant amount he was requesting, Chinese aid in this instance was not forthcoming.[77] Nevertheless, China increasingly became a lender of last resort for Pakistan. In November 2019, the Pakistani minister for planning, Asad Umar, remarked, "As far as the money taken from China is concerned, it was taken at such a time when our trade deficit was dangerously high and our reserves were falling. We were unable to easily procure loans from other sources. This was the hallmark of China's friendship with Pakistan that in such a time of crisis, it provided us loans from its commercial banks."[78]

As US assistance declined following its peak in 2010 in the context of the US war in neighboring Afghanistan and Pakistan's cooperation with the global war on terror, China's military and economic influence only rose further, with the country becoming Pakistan's largest bilateral trading partner, largest source of foreign direct investment (FDI), and top arms supplier. In November 2006, China and Pakistan concluded a free trade agreement, which went into effect the following year and helped to strengthen the economic relationship between the two countries. China's FDI in Pakistan increased from $2.6 million in 2006 to $718 million in 2007, comprising 12.85 percent of the total FDI in Pakistan. By 2017, Chinese FDI in Pakistan grew to $1.4 billion, or 55.6 percent of the total.[79] However, this has largely been a one-way street. By 2019, 87 percent of trade between the two countries consisted of Chinese exports to Pakistan.[80]

The growth in Chinese investment in Pakistan was increasingly directed toward expansion of the country's infrastructure, such as roads, power plants, and gas lines. In April 2015, Chinese President Xi Jinping traveled to Pakistan to sign several agreements formally establishing CPEC, the flagship project of the BRI, but based around several existing projects already launched within Pakistan. Initially, CPEC's fundamental purpose was to be a transportation corridor connecting Kashgar in China's western Xinjiang Province with Gwadar Port on Balochistan's coast, giving China direct access to a deepwater port on the Arabian Sea. However, it quickly grew in scope and ambition, encompassing a wide range of development projects with the aim of connecting the Chinese and Pakistani economies. China's foreign minister at the time, Wang Yi, stated, "If One Belt One Road is like a symphony involving and benefitting every country, then construction of the China-Pakistan Economic Corridor is the sweet melody of the symphony's first movement." This agreement helped to cement China and Pakistan's "all-weather strategic cooperative partnership." With CPEC intended to link markets in China, Central Asia, and South Asia, Pakistan's planning minister, Ahsan Iqbal, added, "If we become the bridge between these three engines of growth, we will be able to carve out a large economic bloc of about 3 billion living in this part of the world . . . nearly half the planet."[81] The Chinese government hoped to use its experience with developing CPEC to promote the BRI in other countries.[82]

That same year, Pakistan's Ministry of Planning, Development, and Reform released a report, *Ascending the Saga of National Progress*, portraying CPEC as a "fate-changer for Pakistan" through a "comprehensive package of cooperative initiatives and projects" covering a variety of key areas such as an expansion of the country's information and network infrastructure, energy projects, industries and industrial parks, agricultural development, poverty alleviation, tourism, financial cooperation, and further developing Pakistan's municipal infrastructure, education, and public health.[83] CPEC's Long Term Plan, agreed to by both Pakistani and Chinese governments in November 2017, outlined seven key areas of cooperation: connectivity, energy-related fields, trade and industrial parks, agricultural development and poverty alleviation, tourism, those concerning people's livelihoods and nongovernmental exchanges, and finance.[84] To begin with, the plan argued that expanding transportation infrastructure, such as road networks, railways, ports, and airports, would serve as the foundation for the expansion of CPEC and its accompanying development projects.[85] Within Balochistan, this aspect of the plan would focus on Gwadar, including the construction and development of Gwadar city and its port facilities, an expanded transport system, accelerating the construction of Gwadar's East Bay Expressway and a new international airport, and promoting the competitiveness of Gwadar's free trade zone. In addition, the plan called for expanding the energy infrastructure along the CPEC route, including the development and utilization of oil, gas, and coal resources within Pakistan, constructing thermal power, hydropower, coal gasification and renewable electricity facilities, and supporting power transmission networks to enhance power transmission and supply reliability.[86] The plan also outlined financing mechanisms for expanding the number of projects along the CPEC route, including via the use of government funds, indirect financing of financial institutions such as the Silk Road Fund and the China-Eurasia Economic Cooperation Fund, encouragement of Chinese enterprises and the private sector to make direct investment in CPEC projects, and China's support for Pakistani cooperation with the Asian Infrastructure Investment Bank and other international financial institutions within China.[87]

CPEC's anchor in Balochistan would be Gwadar Port, with more than half of the corridor's projects in the province taking place in the Gwadar area. In November 2016, Prime Minister Sharif presided over the opening of Gwadar Port operations, having transferred control of the 2,281-acre Gwadar free trade zone to the Chinese Overseas Ports Holding Company the previous year under a forty-three-year lease.[88] The opening ceremony coincided with the arrival of an overland trade convoy that departed the city of Kashgar in western China on October 29 and reached Gwadar on November 12, the first such trade convoy traveling along this route. Sharif referred to its arrival as a "watershed event." China's ambassador to Pakistan at the time, Sun Weidong, told the gathered VIPs, "It proves the connectivity of the local roads and the realization of the concept of one corridor with multiple passages." Sharif added, "The newly-constructed roads in Balochistan have opened up new areas that were inaccessible and deprived of development . . . and have brought peace to a volatile region."[89]

Pakistani officials saw the regional connectivity brought by CPEC as creating opportunities to exploit the country's natural resources and supporting domestic markets, especially in underdeveloped regions, and thereby allow Pakistan to grow into a "tiger of Asia."[90] However, the route CPEC would take through Pakistan was not a settled issue at the time, and debates quickly emerged over which route it should follow between

Kashgar and Gwadar. Criticism was mounting, especially from the political opposition, that CPEC would likely favor the eastern but longer route through the Punjab, which already had established infrastructure and transportation networks and served key constituencies of the Punjabi-dominated Pakistan Muslim League-Nawaz government in power at the time, at the expense of the western route through Balochistan. Indeed, a number of the early CPEC projects completed were located in the Punjab and Sindh.[91]

However, several Pakistani officials pushed for the western route through Balochistan, hoping that it would spur development in the underdeveloped periphery. In 2015, Imran Khan, the cricket superstar turned politician who was head of the opposition Pakistan Tehreek-e-Insaf (PTI) party, stated that Pakistan needed to build "a shorter and better route of the CPEC instead of opting for the eastern route, which will create resentment in other provinces against the Punjab."[92] Dr. Ishrat Husain, the former governor of the State Bank of Pakistan, argued,

> The Western route would open up the backward districts of Balochistan and Southern KP [Khyber Pakhtunkhwa] and integrate them with the national markets. The communities living along the route would be able to produce and sell their mining, livestock and poultry, horticulture, fisheries output to a much larger segment of consumers. Their transportation costs would become lower, the proportion of perishables and waste would go down, cool chains and warehousing would become available and processing would become possible in the adjoining Industrial zones. . . . Fibre optic network would allow the citizens of these deprived districts access to latest 3G and 4G broadband internet connections.[93]

Moreover, with many Pakistani officials hoping CPEC would be the answer to the country's energy crisis, Chinese-led energy projects along the western route, which could take advantage of Balochistan's many natural resources, were seen to be a key part of the corridor's success. However, continued insecurity in Balochistan would become a major hurdle to the expansion of CPEC projects within the periphery.

Nevertheless, Nawaz Sharif's government, which saw infrastructure and development projects as political tools to generate support, saw CPEC as essentially a panacea for many of the country's economic and political problems as it struggled with low foreign investment, continued insecurity, and endemic corruption, all of which scared away potential investors. Minister Iqbal stated, "No one wanted to invest here—the Chinese took a chance."[94] The original estimate for CPEC's total cost added up to $46 billion. By 2020, this figure had ballooned to $87 billion, two-thirds of which was directed toward the energy sector as Pakistan faced an energy deficit of approximately 3,000 megawatts of generating capacity. In early 2020, however, only 32 of the 122 announced projects, worth an estimated $20 billion, had been completed.[95] By this point in time, Chinese-held loans comprised 24.3 percent of Pakistan's total public debt burden, with CPEC-related projects making up 6.6 percent of that figure.[96]

Following the PTI's July 2018 electoral victory and its subsequent formation of a government under Prime Minister Imran Khan, public enthusiasm among Chinese and Pakistani officials for CPEC's potential did not wane. Khan told the Chinese ambassador in Islamabad that, after he assumed office and his party gained control of the government, he would "fully cooperate with China and promote the persistent development and deepening of . . . bilateral relations," with the Chinese government immediately making a $2 billion credit line available to Pakistan.[97] During Khan's November 2018 visit to Beijing, a joint statement from the Pakistani and Chinese governments "reaffirmed their complete consensus on the future trajectory of the CPEC . . . [as well as] their commitment to CPEC and agreed that it was a win-win enterprise for [the] entire region and would bring regional prosperity and development through enhanced connectivity." Regarding Gwadar, China and Pakistan recognized its significance as the central pillar of CPEC and agreed to speed up development of the port and its auxiliary projects. The joint statement further pledged, "Both sides dismissed the growing negative propaganda against CPEC and express [their] determination to safeguard the CPEC projects from all threats. Pakistan recognized the immense contribution of the Chinese personnel working on various economic projects in Pakistan. The Chinese side expressed its appreciation for the measures taken for the security of Chinese personnel and projects in Pakistan."[98]

Speaking at an international security conference at the Marriot Hotel in Islamabad the following month, Chinese Ambassador Yao Jing echoed these sentiments about CPEC's economic potential and the bonhomie between China and Pakistan. In his remarks, he stressed that the BRI was an economic initiative based on the "principle of mutual consultation and mutual sharing," with CPEC as its "leading project . . . decided by consultation between [the] Chinese and Pakistani governments." He described China as "willing to be a reliable partner in development." This was a "new trend in state-to-state relations," he stressed to the audience, focused on "dialogue, political negotiations, and communication." The Chinese ambassador added that China and Pakistan also share "common ground" in dealing with security challenges and development and can work together to address various security issues. He recognized that security is a basic need for CPEC's success and praised Pakistan's effort in providing security for the projects. He concluded by highlighting that China and Pakistan have a "common history" related to the Silk Road dating back two thousand years and "will be neighbor's forever." Ambassador Jing's remarks were followed by those of the conference's chief guest, Pakistani Foreign Secretary Tehmina Janjua. She referred to China as "one of our closest friends" and a partner "with whom we discuss everything and come to consensus on almost everything." Secretary Janjua stated that the two countries have a "shared future" marked by "shared prosperity." She hoped that with CPEC, Pakistan would "become a center of global economics." Speaking the following day, then–President of Azad Kashmir Masood Khan (who was later appointed Pakistani ambassador to the United States) called CPEC a "catalyst" for Pakistan's economic development, while also recognizing that it is not a "panacea." He stressed that the absolute priority for Pakistan should be its economy.[99]

Many CPEC supporters within Pakistan have highlighted the corridor's potential to bolster overall economic growth in the country. One Karachi businessman called CPEC a "win-win" providing "much-needed project financing lines to make up for its infrastructure shortages" and attracting additional foreign investment in Pakistan.[100] Pakistani journalist Imtiaz Gul explained the benefit of Pakistan's relationship with China through the framework of its then declining relationship with the United States. "Obviously Pakistan's reliance on China has increased," he stated. "And it has, I think, given Pakistan greater strength and confidence. And . . . convinced Pakistan that our relationship with the United States will remain transitory, particularly after its tilt toward India. . . . So we needed a shoulder, Pakistan needed a shoulder, and that shoulder is China. And perhaps to the good luck of Pakistan, China had been long thinking about Gwadar and this corridor."[101] Even some outside commentators were caught up in the enthusiasm over CPEC's potential to promote long-term stability and economic growth in Pakistan. In 2019, American journalist Robert Kaplan wrote, "Nothing since independence in 1947 has [had greater] potential to help stabilize Pakistan—calming its frontier insurgencies—than the completion of this project." He also noted that "nothing would do more to firm up China's domination of its own steppe-land periphery."[102] In May 2018, Moody's Investors Service maintained Pakistan's annual credit rating as B3, or stable, meaning that the country's economy is speculative for investors in earning return on investments with high credit risk but with a low likelihood of rating change over the medium term. Nevertheless, Moody's pointed out in its announcement that "there is potential for a further strengthening in Pakistan's growth beyond Moody's current expectations, because successful implementation of CPEC can transform the Pakistani economy by removing infrastructure bottlenecks and stimulating both foreign and domestic investment."[103] Many Pakistanis, as one journalist noted, have "unrealistic expectations" of China, believing that increased Chinese investment in Pakistan will fix everything. This view, he stated, is "unrealistically hopeful."[104]

Not all within Pakistan have been convinced of CPEC's economic promise, however. Some Pakistanis see CPEC-related infrastructure projects as simply vehicles for loading Pakistan with additional debt, with China at times demanding a risk premium and high returns on equity. Researchers at the College of William and Mary noted that Chinese loans to Pakistan have typically averaged a 3.76 percent interest rate, with a maturity period of 13.2 years and a grace period of 4.3 years. On the other hand, loans from lenders within the OECD Development Assistance Committee, such as France or Germany, typically have a 1.1% interest rate and a repayment period of 28 years. However, for many of China's overseas loans, their terms and payment obligations are frequently undisclosed, heightening the possibility of the recipients of the loans falling into a debt trap and potentially forcing them to relinquish key assets to the Chinese government.[105]

CPEC's critics within Pakistan have also noted the lack of transparency for the various projects and agreement between the governments. In December 2015, the governor of the State Bank of Pakistan, Ashraf Mahmood Wathra, stated, "I don't know out of the $46 billion how much is debt, how much is equity and how much is in kind."[106] The Chinese embassy in Islamabad has even reportedly pressured the Pakistani government to keep CPEC deals a secret, promising bilateral loans to give Pakistan's finances a boost in return.[107] "We still know very little about CPEC," journalist Khurram Hussain stated in 2017. "The material that would tell us more is still vigorously concealed."[108] Moreover, the management of CPEC has been highly centralized within Islamabad, adding to the lack of transparency. This was influenced by several factors, including the Chinese officials' preference for government-to-government engagement and a centralized decision-making process, which they saw as a more effective approach rather than dealing with provincial politics or other economic actors.[109] Beginning in 2017, there was a push within provincial governments for greater involvement in the decision-making process around CPEC, especially over concerns at the time that Prime Minister Sharif sought to extract whatever political benefit could be gained by supporting CPEC's construction, and that any scrutiny of the development projects would reveal the "hollowness of overblown claims."[110] Additionally, as a Pakistani official explained, "The pressure from the Chinese side to move quickly did not allow the federal government time to fully integrate the provinces initially."[111] Referring to such concerns, a Pakistani senator remarked that "another East India Company is in the offing."[112]

Others within Pakistan also pointed to the danger that China poses to the country's fragile democratic institutions, particularly as Chinese officials have demonstrated their preference for working with a highly centralized governing authority. Muhammad Amir Rana, the director of the Pak Institute of Peace Studies in Islamabad, referred to the impact on democracy as the "dark side" of the Chinese relationship, particular with China preferring stability over democracy, with little interest in the protection of political and civil rights. He further observed, "With China, we can't demand. Even, we can't negotiate or renegotiate our partnership with China. Our relationship is somehow different. With the United States, we can demand equality. But with China we cannot. And China has broader designs."[113] Yet, as Pakistan and China continued to develop and expand their plans for CPEC, they would come to face the most stringent opposition in Pakistan's western periphery.

5

CPEC AND THE BALOCH INSURGENCY

In early 1962, President John F. Kennedy dispatched Henry Kissinger, then serving as a consultant to the National Security Council, on a fact-finding trip to Pakistan. It was a period of high tension between the United States and the Soviet Union. Making the politics of the region even more complicated, the Soviet Union and China were undergoing an ideological and political split, with the upshot that the Chinese government was becoming increasingly expansionist and aggressive and would soon launch a military invasion into northeastern India. Amid these geopolitical tensions, Pakistan was a key treaty partner for the United States; the South Asian country was a member of both the Central Treaty Organization and the Southeast Asia Treaty Organization at the time. During his visit, Kissinger engaged with Pakistan's military leaders, discussing their readiness and broader strategic issues in the region. Despite Kissinger's best efforts to evade the press, Pakistani journalists hounded him for his views on several sensitive issues facing the country.[1] One local reporter pressed him for the US position on the recent insurgency that had broken out in Pakistan's western province of Balochistan. An exasperated Kissinger famously responded, "I wouldn't recognize the Balochistan problem if it hit me in the face."[2] Kissinger's display of ignorance vis-à-vis Pakistan's largest province by territory and its long-standing political problems echoes a common theme among foreign observers, and even among some Pakistanis themselves. A 2014 *BBC Urdu* report featured residents of Punjab's capital city of Lahore who were not only unfamiliar with Balochistan's history and culture, beyond crude and often inaccurate stereotypes, but could not name a single city located in the province.[3]

This sparsely populated province is Pakistan's largest geographically, comprising 44 percent of the country's total territory, but possesses the smallest population at only 12.3 million people, or approximately 5.7 percent of the total population of Pakistan (almost a quarter of Balochistan's population resides in the capital city of Quetta). With a lengthy border with Afghanistan and Iran, an Arabian coast eyed by global powers, and vast mineral, oil, and gas deposits, Balochistan has long been viewed by the Pakistani government through a strategic lens. Akbar Ahmed, a former senior member of the Civil Service of Pakistan who served consecutively as commissioner for three of Balochistan's divisions (Quetta, Sibi, and Makran) during the 1980s, explained,

> The problem for Pakistan is that not only is Balochistan poorly understood but the central structural conundrum in the relationship remains irresolvable: while Balochistan has a population of some 12 million people of the 210 million Pakistanis, its area comprises almost 50% of the land mass. Besides, Balochistan has rich, untapped mineral, oil and gas deposits. It also has a large coast, which gives it access to the sealanes of the Persian Gulf, and has long borders with both Iran and Afghanistan, placing it in one of the most sensitive geopolitical regions of Asia. It is quite clear that while Pakistan will find it difficult to survive without Balochistan, Balochistan could easily survive without Pakistan.[4]

This tension between the central government and its western periphery has plagued Pakistan since the earliest days of independence and has only been exacerbated by Baloch grievances over alleged political repression and economic exploitation. Beginning in August 1947, the newly established Pakistani government faced the challenge of integrating a plethora ethnicities and cultures into a single nation that had no historical territory, unifying traditions, or other historical basis

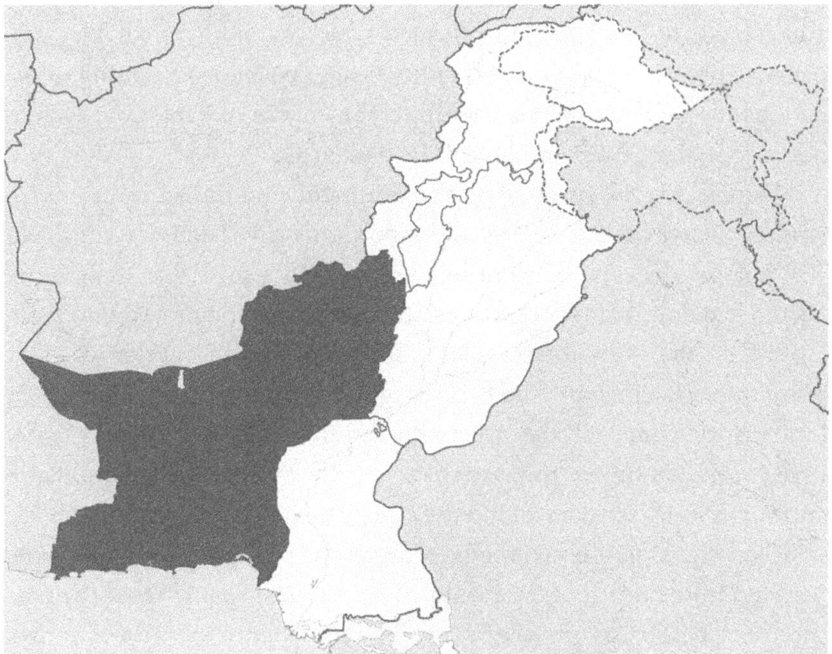

FIGURE 5.1 Pakistan's Balochistan Province. (Courtesy of Wikimedia Commons, CC BY-SA 3.0.)

beyond those of the Islamic faith to draw upon to help unify the disparate social groups within its borders, haphazardly drawn by Sir Cyril Radcliffe around the Muslim-majority areas of British India. What emerged was a state in two parts (West Pakistan and East Pakistan) with thirteen hundred miles and a rival state dividing them. Pakistan's founding father, Muhammad Ali Jinnah, and other leading Pakistani officials understood the importance of forging a new national identity in the face of intersecting domestic and international forces that could tear the new country apart. Hostile neighbors could exploit internal dissent to weaken the country. The centralization of the Pakistani state was thus driven by the necessity of forming a strong and unified state to simultaneously confront external threats, with the burgeoning rivalry with India looming large in leaders' minds, and internal divisions among the new country's five main ethnic groups at the time, which could bolster separatism within Pakistan. In April 1979, the British ambassador to Pakistan, John Bushell, observed in his valedictory despatch, "For Pakistan, internal fragility is aggravated by alarming external changes, for the most part still in the course of evolution. Neighbours look dangerous or liable to be dangerous."[5]

Historically, the reach of any government into Balochistan's harsh landscape, whose arid deserts and mountains have been described as a veritable moonscape, was limited, leaving space for tribal leaders and customs to dominate for centuries.[6] British forces first moved into Balochistan in the 1830s to secure the Bolan Pass as an alternative entry point into Afghanistan. The British signed a treaty with the khan of the local princely state of Kalat, eventually installing a British-friendly leader in 1840 and stationing troops in the state. However, the British military's entry into Kalat sparked an intense conflict with the independent Bugti tribe on the state's eastern edge. The fighting lasted until 1847 and resulted in the death of the local British political agent.[7] Over the next three decades, tribal unrest and rebellion persisted as local Baloch tribal leaders, known as sardars, opposed the British-backed khans, with the British periodically supporting and encouraging the centralization of the khans' power to establish control over the region's tribes. The British government's own efforts to pacify the area proved to be futile, with punitive military actions having little lasting impact on tribal raiding into British-held territory. Balochistan's frontier remained a terra incognita from the perspective of colonial officials in Calcutta, with the British government having no official relations with the frontier tribes until 1867.[8]

It was not until December 8, 1876, that Robert Sandeman, on behalf of the British government, signed a new treaty with the khan of Kalat officially bringing the princely state and the broader Baloch region firmly within the British political sphere. The purpose of the treaty was to ensure security on the frontier and protect trade routes with Afghanistan.[9] Ultimately, Kalat's primary value to the colonial government was as a buffer state in support of the British forward policy of frontier defense, as London feared that Balochistan could provide the competing Russian Empire a more accessible route into India. Following the signing of the 1876 treaty, British officials argued for the necessity of their presence to ensure peace between the khan and the sardars, whose status was also recognized under the new treaty, and bring a halt to tribal raiding into the Punjab, particularly the "troublesome" Marri and Bugti, over whom "no Khan has ever been able to exercise any really effective control," without resorting to costly military expeditions. "The direct interference of the British Government, acting as a paramount power," Sandeman stated, "is absolutely necessary, and must be maintained" as this would provide the British government a strategic advantage in case of future action in Afghanistan.[10] In early 1877, Lord Lytton appointed Sandeman the agent to the governor-general in the Balochistan Agency, based in Quetta, after which Sandeman undertook a concerted effort to slowly expand British reach into the various unadministered tribal regions of Balochistan.

Following the demarcation of the border with Afghanistan in 1893, known as the Durand Line after British India's foreign secretary, Mortimer Durand, Balochistan became an administrative mix of the princely state of Kalat and its feudal territories; areas leased by the British government from the khan of Kalat, including the Quetta, Bolan, and Chagai Agencies; various tribal areas; and British-ruled Balochistan, consisting of areas granted to the British from Afghanistan under the 1879 Treaty of Gandamak signed during the Second Anglo-Afghan War. The Marri and Bugti tribes, with their history of raiding and tribal resistance, remained of particular concern for British authorities as the primary source of unrest among the Baloch.[11] These two tribal groups resided within areas only indirectly governed by British authorities, with British political officers on the frontier observing into the 1920s that the government exercised little interference in the internal affairs of the tribes, which were managed by their own leaders.[12] This on-the-ground reality limited the influence of local British political officers. An 1880 report by Sandeman on the two tribes observed, "The only title to independence they possess is like that of the pirate or highway robber, having cut themselves adrift from all wholesome governing authority, and thereby having obtained a license to cut throats and plunder their neighbors."[13] Such unrest on the western frontier abutting Afghanistan was always concerning to British authorities given the potential for exploitation by outside rivals, foremost among them imperial Russia.

The "Great Game," the contest between Britain and Russia for political influence and control within Central Asia, is thought to have ended with the Anglo-Russian Convention, signed amid great secrecy in St. Petersburg in August 1907. Yet, Balochistan, on British India's western periphery, remained strategically vulnerable to the incursions of other European powers. During World War I, reports reached British officials in Quetta that a group of Germans led by Lieutenant Erich Zugmayer, who had traveled widely through the region before 1914, were attempting to stoke an anti-British holy war among the Baloch tribes.[14] While these German plans ultimately failed, British authorities worried nevertheless that the German government could exploit tribal unrest in Balochistan for its own ends. In 1916, the British government dispatched Brigadier General Reginald Dyer, who three years later would bear responsibility for the deadly Amritsar Massacre, to "bring the restive Baluchis to heel."[15] Problems with Balochistan persisted throughout World War I. In 1918, fighting broke out between the Marri and the British military when tribal leaders refused a request to provide recruits for the Indian Army. Another Indian Army regiment recruited from Balochistan had mutinied before being deployed to Mesopotamia to bolster the fight against the Ottoman military, killing their commanding officer in the process.[16]

Ultimately, the British government held Balochistan as a strategic territory. Little effort was made in wide swaths of the region to introduce any meaningful development or engagement with local communities beyond those necessary to protect British strategic interests. This hands-off approach persisted after independence. As late as the 1970s, the Pakistani government remarked that its writ,

> until recently, ran in not more than 134 square miles of Baluchistan. That is one-thousandth part of the province. Outside this tiny island, where the nation's penal and civil laws and procedures are in force, administrative difficulties were compounded by the vast distances over one of the most arid deserts of the world. The long, barren and almost

> impregnable mountain ranges, reaching out into the desert like a hand with many fingers, have not only shaped an insular tribal psychology but barred the entry of the people into the modern age.[17]

Following the creation of Pakistan in 1947, many in Balochistan complained of continued political marginalization and economic exploitation of its many natural resources, especially its gas fields. With Balochistan chronically lagging other regions of Pakistan in education and development, it has remained the poorest of the four provinces. By 2006, only 20 percent of Balochistan's residents had access to safe drinking water, as compared to 86 percent in the remainder of the country; electrification had only reached 26 percent of Baloch villages, with electrification as high as 75 percent elsewhere; and Balochistan's infant mortality rate, 108 per 1,000 people, was higher than the national average of 100. Over 50 percent of Balochistan's residents lived below the poverty line.[18] Pakistani government support for Balochistan has also trailed behind that provided to other provinces given its smaller population size, despite Balochistan's lack of development and poor financial position frequently leading to shortfalls in provincial revenues.[19]

This comparative lack of development and educational opportunities, combined with the strength of local identities, has planted the idea among many within the periphery that "deep down the Baloch don't consider themselves Pakistanis."[20] In a 2010 episode of the Pakistani television show *Policy Matters with Nasim Zehra* during which the host interviewed Baloch students about ongoing conflict within the province, one young Baloch woman prefaced her comments by stating, "The first thing I want to tell you is that I am not Pakistani. My identity is Baloch."[21] In an interview with *BBC Hindi*, Baloch activist Mazdak Baloch, speaking from India, where he was in exile, likewise stated, "We are not Pakistani. We are not of any concern for Pakistan. We are Pakistan's colony."[22] He said in an earlier interview, "Call me a dog, but not a Pakistani. I am a Baloch." He went on to explain: "Because there is no education, there are no jobs. A common Balochi can find only menial job[s]. Islamabad has appointed Pakistani Muslims in all important positions in Balochistan. Its army has created a mess in the entire region. The economic resources of our land are plundered."[23] Baloch nationalists and insurgents often exploited this lack of development to gain supporters for their cause. The combination of Baloch identity and historical glorification of independence, government policy teetering between neglect and oppression, and Balochistan's harsh and inaccessible terrain created, as US diplomat and writer James Spain noted, "almost ideal conditions for resistance to authority," with the region experiencing successive periods of antistate violence dating back to the earliest years of independence.[24]

With China's growing investments in Pakistan over the past two decades, Balochistan has taken center stage with the development of the China–Pakistan Economic Corridor. Yet, Chinese investments in CPEC have landed in the middle of a difficult security environment, with a new era of insurgency and rebellion plaguing the region since 2006. Chinese and Pakistani plans to increase infrastructure and investment along the CPEC route have only exacerbated the tensions between the Pakistani state and the Baloch periphery as this has increased government penetration within the periphery and heightened opposition to the further exploitation of Balochistan's resources. With various Baloch militant groups increasingly targeting the expanded Chinese and Pakistani presence in Balochistan, the Pakistani government has been drawn into a security dilemma whereby actions to improve security and protect CPEC projects have provoked greater violence, with militant groups expanding their attacks outside of Balochistan in recent years. Despite the increased investment in Balochistan's economy and infrastructure, Baloch voices point to the fact that the underlying drivers of conflict, including economic inequality, lack of opportunity, and political underrepresentation, have not been addressed in any meaningful way. As the government has further opened the region to outside investment, longstanding tensions between center and periphery, in many cases dating back to British colonial rule, have only been exacerbated with opposition to Chinese investments and broader instability in the region persisting.

Given the history of conflict between the central government and the Baloch periphery, it is unsurprising that the expansion of Chinese investments in Gwadar Port and the development of other CPEC projects within Balochistan have provoked intense opposition, especially as such development has increased the government's presence in the region. While Pakistani officials highlighted the potential for CPEC to serve as a catalyst for economic growth and social development within the chronically underdeveloped province, many Baloch communities have complained of being excluded from the planning process for Chinese-led development and argue that these projects are intended to provide benefits to local communities. Rather, in the view of many Baloch, they are simply meant to bolster the center's exploitation of the region's land and resources. By increasing the ire of local communities, expanded development has been met not only with heightened political opposition within the periphery but also rising levels of violence from several Baloch militant groups. This has spurred the increased militarization of the province to protect the various infrastructure projects and their Chinese workers. By landing in the midst of an already difficult security situation, CPEC has aggravated the existing tensions between center and periphery.

Several Baloch leaders attributed the current problems between the Baloch and the Pakistani government in part to the launch of various infrastructure projects in the early 2000s, including those associated with the Gwadar Port. They argued the projects were launched without consulting local political leaders during their planning and implementation. "The mega projects were so alien to the people of Balochistan that no one owned them," Baloch Senator Sanaullah Baloch argued. "We told the government that the strategy, not the mega projects, was faulty. Let's sit and talk about the reservations of the nationalist forces. On the other hand, the government viewed us as a minority ethnic group and initiated a military operation which led to unprecedented and irreparable losses in the province."[25] Rather than spearheading increased local development and further integrating the periphery into the state, the Chinese-led development projects have only served to exacerbate existing grievances within a region plagued by a history of underdevelopment and violence.

BALOCHISTAN IN PAKISTAN: A HISTORY OF REBELLION

Since Pakistani independence, Balochistan's turbulent history has been marked by tension and conflict with the Pakistani government. The journalist Mahvish Ahmad described the history of Balochistan since 1947 as a history of betrayals by the Pakistani state, which further fanned the flames of Baloch nationalism.[26] As a result, the region has been rocked by five different periods of rebellion over the past seven decades, with the seeds of the first rebellion planted even before Pakistani independence on August 14, 1947. Initial Baloch opposition to Pakistan emerged around the status of the princely state of Kalat. In the lead-up to Partition in 1947, Kalat's political leadership had been lobbying the British government for independence rather than acceding to a sovereign India or Pakistan. Before the decision to establish Pakistan was finalized, the khan of Kalat at the time, Mir Ahmad Yar Khan, intended to maintain a treaty relationship with the British government rather than accede to an independent Indian Union, a position opposed by Nehru and the Indian National Congress given the strategic importance of the frontier. As it became clear that British India would be partitioned into two states, the khan maintained his interest in pursuing independence for Kalat. Despite many within the princely order as well as several British officials arguing that princely states held the legal right to choose independence rather than join India or Pakistan, British Viceroy Lord Mountbatten, in an August 4, 1947, meeting with the khan of Kalat in New Delhi, maintained that it would be most appropriate for Kalat to accede to Pakistan.[27]

On August 15, 1947, the khan of Kalat rebuffed Mountbatten's advice and declared his state's independence while also promising to work toward a unified Balochistan. In defense of his declaration, the khan claimed that, given its position on the frontier, Kalat's status and relationship with the British Indian government was more akin to that of the kingdoms of Nepal and Sikkim rather than a princely state firmly within the British Raj's domain. As Kalat's political leaders debated the prospects of joining Pakistan, Ghaus Bakhsh Bizenjo, the leader of the

National Party of Kalat, asked, "Why should we be asked to join Pakistan, merely, because we are Muslims? For that matter, then Iran and Afghanistan, as they are Muslim countries, must also join Pakistan. Under no circumstances would we join Pakistan and sign the death warrant of 1.5 crore [15 million] Baloch of Asia. We have unlimited resources and if we are forced, we will fight back to preserve our independence."[28]

Whereas Jinnah had followed a laissez-faire approach to the princely states before the transfer of power, now facing the prospect of Kalat successfully asserting its independence, he feared the trouble that an independent state on a strategic frontier could have on Pakistan's security as well as the ramifications on other social or political groups' relations with the Pakistani central government, such as the Bengali-majority East Pakistan which was separated from West Pakistan by over a thousand miles of Indian territory.[29] In March 1948, Kalat's three constituent feudatory states—Kharan, Lasbela, and Makran—acceded to Pakistan. This shrunk the state's territory by half and cut off its access to the sea. The Pakistani government soon dispatched the military into the newly acceded territory to secure lines of communication, guard against potential for political unrest and other law-and-order challenges, assert the sovereignty of the Pakistani government, and apply further pressure to the khan of Kalat.

Later that month, however, the precipitating event that ultimately forced the khan to accede to Pakistan came from an unexpected source. On March 27, 1948, All India Radio broadcasted a story about Kalat's alleged overtures to India in which it incorrectly stated that the khan had requested accession to India; in reality, he had reached out to Indian authorities regarding the positioning of a trade representative in New Delhi as a recognition of Kalat's independence. Even though Ahmad Yar Khan denied the report, Pakistan, already locked in conflict with India over the disputed princely state of Jammu and Kashmir, saw this as a dangerous development on its southwestern frontier. There were even reports that the Pakistan Army had ordered the local garrison commander to march into Kalat and threaten to arrest the khan unless he signed the Instrument of Accession.[30] Only seven months after declaring independence, the khan was forced to capitulate and accede to Pakistan.

Prince Abdul Karim, the brother of the khan who had been serving as governor of Makran, refused to follow his brother's decision and launched a rebellion in May 1948, just over a month after Kalat joined Pakistan. Karim saw the new Pakistani government simply as a vehicle for the Punjabi domination of Balochistan. In a letter to his brother, he wrote, "From whatever angle we look at the present Government of Pakistan, we will see nothing but Punjabi Fascism. The people have no say in it. It is the army and arms that rule. . . . There is no place for any other community in this government, be it the Baloch, the Sindhis, the Afghans or the Bengalis, unless they make themselves equally powerful."[31] Karim initially crossed into Afghanistan to attempt to gain the backing of the Afghan government, which refused to provide any direct support to the prince and his followers. Pakistani troops were quickly deployed to the border region to challenge Karim and his forces, and they soon arrested the prince alongside 126 of his men. Karim was given a seven-year prison sentence, and he and his men subsequently became rallying symbols for Baloch nationalism.[32]

In 1952, the Pakistani government combined Kalat with Kharan, Lasbela, and Makran to form the Balochistan States Union (BSU), an administrative unit distinct from the northern regions of Balochistan, then known as the Chief Commissioner's Province of Balochistan, retained by the Pakistani government following Partition. Mir Ahmad Yar Khan was appointed the head of the BSU and given the title of *khan-i-azam*, a conciliatory gesture by the state.[33] The BSU and Chief's Commissioner's Province were dissolved in October 1955 with the introduction of the One Unit scheme, joining the two areas of Balochistan with Punjab, Sindh, and the NWFP into the single administrative unit of West Pakistan, an idea introduced as early as March 1949 in the Constituent Assembly. The new administration was meant to be a counterweight to the numerical superiority of the Bengali population in East Pakistan.

Mir Ahmad Yar Khan and several Baloch sardars opposed this move due to concerns that it diluted their political power and the autonomy of the Baloch tribes. Stoking further resentment among the Baloch, the central government appointed a Pashtun from the NWFP as administrative head of Balochistan under the One Unit scheme. By 1958, only 10 percent of positions within the government and 20 percent of the police force within Balochistan were filled by local Baloch.[34] As the government centralized political control over the periphery, tribal resistance persisted, with many leading Baloch political figures calling on local communities to "cast off their weakness and backwardness and to begin to assert themselves politically."

In October 1958, shortly before General Ayub Khan's military coup, the government dispatched troops to Balochistan to arrest the former khan on sedition charges, along with three hundred other Baloch political leaders. The government accused him of conspiring with Afghanistan to launch a full-scale rebellion against the state. Yet, it was this government action that helped to provoke an antistate insurgency led by the octogenarian head of the Zehri tribe, Nawab Nauroz Khan, who took to the hills with a thousand tribal fighters. They launched a series of attacks against government targets in the region and demanded the release of Mir Ahmad Yar Khan, the dissolution of the One Unit scheme, and respect for Baloch honor and traditions. It took the Pakistan Army over a year to suppress the rebellion. Nawab Khan was arrested, given a life sentence, and died in prison in 1964, with his son and five other followers executed by the state in July 1960.[35]

Following the suppression of this rebellion, the Pakistani government grew increasingly concerned with the Baloch tribes' ability to bog down numerically superior and well-armed security forces and correspondingly increased the number of garrisons within Balochistan's interior. The expanded presence of the military, however, provoked further tribal unrest, with raids and guerrilla attacks against Pakistani military positions continuing throughout the 1960s. One tribal leader, Sher Mohammed Marri, recalled in a later interview, "At first we had a simple objective. We were struggling to save the Baluch nation, which was being crushed by the Pakistani government. We did not define our long-range objectives at that time on the question of independence or autonomy within Pakistan, because we were too busy concentrating on our immediate objective, namely, ousting the Pakistan Army from Baluchistan."[36]

In March 1969, Ayub Khan resigned as head of state following mass demonstrations against his military government and handed the reins of power to the commander in chief of the army, General Yahya Khan. Shortly after, General Yahya dissolved the One Unit scheme and elevated Balochistan to a province, fulfilling a key demand of Baloch groups over the previous fifteen years. However, Baloch leaders continued to push for space to protect what they saw as Baloch political interests. In the 1970 elections, several Baloch political leaders—including Ghaus Bakhsh Bizenjo, Nawab Khair Bakhsh Marri, Sardar Attaullah Mengal, and Nawab Akbar Khan Bugti—joined the National Awami Party (NAP), aligned with the Awami League based in East Pakistan, to contest the elections and to safeguard Baloch identity and rights. The NAP emerged as the leading political party in Balochistan, winning a plurality of the seats in the provincial assembly and therefore the right to form a provincial government.

At the national level, the Bengali Awami League won a majority of parliamentary seats, and more than twice the number won by Zulfiqar Ali Bhutto's Pakistan People's Party (PPP). With the Awami League leader Mujibur Rahman set to become prime minister, General Yahya intervened to delay the transfer of power between political parties, causing widespread demonstrations in East Pakistan. In response, General Yahya deployed the Pakistani military in March 1971's Operation Searchlight to restore law and order in East Pakistan, which only served to further stoke unrest and an antistate insurgency. Following reports of widespread atrocities by the Pakistani military against Bengali civilians in East Pakistan, with estimates of the numbers killed ranging from 300,000 to 3 million, India militarily intervened in December 1971, resulting in East Pakistan's independence from West Pakistan and the formation of Bangladesh.[37] On December 20, 1971, General Yahya resigned and handed power to Bhutto as the new martial law administrator and president, who in turn appointed loyalists as governors of the four remaining provinces of Pakistan. The NAP, which was previously banned by General Yahya, continued to agitate for the lifting of martial law and moving forward with establishing a NAP-led provincial government in Balochistan. Following an agreement between the PPP, NAP, and the Jamiat-e-Ulema Islam, government authorities lifted martial law in April 1972, with Ghaus Bahsh Bizenjo appointed governor and Sardar Attaullah Mengal selected as chief minister of Balochistan. After the adoption of the 1973 constitution, enshrining a parliamentary-style democracy, Bhutto was sworn in as prime minister. With the loss of East Pakistan, the dangers of the periphery undermining the unity of the state continued to loom large for officials in Islamabad. In a February 22, 1973, parliamentary speech, Bhutto warned, "If you think that the story of East Pakistan will be allowed to be repeated here [in the West] you are sadly mistaken."[38]

Balochistan's NAP-led provincial government quickly made efforts to strengthen its political position. This included removing those it saw as outsiders, especially Punjabis, from government positions in the province and, to Islamabad's dismay, creating a new local police force, Balochistan Dehi Muhafiz, comprised of ethnic Baloch; only 3,000 of the 12,000 government employees and 10 percent of the Frontier Police in Balochistan were ethnic Baloch at the time, with many Punjabis holding key civil service positions within the province.[39] With the NAP government further emboldening Baloch nationalists, the latter pushed the idea that Balochistan had been forced to accede to Pakistan in 1947, subjecting the Baloch people to domination by the Punjabi-majority establishment. Attaullah Mengal later proclaimed, "If Pakistan is meant to be the land of one nationality and the smaller units are treated as slaves, then I am not a Pakistani and I don't wish to be called a Pakistani. . . . Pakistan cannot survive without us for a single day. The whole country is dependent on our resources. The rest of Pakistan is thriving and becoming more prosperous by utilising our natural resources while we are being deprived of our wealth."[40] Pakistani officials continued to see the potential of Balochistan's natural resources, especially gas and oil, to fuel Pakistan's economic growth. Large natural gas reserves were discovered in the province in 1952 and were vital to the Punjab's industrial sector, but Baloch leaders argued that the exploitation of these resources provided little benefit to local Baloch communities. One Baloch political leader joked, "Pakistanis do not value us. We have so much gas that if Dera Bugti was located in a Gulf country, all these Bugtis would have to add 'Sheik' with their names."[41]

Problems between the center and periphery only increased after the provincial government failed to quell further unrest among the Bugti, Jamote, Mengal, and Marri tribes, including attacks against Punjabi settlers in the region. The central government deployed the army to deal with the recalcitrant tribes, operations that were taken under the personal direction of the president.[42] At the time, a senior Pakistani official confided to the Iranian ambassador that Bhutto was sitting on a "powder keg" in Balochistan.[43] In February 1973, long-standing tensions with the Baloch tribes boiled over when the Pakistani government claimed it had discovered Soviet arms during a raid of the Iraqi embassy in Islamabad and that these weapons were intended for Baloch insurgents to support their fight against the Pakistani government. A US diplomat who happened to be on a stroll by the embassy at the time of the raid recalled that "all hell broke loose" as Pakistani security forces charged the embassy grounds, with military helicopters hovering overhead. After an hour within the compound, they hauled out "truckloads" of small arms, submachine guns, rifles, and ammunition. Bhutto accused the Iraqi ambassador of supplying "enemies of Pakistan" and declared him persona non grata.[44] Over the previous five years, the Iraqi government had in fact been providing weapons to the Baloch rebels in southeastern Iran to stir an antistate rebellion, reportedly in response to Iranian support for Kurdish militants in Iraq.[45]

Seeing the threat of armed resistance growing in the province, and wary of Balochistan going the way of East Pakistan, Bhutto intended to establish firm central government control over the periphery. Following the announced discovery of the cache of weapons in the Iraqi embassy, he soon dismissed Balochistan's provincial government, instituted a thirty-day period of presidential rule over the province, and installed Nawab Akbar Khan Bugti as governor. Opposition politicians further asserted that the Iraqi embassy raid was only a pretext for action against the provincial government, with Bhutto intending to move against it even before the discovery of the cache of weapons.[46] The government also jailed three key Baloch leaders—Marri, Bizenjo, and Mengal—and charged them with planning and fomenting an antigovernment insurgency. Following the dismissal of the provincial government, Marri, the leader of the 113,000-member Marri tribe, unequivocally declared, "The foremost thing is that Punjabis should quit Balochistan. . . . I can coexist with a pig but not with a Punjabi."[47]

Rather than suppressing Baloch opposition to the government, Bhutto's move sparked an insurgency largely from among the Marri and Mengal tribes, with Islamabad accusing Baloch officials of supporting lawless actions by the tribesmen and bolstering Baloch and Pashtun separatist movements.[48] Soon after the dismissal of the provincial government, Baloch insurgents began attacking Pakistan Army convoys and civilian officials in Balochistan. With the central government's precarious hold over the province, insurgents were able to establish effective control over large swaths of territory and almost managed to cut Balochistan off from the rest of the country, disrupting coal shipments to the Punjab and oil and gas surveying and drilling. Bhutto dispatched around 70,000 troops to quell the insurgency, with the Pakistan Army used as one of the government's "prime implements in this contest." The chief of army staff, General Tikka Khan, stressed that the army would not allow future "Bangladeshs" to undermine the integrity of the state.[49] The army commander in Balochistan, Lieutenant General Jehanzeb Arbab, further stated, "The hostiles were becoming quite bold as the year progressed. They thought they had reached the stage of the confrontation with the armed forces in which they would actually be able to drive us out of Baluchistan. They were determined to stop oil exploration. We knew that we had to respond very forcefully or we would simply be unable to bring the situation under control."[50] As part of the operations within the Marri tribal areas, the military worked to open up previously inaccessible terrain through the construction of roads linking Sibi with Talli, Maiwand, and Kohlu. Army engineer units were re-tasked from work on the Karakoram Highway connecting Pakistan with China to focus on these priority projects within Balochistan.[51]

Estimates of the total number of insurgents varied from 11,500 fighters up to 55,000, with many operating from camps within neighboring Afghanistan.[52] The insurgency increased tension between Pakistan and Afghanistan, as Baloch insurgents were able to exploit the porous border to evade Pakistani military operations. Bhutto even hinted that the Afghan government was behind the violence, with Pakistani intelligence arguing that Afghan officials provided Baloch fighters with access to the country, where they received money, arms, and ammunition before being sent back into Pakistan.[53] Afghan leaders deepened these suspicions with a propaganda war against Pakistan in which they called for an international commission to investigate reported atrocities committed by the Pakistan Army in Balochistan.[54]

The fighting was most intense in the first two years of the insurgency, when the army was backed by both the Pakistan Air Force and the Iranian military; officials in Iran were concerned with the potential for unrest to spill across the border among its own Baloch periphery in Sistan and Baluchestan. Sporadic fighting continued until 1977, with Pakistani military operations ultimately killing almost 6,000 insurgents, alongside 3,300 security personnel killed in 178 major engagements and 167 lesser incidents.[55] The United Democratic Front (UDF), a coalition of opposition political parties formed in 1973, further accused the military of imprisoning over 10,000 people, including women, the elderly, and children, in what were essentially open-air concentration camps in Kohlu, Loralai, Quetta, Jhalawan, and Chamalang, where they were subjected to "the indignities, privations, and cruelties of prison" along with starvation and disease. The UDF also reported that the military had engaged in indiscriminate violence and committed widespread massacres of innocent civilians during its operations under the pretext of hunting for rebels. These actions were, according to the UDF, "a virtual war of extermination" in Balochistan.[56]

In November 1973, following the outbreak of hostilities, Nawab Bugti resigned from his position as the province's governor after a falling-out with Bhutto and was succeeded by the former khan of Kalat, Mir Ahmad Yar Khan, in January 1974. On the same day that his resignation was made public, Bugti spoke at the Pakistan Army's Command and Staff College in Quetta about the numerous security and development challenges within Balochistan. He ended with a warning about the failure of the government response to address the underlying causes of conflict in the periphery. He stressed, "Let me tell you that the end of one insurgency will only be the beginning of the next. Escape, evasion and if necessary dormancy will not end matters. So long as the aspirations of the people are not met and they have the will, the space and the time there can be no scope for optimism. They have the shown the will, they have the space, and time stands still for them."[57]

However, Bhutto ultimately lay the blame for the chronic underdevelopment within the region, and implicitly the resulting unrest, firmly at the feet of the tribal sardars, claiming that their resistance to political progress and modernization resulted in a clash between "the forces of progress and those of reaction."[58] In several ways, the autocratic sardars, who wielded almost absolute authority within the tribe, had inhibited the expansion of democratic institutions and development, which a number of them saw as potentially undermining their authority. While at times deriding the central government's neglect and oppression of the Baloch, many also exploited state and provincial political institutions to consolidate their power and control the region's resources to bolster their customary authority.[59]

In 1976, Bhutto officially abolished the institution of *sardari*. Despite this new law, which even prescribed criminal penalties in cases where sardars exercised their authority, several were able to maintain their status by working with the government, and sardars more broadly continued to hold informal influence within their tribes. The prime minister described the underlying motives for the 1976 law in the following terms:

> I recognize the *sardari* system is a symbol of their identity for many Baluch. You can't get rid of it overnight without putting something in its place, something substantial in the form of economic modernization. This is what we have been trying to do and the *sardars* realize they

> are done for if we can do it, if we can get roads in, schools in, hospitals in. That is why they are opposing us. They know that if we destroy the *sardari* system, we will destroy Baluch identity, or at least begin the process of destruction.[60]

He even declared a public holiday throughout Pakistan in celebration of the end of this tribal system and the dawn of a new era of progress for the Baloch people.[61] In defense of his actions, Bhutto accused the sardars of believing themselves to be above the law and attempting to halt road construction through the province and other development activities. As an example of the new direction it wanted for the periphery, the Pakistani government increased the availability of development funds for the impoverished province by reallocating the royalties and excise duties from the Sui gas field in the Bugti tribal area, with provincial revenues rising from 88 million rupees in 1974 to 226 million rupees in 1975.[62]

To support the government's development plans as a means of addressing unrest, the Pakistan Army remained in Balochistan to play a dual role in implementing development projects and providing expanded security to "save [local communities] from those who had gone to the mountains and are operating from there against the country."[63] Given the difficulty of the terrain, the government justified the military's presence as the only organization with the requisite manpower and logistical support to implement construction projects throughout the province.[64] Balochistan's governor, Mir Ahmad Yar Khan, argued that the army's role in development was essential for expanding access to water, electricity, medical facilities, and communications in the more remote parts of the province.[65] However, Baloch nationalist leaders insisted that government spending in Balochistan was ultimately aimed at bolstering military operations and extracting raw resources, and thus offered little benefit to local communities.[66]

The central government had frequently sought to use increases in development funds as a conflict-resolution strategy in previous episodes of violence, but often with little positive effect. In the words of a 1980 review by Pakistan's Information Ministry,

> It has been the general practice of the previous governments to hurriedly draw up a panel of development schemes sector-wise, supported by guess estimates of costs, and to launch them without undertaking proper studies. As a result, a number of schemes used to drag on for years without achieving the targets. And when, at long last, some schemes reached a stage of fruition, these were found to be faulty and economically unsound or completed at tremendous expense to the state with enormous leakages through corrupt practices.[67]

Due to these issues, funds allocated to development projects within Balochistan were routinely underspent by as much as 50 percent each year.[68] Moreover, the Baloch continued to be underrepresented in the province's civil service, leaving key political and economic decisions, including how to disperse development funds from the central government, in the hands of non-Baloch officials. In 1979, for instance, out of 830 high-level civil service positions, locals only held 181, and these were largely minor positions.[69]

In 1977, Bhutto's actions to reshape Balochistan's political landscape were brought to a halt when the army's chief of staff, General Muhammad Zia-ul-Haqq, seized control of the government in a military coup. General Zia not only sought a greater centralization of political power but was also a devoted follower of the Deobandi group Jamaat-e-Islami and embarked on a process of Islamization within the country. He understood the Islamic faith as the key to Pakistan's national integration and felt that this unifying force should serve as the basis of the government and its policies. From the perspective of the smaller provinces, however, many feared that his Islamization policies, which had the strongest support within the Punjab, were simply an expression of continued Punjabi dominance within the government and military ranks and would undermine the strength of distinct regional political and ethnic identities.[70]

Despite these fears, General Zia took a more conciliatory approach to Balochistan after taking power. He released Mengal, Marri, and Bizenjo from prison, along with six thousand other Baloch prisoners, and established an uneasy truce with Baloch leaders, bringing violence in the province to an end.[71] He declared a general amnesty for Baloch insurgents and ended Pakistani military operations in the province. Yet, Baloch leaders continued to press for a full withdrawal of the military, arguing that the army was still active within Balochistan. Marri insisted that the Baloch could not support the new military regime unless the armed forces were fully withdrawn from Balochistan, the government declared a general amnesty for all political prisoners, and compensation payments of at least $10 million were provided to victims of past military atrocities. Zia rejected such demands. Bizenjo remarked that Zia was simply reinforcing the sentiment among the Baloch people that they were second-class citizens within Pakistan, regardless of who held the reins of power. "Before, we could say that it was just Bhutto," he asserted, "but now they can see that the Pakistani government and the Punjabis are all the same, regardless of who is in power."[72]

Engagement on various internal political and social problems in Balochistan was quickly overshadowed by the Soviet invasion of Afghanistan in 1979 and the resulting influx of Afghan refugees across the Durand Line, which monopolized the Pakistani government's attention. With Russian military operations across the border and long-standing concerns with Russian interest in a warm-water port on the Arabian Sea, Balochistan became much more of a strategic concern for the government. In conversations with American journalist Selig Harrison, Zia distinguished between the importance of Balochistan as a strategic territory and the problems with the Baloch, which he argued had been exaggerated by foreign observers. He dismissed the idea of a multinational Pakistan with distinct regional identities. "I simply cannot understand this type of thinking," he told the American journalist. "We want to build a strong country, a unified country. Why should we talk in these small-minded terms? We should talk in terms of one Pakistan, one united, Islamic Pakistan."[73]

In engaging with Pakistan's western periphery, Zia understood Balochistan as strategically and militarily valuable due to its ample resources and the threat of a possible Soviet invasion across the border from Afghanistan by way of the Khojak or Bolan Passes to reach the region's Arabian coast, using Afghanistan as a base and staging area for intervening in Baloch affairs. In the past, the Soviet Union had even expressed interest in building a port at on the Balochistan coast at Gwadar. Moreover, the separatist tendencies and widespread disaffection in the province could provide a fertile ground for various kinds of Soviet subversion and expansion of Soviet influence, further contributing to political instability, not only in Balochistan but in Pakistan as a whole. In March 1979, a senior Pakistani official stressed to a US diplomat that there were real concerns among Pakistani leaders that KGB agents would begin concrete work in Balochistan in support of the "incitement of ethnics." He saw Balochistan as a "target of opportunity for the Soviets" and described several Baloch leaders, such as Bizenjo, as "pro-Soviet."[74]

However, there were divided opinions among Baloch leaders regarding the utility of Soviet involvement in the region. Attaullah Mengal flirted with the idea that a Soviet intervention into Balochistan could even benefit the Baloch. Continued Punjabi domination, he argued, means "tens of thousands of them coming in [and] civil servants and army fellows telling you what to do, people from Lahore buying up our farms, buying the best lands in Quetta, more and more of them crawling all over us, annihilating us. We Baluch must choose, losing our identity at the mercy of the Punjabi or stretching our hands to others." With the Russians, he stated, "we might at least have some kind of conditional freedom. They may send their technocrats and their soldiers, but they would not send a whole population to occupy Balochistan as the Punjabis are doing, step by step."[75]

Other Baloch leaders, witnessing the violence across the international border, were convinced that the Soviets represented a greater threat than the Pakistani state and that a military invasion could lead to increased suffering for the Baloch people, not to mention sparking additional interference from Islamabad to protect the country's southwestern flank, which would ultimately threaten Baloch political interests. They saw events in Afghanistan as having strengthened the position of Zia's government and felt that any further attempt at raising rebellion would ultimately be counterproductive. Instead, they pushed for the Baloch to move closer to Islamabad while continuing to advocate for greater political autonomy. At any rate, the shadow of Soviet intervention, many Baloch leaders recognized, could be used as a key point of leverage for applying political pressure on Islamabad.[76]

In response to these concerns, the central government allocated funds to improve transportation and communication infrastructure aimed at strengthening its border defenses and expanding the ability to exploit the region's natural resources.[77] Senior Pakistani officials felt that the presence of military cantonments in Balochistan was now, more than ever, necessary with the Russian presence across the border in Afghanistan.[78] Pakistan also developed a new special development plan for Balochistan in 1980, focused largely on the transportation, communication, minerals, energy, and water sectors. These planned projects added up to nearly 20 million rupees over a period of four years. However, the government also recognized that limited resources at both the federal and provincial levels restricted its ability to support sufficient economic and social development in the near term, which would require significant levels of financing from international donors.[79] Paired with government development plans, it also introduced incentives to attract private investment, such as guaranteeing businessmen who invested in certain areas of Balochistan a ten-year tax holiday.[80]

Some Baloch saw any efforts to support development projects within the region as a positive measure that would contribute to raising the overall standard of living. Others saw them as simply the government asserting its control over the periphery and contributing to the ability of military forces to operate in the province. Marri argued, "Of course we want to do these things, to modernize and to develop in ways and at a speed that we think make sense under our conditions. We were starting to do this when we were in power. But they don't want us to carry out modernization under our own control. They want to modernize us in their own way, without listening to us." Road construction in Balochistan, he added, was "not for our benefit but to make it easier for the military to control us and for the Punjabis to rob us. The issue is not whether to develop, but whether to develop with or without autonomy. Exploitation has now adopted the name of development."[81] Leaders in Islamabad, on the other hand, were dismissive of Baloch demands for a greater share of provincial resources, citing their low population and lack of industrialization. They further saw Baloch demands for greater autonomy as, according to Selig Harrison, "at best, a thinly disguised form of blackmail designed to extort a disproportionate share of the benefits of economic progress or, at worst, a prelude to eventual secession."[82]

During the 1980s and 1990s, the Baloch nationalist movement went into decline, often unable to overcome traditional tribal divisions and factional infighting, which limited the ability of different groups to coordinate their efforts and for the Baloch to speak with a single, unified voice. The central government continued to crack down on civil society and arrested members of Baloch rights advocacy groups, such as the Baloch Students Organization. Some key nationalist leaders, including Mengal and Marri, moved abroad. Following Zia's death in a plane crash in 1988, and the return of democratic rule under Prime Minister Benazir Bhutto, several notable Baloch leaders were prepared to compromise with the central government and participate in elections with the goal of accruing benefits from the new political system. However, conditions in Balochistan failed to improve as many of the underlying problems between center and periphery remaining unresolved, especially issues around the exploitation of the province's natural resources. In the coming decades, growing Chinese investment in the region, especially support for the development of CPEC, would help to bring national and international attention back to the Baloch periphery while accelerating Baloch opposition to the Pakistani government.

BALOCH OPPOSITION TO CHINESE-LED DEVELOPMENT

Tensions between center and periphery flared once again in the early 2000s as the Pakistani government began granting licenses to international companies for gold and copper mining within Balochistan. In October 2002, Pakistan granted a ten-year license to the Metallurgical Corporation of China (MCC) for the Saindak mines in Chagai District, one of Balochistan's poorest and most undeveloped areas, to extract its abundant gold and copper reserves (the license was renewed for a period of five years in 2012, and again in 2017). In 1961, the Geological Survey of Pakistan first discovered copper deposits within the Saindak area, and, by April 1974, the Pakistani government had set up a government-owned and -managed mining corporation, the Resource Development Corporation (later Saindak Metal Limited), to begin mining for gold and copper. Yet, it was not until agreements were signed with the MCC that large-scale mining operations began, with Chinese state media portraying this venture as a model for economic cooperation between China and Pakistan.[83] By 2010, the Saindak mines processed around 15,000 metric tons of ore per day.[84] The government also established an Export Processing Zone Authority to facilitate the export of the mines' product. Between 2003 and July 2017, 290,000 metric tons were exported at a value of approximately $2 billion. In 2017, the MCC leadership expressed interest in expanding the company's projects within Balochistan, including searching for new sites to exploit within the resource-rich Chagai District.[85] In June 2020, the government renewed MCC's license for a further fifteen years, with MCC pledging to invest another $45 million in the project.[86]

Despite claims in Chinese state media that Saindak was "winning hearts and minds of families in Pakistan," local Baloch leaders complained that they were not consulted before the mining license was granted and the resulting contracts were set at "giveaway prices."[87] While the licenses did have a corporate social responsibility component requiring contributions toward the alleviation of poverty in the area and support for local communities, very little of the profits from the mines actually trickled down for this purpose, limiting their broader economic impact. Despite promises to the contrary from the MCC and the Pakistani government, surrounding villages in Chagai have complained about the lack of electricity, paved roads, adequate public health resources, education facilities, and employment opportunities. As one journalist noted in 2018, "As opposed to what the Chinese have been told, locals of Saindak are only given labour, security, and other menial jobs." Chemical spill-off from the mining project has also negatively impacted water sources. One local remarked, "The project has done nothing for us; our agriculture is finished and our date exports are finished. As a result, people have migrated away from Kachao [a neighboring village]."[88]

Similar problems have arisen with the development of the Gwadar Port and other associated energy and transportation projects in Balochistan. Baloch political leaders have argued that large-scale infrastructure projects are intended to boost overall economic growth. However, many in the periphery point to the fact that profits will simply be diverted elsewhere within Pakistan and abroad. According to the agreement between China and Pakistan for the development of Gwadar Port, the Chinese corporation operating the port will claim 91 percent of the revenue from operations, leaving 9 percent to Pakistan and nothing for the Baloch provincial government.[89] In 2018, Balochistan Chief Minister Mir Abdul Quddus Bizenjo complained at the National Press Club in Islamabad that while trillions of rupees were being spent on CPEC, Balochistan was not even receiving 1 percent of the costs. He stressed, "We have to see what benefit the people of Balochistan will get from the CPEC."[90]

In addition to limited financial benefits, local workers have complained about the lack of economic opportunities from Gwadar Port and the various other CPEC projects in the region, with the upshot that it has increased the presence of outsiders within Baloch areas. They have raised concerns that their exclusion from the numerous jobs created by the development projects has led the government to rely on Punjabi and Chinese labor instead. The military's Frontier Works Organization, which has played a leading role in several construction projects associated with CPEC, has largely recruited laborers from central and northern Punjab.[91] In a 2006 interview, Balochistan's first chief minister, Sardar Attaullah Mengal, explained that the Baloch are not opposed to the construction of Gwadar Port, or the development of any other part of Balochistan, as such. Their concerns stem from the way in which the port was being developed, including the resulting influx of outsiders and the lack of benefits for local communities:

> Since Gwadar is a small coastal town, the influx of a large number of outsiders when the Port becomes operational will result in serious demographic changes. The total population of Balochistan is half of Karachi's population. The government is planning to set up another Karachi at Gwadar. We will be outnumbered. We have asked the government to debate the entire proposal with us. We want to know who is going to benefit from this mega project. If the project is meant to bring economic prosperity to others at our cost, we won't let that happen. The government should not give outsiders the right to vote in Gwadar. We welcome anyone who is interested in investing in Gwadar. But they should pay taxes to the government of Balochistan. Moreover, the revenue collection against imports and exports from Gwadar Port should go to Balochistan. The federal government mustn't interfere in the matters of the Port. It should be up to Balochistan to decide how much it wants to contribute to the divisible pool.[92]

In addition to the presence of Punjabi workers, Dr. Abdul Basit Mujahid, the head of the Balochistan Intellectual Forum, stated that there is a "flood of Chinese with CPEC" in Balochistan and the rest of Pakistan.[93] The use of Chinese workers in place of local labor has been a common feature of Chinese assistance overseas over the past half century. Chinese-supported development projects, largely focused on transportation infrastructure and light industrial projects, relied on Chinese personnel, both semiskilled and skilled labor, rather than local workers, which helped to speed up their completion. With this approach to international development, the number of Chinese technicians working in developing states increased from as little as 25 in 1957 to around 20,000 in 1972, 90 percent of whom worked in Africa. The Chinese government largely covered the expenses for these Chinese workers, leaving only room and board and minor local costs to the host government, with Chinese workers living at the same standard as their local counterparts.[94] In many respects, planning for the BRI has been no different; 89 percent of Chinese-funded projects have relied upon Chinese contractors for completion.[95] With China home to the ten largest construction companies in the world, which together employ millions of workers, one analyst referred to the BRI as these companies' "safety net."[96]

By 2017, the total number of Chinese nationals working on CPEC projects in Pakistan reached 19,583 with around 71,000 Chinese visiting Pakistan per year, often for business or to work on other projects in the country.[97] However, the Chinese and Pakistani governments were planning for a larger influx of Chinese workers, especially into Balochistan as they made plans to expand work on the corridor, including introducing a special visa category for Chinese workers coming to Pakistan with CPEC projects and opening a dedicated counter at the Islamabad International Airport for those arriving on a CPEC-related visa. In 2018, the China-Pak Investment Corporation purchased 3.6 million square feet of land in Gwadar to construct a Chinese-only gated community for the 500,000 Chinese workers expected to settle there, at an estimated cost of $150 million.[98] In 2016, the Federation of Pakistan Chambers of Commerce released a report arguing that, if the current influx of Chinese workers into Balochistan persists, they could outnumber the Baloch by 2048.[99]

Whether or not these predicted numbers of Chinese workers are ever actually reached in the future, such assessments played into Baloch fears of being displaced by outsiders. In July 2007, Nawab Aslam Raisani, a member of the Baloch provincial assembly, stated, "Mega-projects have created nothing but mega problems. Eight million people from outside will be settled in Gwadar and a similar number in Somiani [on the Balochistan coast]. Where will we Baloch go?"[100] In early 2021, in response to the growing presence of Chinese and Pakistani investors displacing locals within Gwadar, the leader of the Balochistan National Party, Aziz Baloch, reiterated, "It is strange [that the security forces] are fencing an entire town to protect the business and interests of people coming from outside. The decision to fence an entire city is certainly part of a dubious plan. This is the beginning of sweeping demographic changes."[101]

The expansion of development projects and the need for land have already led to several communities being relocated or forcibly displaced. With the expansion of the port facilities in Gwadar, for instance, property speculators and developers have bought up land, which has drastically driven up real estate prices and priced out many local residents. A senior Gwadar official acknowledged that rumors that residents could be forced out of their homes was "not a myth."[102] In and around Gwadar, the central government also has expropriated land under the Land Acquisition Act, first introduced by colonial authorities in 1894 and retained after Pakistani independence in 1947. This law authorizes the government to acquire land for public purposes, including some of the most attractive land around Gwadar's bay.[103] However, residents in the area say that the government acquired land without providing advance notice, as required by section 6 of the act. In late 2017, an urban planner admitted that the government had held no consultations on land acquisitions with local officials or local residents, "not even a cosmetic consultation."[104] This process expropriated an estimated 290,000 acres around Gwadar, with residents reportedly receiving little more than a notification from the government with the threat of forced resettlement.[105] The development of the coastline has hit fishing villages particularly hard, as fishermen have been forced to move farther and farther away from the sea. Many local fishermen have already raised concerns over the expanding presence of commercial Chinese trawlers that have depleted fish stocks in the region.[106] The displacement crisis throughout Balochistan was worsened because of the growing antistate violence in the region and Pakistani military operations, forcing many Baloch into other parts of Pakistan and neighboring Afghanistan.[107]

Local communities also have expressed concern with large-scale projects' consumption of the region's limited resources, especially water. The Mirani Dam in Turbat, near Gwadar, was originally inaugurated in 2008 to provide irrigation for 30,000 acres of surrounding agricultural land. Instead, the dam has largely been used to funnel water to Gwadar. This has provoked anger among local communities and even attacks on water tankers delivering water.[108] As a result, Gwadar residents complained that tankers only made the two-hour drive from Mirani once or twice a month. And when they did arrive, according to Balochistan's planning and development secretary, Muhammad Ali Kakar, tankers only carried two million gallons of water, against Gwadar's total daily demand of 6.5 million gallons.[109] By 2018, the Pakistani military, with Chinese technical assistance, began to construct desalination plants in Gwadar to help address water shortages. By early 2019, the plants had been installed but failed to properly function, in part due to unreliable access to grid-based power.[110] A parliamentary inquiry report also blamed the misappropriation of funds and interference by "tankers mafia" opposing the construction of desalination plants, fearing that their successful implementation would disrupt their business.[111]

On the other hand, local Gwadar residents have argued that increased water access only benefits port operations, and water delivery services have not been used to provide potable water for the broader city. In 2011, freshwater shortages forced twenty thousand people to leave Gwadar.[112] In recent years, this problem has been exacerbated by the declining levels of rainfall. One local fisherman complained, "We are dying from thirst, there are no doctors in our hospitals, the electricity comes and goes and there is garbage everywhere as no one collects it."[113] Another Gwadar resident stated, "They say that Gwadar will be a major hub of industry; for the people who live here, it is Karbala," referencing an Umayyad commander blocking Imam Hussain and his followers' access to the Euphrates River to force them to surrender ahead of the Battle of Karbala in 680 CE.[114] In November 2021, protests erupted in Gwadar against the Chinese-led development projects. Local residents demanded access to clean drinking water along with unrestricted access to fishing grounds and a halt to deep-sea trawling. By early December, the protestors had blocked the highway connecting the port city to Karachi, leading to the deployment of more than five thousand riot police to the region to quell the unrest.[115]

A Baloch researcher in attendance at a December 2018 security conference in Islamabad, at which the Chinese ambassador to Pakistan and the Pakistani foreign secretary highlighted the many benefits of CPEC and the strong Chinese-Pakistani relationship, stated that many people in Balochistan are opposed to CPEC and the growing Chinese presence in the province. But, he added, "You'll never hear about such opposition at any event like this conference or from think tanks with official connections."[116] A Pakistani scholar based in Islamabad further described the trip he took to Gwadar with a group of academics and the official efforts he and his colleagues faced to limit their contact with locals who could potentially express such opposition. He said that they flew down on an AC-130 plane and were accompanied by government representatives wherever they went. Whenever he moved around the port city and its markets, the accompanying officials tried to stop him from interacting with locals. When he was able to talk with them, the locals complained about the infrastructure projects taking land and displacing local communities.[117]

Besides the absence of local economic benefits, there are concerns among Baloch that Gwadar and other CPEC projects will simply be used to expand and consolidate the Pakistani military's position in Balochistan.[118] In 2004, the Pakistani chief of naval staff described Gwadar as "the country's third naval base," which would "improve the country's defence in deep sea waters."[119] There have also been ongoing rumors and concerns over the Chinese navy's use of Gwadar for its ships. In 2013, the Chinese ambassador to Pakistan, Pei Yuanying, explained there was no intention to turn the port into a Chinese naval base, but he admitted, "Gwadar port will become a logistics support base for supplies and maintenance along the route . . . when the Chinese naval fleet goes to the Suez Canal, the Mediterranean, and the Gulf of Aden." In this way, Gwadar would serve a similar use as the Karachi port as a repair facility, with the added advantage of increased distance from India.[120] Ultimately, Pakistan continued to frame CPEC not only through a development lens but through a strategic one. As one Pakistani journalist noted, "The military sees CPEC as a counterforce to a hostile U.S. and India. It will latch on to China even if the deals [under CPEC] are unfair to Pakistan."[121] A member of the Pakistan Business Council further argued, "CPEC is primarily a geopolitical project. Economics have merely been added on to it."[122]

THE BALOCH INSURGENCY ERUPTS

Renewed violence between Baloch militants and the Pakistani state erupted in 2006 in the wake of the Pakistani military's killing of Nawab Akbar Khan Bugti, the seventy-nine-year-old head of the Bugti tribe and former governor and chief minister of Balochistan who had dominated Baloch politics since independence. Even before this killing, there had been growing tension between the Bugti tribe and the Pakistani government as the Bugti were clamoring for a greater share of the revenue from the Sui gas field within their territory, which provided around a third of Pakistan's energy, and a moratorium on the construction of military cantonments in the area. Revenues from the Sui gas field had long been a point of contention between the government and the local tribesmen, dating back to the discovery of natural gas deposits in 1952 and the construction of a 347-mile pipeline connecting the gas field to industrial areas in Karachi and Hyderabad.[123] Bugti leaders argued that the gas field largely benefited outsiders while the needs of local communities were ignored. They cited the fact that the gas was piped to the Punjab as early as the 1950s, while Quetta only had access to it beginning in the 1980s.[124] Despite being the largest gas-producing district, Dera Bugti, where the Sui gas field is located, ranked last among Pakistan's districts in the Human Development Index in 2003.[125]

The tensions grew when the agreement for royalty payments to the Bugti tribe lapsed on December 31, 2002, and there were subsequent delays in renewing it. Unsatisfied with the government's offer, which Nawab Bugti dismissed as "peanuts," he ordered his men to sabotage gas pipelines to pressure the government to accept his demands, a traditional tactic of the Baloch tribes.[126] In September 2004, Bugti forwarded to National Security Advisor Tariq Aziz fifteen demands that the federal government would need to fulfill to resolve the worsening situation:

- Provincial autonomy to the satisfaction of the people
- Baloch people should be the owner of their natural resources and wealth besides running their own affairs
- The Balochistan government should have powers to execute administrative, financial and planning matters related to mega projects including Gwadar and coastal-belt schemes
- The provincial government should control the revenue of the mega projects
- Employment in the projects should be the right of the local population

- The planned cantonments should be abandoned and land acquired by force be returned to owners
- Rectify the revenue record
- Senate should represent the four federating units and [the] inclusion of Islamabad and Fata in the Upper House [should be revoked]
- The levies force of 1,000 men recruited by the [Inter-Services Intelligence] and the [Military Intelligence] in the Marri area to suppress tribesmen should be disbanded
- All armed forces from interior Balochistan should be withdrawn
- The provincial government should control all civil armed forces
- The provincial assembly should have the authority to frame laws for Balochistan
- In the federating units the federal law should not override the provincial laws
- Problems of gas companies should be resettled
- All prisoners kept under various pretexts (political reasons) should be released.[127]

Subsequent negotiations between Baloch political leaders and the central government, however, failed to make any headway. Sardar Akhtar Mengal added further pressure by announcing that "no self-respecting Baloch leader would talk to Islamabad at gun point."[128]

The precipitating event that pushed this standoff into direct and violent confrontation was the January 2005 rape of a female doctor serving on a base in the Bugti territory by a Pakistani army officer. As the doctor was working in the Bugti Agency, the Bugti tribe viewed her as a guest under their protection, according to their code of honor. Moreover, the military alleged that a Bugti tribesman was responsible, insulting the honor of Nawab Bugti and the broader tribe.[129] When Nawab Bugti claimed that the doctor's rape was a violation of Baloch honor, President Musharraf supported his fellow army officer, and a military court ultimately found him innocent. Members of the Bugti tribe, led by Nawab Bugti's twenty-two-year-old grandson Brahumdagh Khan Bugti, responded by attacking the Sui gas field with rockets, mortars, and small arms fire. Brahumdagh later stated, "Our homeland is not a brothel for the Pakistani army."[130]

The response from the government was swift. Musharraf dispatched tanks, helicopters, and an additional forty-five hundred soldiers to safeguard the gas installation and threatened the Bugti tribesmen in a television interview. "Don't push us," he warned. "It isn't the 1970s, when you can hit and run and hide in the mountains. This time you won't even know what hit you."[131] The equally defiant Nawab Bugti responded, "As long as the perpetrators of this heinous crime are not dealt with, there can be no talks."[132] Two months later, violence erupted between Bugti tribesmen and members of the Frontier Corps in Dera Bugti, resulting in the shelling of the ancient fort in which Nawab Bugti resided. The bombardment killed sixty-seven civilians, including reportedly women and children, in the fort's surrounding lanes.[133] Afterward, Nawab Bugti announced that his residence was the main target of the assault, which intended to eliminate him and to warn off others pushing for Baloch rights.[134]

Alongside the Bugti, unrest was similarly spreading among the Marri tribe, who opposed government plans to expand oil exploration and construct a new military base in their territory. In December 2005, Musharraf visited Balochistan's Kohlu District, the stronghold of the Marri, to signal the government's resolve. In a speech, he stated, "Saboteurs and anti-development elements cannot deter the process of socio-economic progress as the masses want to move forward," and pointed out that increased oil and gas exploration and the opening of the Gwadar port would speed up development in Balochistan. For Kohlu, Musharraf promised a 40.5-million-rupee network of new roads, electrification of villages at a cost of 210 million rupees, the upgrading and building of new schools, a 50-million-rupee water supply scheme under which twenty-three tube wells would be installed, the revamping of the district hospital in Kohlu, and the construction of water storage dams.

However, Marri tribal leaders refused to participate in a gathering with the president during his visit. Instead, while Musharraf was in Kohlu, the Balochistan Liberation Army (BLA), a Baloch nationalist militant group formed in 2000 whose membership was largely drawn from the Marri and Bugti at the time, launched rockets from the nearby Jandran mountain range.[135] Shortly after the attack, the Pakistani military conducted operations with around 25,000 troops supported by helicopter gunships and air strikes to target suspected militant hideouts in Kohlu and Dera Bugti. Marri tribesmen claimed that over 50 people, including women and children, were killed and another 100–150 injured in the assault. In addition, over 100 Marri were arrested in Kohlu and Quetta.[136] As clashes escalated between various Baloch tribal groups and Pakistani security forces, Prime Minister Shaukat Aziz stated that the government was not considering an amnesty for "miscreants in Balochistan" and warned, "Stern measures will be adopted against violators of the law and the writ of the government will be ensured at every cost."[137] The elderly Bugti, who had supported the creation of Pakistan in 1947 as a young man, and was even photographed shaking hands with Jinnah during his visit to Quetta in 1948, asserted, "The government does not recognize us as Pakistanis and declared us as enemies of the country."[138]

With both sides refusing to negotiate, the elderly nawab found himself fleeing into the Sulaiman Mountains with Pakistani forces in hot pursuit. When the military finally tracked him to the cave in which he was hiding in August 2006, Pakistani troops quickly launched an assault and killed Nawab Bugti, along with thirty-seven of his followers. This triggered riots in several cities across Balochistan, during which rioters tore down symbols of the Pakistani state, including portraits of Jinnah.[139] Musharraf was unwilling to admit responsibility for the attack and, in a two-part article published in Pakistan's *The News*, would later claim that Bugti's killing was "a clear case of a self-inflicted casualty." He denounced the Baloch tribal leaders as "very vicious, unforgiving and decadent," and accused them, especially the Marri and Bugti tribes, of "killing people of other ethnicities (especially Punjabis), blowing up and damaging national infrastructure . . . and challenging the writ of the government."[140] The president further argued, "The *sardari* system is anti-government, anti-democracy and anti the people. It must be finished."[141] Reflective of a broader attitude of contempt for the country's peripheral regions, Musharraf stressed that the government needed to use "an iron hand" to deal with unrest in Balochistan and condemned the Baloch as terrorists.[142] Musharraf viewed unrest in Balochistan as fundamentally a military problem rather than a political one, and he pushed the use of force as the primary means of dealing with opposition to the government.

With the killing of Bugti, the president of the BNP, Sardar Akhtar Mengal, argued that the military "cut our last link, if there was any, with Pakistan."[143] In his conflicts with the central government, Bugti, a periodic ally of Islamabad in the past, had never strayed beyond his parochial tribal demands to stoke broader Baloch nationalism or press for Baloch independence. As one Pakistani scholar surmised, "He lived a Bugti and died a Bugti."[144] However, in death, he became a martyr and a unifying symbol to the Baloch nationalist cause as his killing gave "blood to the Baloch national struggle" and "once again triggered anti-military feelings in the hearts of the Baloch," according to a Baloch politician.[145] Bugti's death served as a catalyst for a full-fledged Baloch insurgency, which moved beyond localized, tribal conflicts and increasingly involved a wider spectrum of Baloch society.

In the wake of the military assault on Bugti's cave, Baloch militants launched a string of attacks against Pakistani military forces, development projects, gas pipelines, power infrastructure, non-Baloch communities associated with the government presence in Balochistan, and other symbols of the Pakistani state; in 2013, the BLA even committed an arson attack on Jinnah's residency in Ziarat, burning the historic house to ground.[146] Terrorist attacks within the province steadily increased between 2007 (with 35 attacks) and 2015 (with 483 attacks).[147] The Bugti tribe even put a price on Musharraf's head, totaling 1 billion rupees ($9.5 million) and a 1,000-acre plot of land, in revenge for their leader's death.[148] Within this context, the BLA emerged as a leading militant group fighting for Baloch independence, with the government banning it in April 2006, under the Anti-Terrorism Act. While the alleged BLA leader at the time, Nawabzada Balach Marri, denied any involvement with the group, he argued that the problems within Balochistan were broader than the actions of the BLA alone. He stated, "The Baloch are fighting a legitimate battle for their rights which they must be granted. The situation is unlikely to improve if I am labeled the head of some militant organisation or another. This trouble will continue unless the government begins to treat the Baloch with honour and dignity."[149]

With the increasing violence, the Pakistani government also targeted Baloch political organizations advocating for Baloch rights. In November 2006, the government arrested approximately seven hundred political workers of the BNP, including its president, Sardar Akhtar Mengal, and secretary-general, Habib Jalib. The arrests followed the BNP's announcement of a long march across Balochistan to protest the ongoing military operations and government plans for the construction of new military cantonments in the province. The cantonments effectively served as a parallel government within Balochistan, extending central state authority as they operated autonomously from the provincial government, whose reach was severely limited (for example, the provincial administration lacked the ability to levy taxes on private property in the cantonments).[150] Shortly before his arrest, Mengal, the son of former Baloch Chief Minister Attaullah Mengal, stated, "We don't want military development but better health and education facilities. Secondly, why should the Baloch allow the construction of cantonments on our land when we have no representation in the Pakistani Army?"[151]

With attacks against the government ramping up, Baloch militant groups also targeted Punjabis in Balochistan, a tactic largely absent in previous periods of violence. A number of Punjabis had settled in the region during British colonial rule, coming as tradesmen, skilled labor, and camp followers of the British Indian government. Many stayed after independence, creating Punjabi communities that would provide a disproportionate number of members of the provincial civil service and leading businessmen within the province, rather than local Baloch, many of whom lacked the requisite skills or education to compete. The Baloch continued to brand Punjabis as settlers and fifth columnists for the government, despite having lived in the region for multiple generations. After Nawab Bugti's killing, insurgents increasingly targeted a wide range of service professions: Punjabi laborers, barbers, tailors, teachers, doctors, lawyers, and civil servants, who they suspected of spying for the security forces.[152] By June 2011, it was estimated that nearly 1,200 non-Baloch had been killed across Balochistan, while another 200,000 were forced to flee the province. The only Punjabis who remained, according to a Quetta businessman, were those who had the protection of Baloch tribes or who worked on government development projects under the direct watch of Pakistani security forces. One resident in Quetta stated, "Almost all non-Baloch are on their hit-list."[153]

In response to the growing violence, the government relied on a military-led approach within the province. The military, however, faced a challenge as its ranks lacked any significant presence of Baloch recruits. As a result, the deployed troops frequently did not speak the local Balochi language and were unfamiliar with the cultural and geographic terrain. Even the local Frontier Corps largely consisted of Pashtun rather than Baloch. They therefore were unable to effectively target the actual insurgents who hid within the difficult terrain of the Marri and Bugti tribal areas, resulting in increased operations within settled areas that they could more easily reach. As the Pakistan Army and local Frontier Corps consisted of non-Baloch (both Pashtun and Punjabis), a Baloch journalist argued that they were also more willing to use brutal tactics against civilians as they did not fear repercussions or acts of blood revenge against their families or clan under the local tribal code of honor.[154]

Amid security operations in Balochistan, human rights organizations reported that local communities faced an increasing problem of forced disappearances of Baloch citizens, with many civilians and suspected armed separatists simply disappearing after being accused of supporting terrorism.[155] According to a United Nations fact-finding team's 2013 report, 14,000 individuals had simply disappeared in the province.[156] Between 2011 and 2016, nearly 1,000 of these missing persons were discovered dead, their bodies often riddled with bullet holes or messages carved into their chests, such as "Pakistan Zindabad" (Long live Pakistan) or "Eid Gift for Baloch."[157] In July 2006, Kachkol Ali Baloch, the leader of the opposition in the provincial assembly, stated that with these disappearances, anti-Islamabad sentiment was drastically increasing among the Baloch people.[158] The president of the Balochistan chapter of the Human Rights Commission of Pakistan, Zahoor Ahmed Shawani, explained, “These people are kept in illegal confinement in inhuman conditions and are routinely tortured. The legal procedure requires that the challan [official paperwork] must be submitted within fourteen days. But in most cases no first information report (FIR) is registered nor are these people produced before a court of law.”[159] By the early 2020s, protests against forced disappearances by Pakistani security forces were taking place in Quetta every Eid.[160]

These actions, according to Baloch journalist Malik Siraj Akbar, who received political asylum within the United States after facing harassment and death threats due to his reporting, were “cultivating the seeds of hatred” among the Baloch population and stoking “revenge that people have in their mind and hearts.”[161] Anwar Sajidi, the editor of a daily newspaper in Balochistan, further stated that even if many Baloch don’t support the insurgency, they are opposed to the government. “The state has so far not treated the residents of Balochistan well,” he explained. “There is scant development, education or health care. In many regions, the state has failed to provide basic services required for a good life today. The state’s conduct is not fair, which leads some to say Islamabad considers Balochistan a conquered territory.”[162]

In the 2008 national elections, which Baloch nationalist parties boycotted, the Pakistan People’s Party rose to power once again, this time under Benazir Bhutto’s husband, Asif Ali Zardari. President Zardari, an ethnic Baloch himself, but from Sindh Province, attempted to reach out to and negotiate with the Baloch insurgents, calling a ceasefire in the process. In February 2008, the PPP government even took the unprecedented step of issuing an apology. “The PPP, on behalf of the people of Pakistan,” the government resolution read, “apologises to the people of the province of Balochistan for the atrocities and injustices committed against them and pledges to embark on a new highway of healing and mutual respect.” While Mir Hasil Bizenjo, the secretary-general of the National Party (formed in 2003 through a merger between the Balochistan National Democratic Party and the Balochistan National Movement) called this a welcome development, the apology did not produce the desired effect. Many Baloch leaders felt that it was essentially an empty gesture that was not paired with substantive action to resolve the deadlock between center and periphery. "A mere apology," one Baloch politician asserted, "could not solve the Balochistan problem." Others recognized that the civilian leadership of the central government, regardless of their intentions, were hamstrung in their ability to resolve the crisis given the strength of the country's military leaders in calling the shots in Balochistan.[163]

In April 2008, a BLA spokesperson responded, "We regard the government's offer for talks as its defeat because previously it was not ready even to recognize the existence of the BLA," adding that the system that resulted in the "genocide" of the Baloch was still intact: the establishment, the army, and the Musharraf-led system.[164] The following year, militants stepped up their attacks after claiming that the central government had not ended military operations, continued targeting civilians, and failed to account for disappeared persons. Yet, Baloch society was polarized over the use of violence; moderates, such as the BNP, pushed for political autonomy within a Pakistani federal system, while militants fought for outright Baloch independence, with the bulk of the insurgency consisting of members of the Marri, Mengal, and Bugti tribes.[165]

Just before the 2013 elections, Sardar Mengal presented to the Pakistani Supreme Court a six-point reconciliation proposal for resolving the situation in Balochistan, which was described in the Pakistani media as "akin to Sheikh Mujibur Rahman's six-points, which had led to the bloody civil war and creation of Bangladesh."[166] His six points were as follows:

(1) All overt and covert military operations against the Baloch should immediately be suspended.
(2) All missing persons should be procured before a court of law.
(3) All proxy death squads operating under the Inter-Services Intelligence (ISI) and Military Intelligence (MI) should be disbanded.
(4) Baloch nationalist parties should be allowed to function and resume their political activities without any interference from intelligence agencies.

(5) Persons responsible for inhuman torture, killing and dumping of dead bodies of the Baloch political leaders and activists should be brought to justice.

(6) Measures should be taken for the rehabilitation of thousands of displaced Baloch living in appalling condition.[167]

He reiterated that the Baloch were only "struggling for our due rights, not charity. The Baloch youth are not sacrificing their lives for packages or for share in the [National Finance Commission] Award. We have been demanding ownership of our own resources since 1947."[168]

Mengal's six-point proposal was criticized for several reasons, including for not mentioning the murder of Punjabis. Others also claimed that he did not have the standing to represent broader Baloch interests, or argued that it was simply too late for any such political effort to succeed in resolving the violence in Balochistan.[169] The military's initial reaction to the proposal was to simply deny the charges, which seemed to provide credence to the final criticism that a political resolution would not be forthcoming. While Mengal stated that the government had agreed verbally to pursue this agenda, he complained the following year that there was no improvement in the situation within Balochistan.[170] Journalist Declan Walsh observed, "Not for the first time, the army was trying to hold Pakistan together by force, crushing its critics instead of talking to them. And not for the first time, in squeezing too hard, it seemed to be pulling the country even further apart."[171]

CPEC AND THE BALOCH INSURGENCY

CPEC landed right in the middle of this difficult security environment. With concerns that Chinese-led development projects expanded the Pakistani government presence in Balochistan, it was not long until Baloch militant groups began targeting Chinese projects and their workers. The first attack against Chinese workers in Pakistan took place in Gwadar on the morning of May 3, 2004. As a van carrying a group of

Chinese engineers turned into the port's construction site, a nearby remote-controlled car bomb exploded, killing three of the engineers and wounding another eleven. At the time, with over four hundred Chinese nationals working on the port, the deputy superintendent of police announced that the purpose of the attack was to terrorize the Chinese workers there. The BLA claimed responsibility for the explosion.[172] Later that month, six rockets were fired at the Gwadar airport.[173] These incidents were followed by a string of additional attacks against Chinese project sites and Chinese workers in the coming years. In February 2006, another three Chinese engineers were shot and killed in Gwadar; in July 2006, a bomb exploded in the headquarters of the Gwadar Development Authority; and, in July 2007, a suicide bombing targeting Chinese workers in the Balochistan's Lasbela District ended up killing twenty-four Pakistanis.[174] Subsequent attacks targeted a hotel in Gwadar frequented by Chinese nationals and a Chinese construction company's camp.[175]

Following the formal announcement of CPEC in 2015, Baloch militant groups—including the BLA and the Balochistan Liberation Front (BLF), a Baloch nationalist group that emerged in the early 2000s to fight for an independent Balochistan—continued their campaigns of violence against the Chinese presence in Pakistan, which exacerbated and reinforced the group's narrative about the exploitation of Balochistan's resources and repression of the Baloch people by the Pakistani state. In early 2016, a spokesman for the BLF, Miran Baloch, announced that the group considered CPEC "an occupation of Baloch territory" and promised that it would target any CPEC workers in the region. "Thousands of Baloch families," he added, "have been forced to flee the area where the CPEC route is planned. [The] Baloch [people] will not tolerate such projects on their land."[176] A former senior adviser to the Balochistan government recognized, "Anywhere the Chinese are working will be perceived as a CPEC project and could hence be subject to attack."[177]

In August 2018, the Majeed Brigade—an affiliated unit of the BLA formed to launch suicide bombings and other attacks against Pakistani security forces and Chinese targets within Pakistan—committed a suicide attack against a bus carrying eighteen Chinese engineers working on the Saindak mining project. Five people were injured in the attack, including three Chinese workers.[178] Later in the year, the unit attacked the Chinese consulate in Karachi, killing two police officers and two visa applicants. After the attack, a BLA spokesperson proclaimed, "The objective of this attack is clear: we will not tolerate any Chinese military expansionist endeavours on Baloch soil."[179] In May 2019, three members of the BLA stormed the Pearl Continental Hotel in Gwadar, where Chinese workers frequently stayed, and killed one security guard in a shootout that lasted several hours. The group later announced that it attacked the hotel to target Chinese guests and other outside investors.[180] A year later, the group also attacked the Pakistan Stock Exchange in Karachi, a leading symbol of Pakistan's economy and an institution in which Chinese investors have a 40 percent stake.[181] After the attack on the Stock Exchange, the BLA chief, Baseer Zeb Baloch, explained that their aim was to send "a message to the world that Pakistan has occupied Baloch land and plundering our resources with the help of China who provides military, economic and diplomatic support to Pakistan. Baloch will not accept the occupation of their land and will not tolerate the nexus of China and Pakistan that are involved in the plundering of Baloch resources."[182] On August 13, 2023, the Majeed Brigade again attacked a convoy of Chinese engineers traveling through Gwadar District, injuring three security officers, with small arms fire and hand grenades.[183] In March 2024, the BLA claimed attacks against Pakistan's Turbat naval air base in Balochistan and a Pakistani government complex at Gwadar Port.[184] Soon after these attacks, a Baloch political analyst asserted, "By attacking the GPA complex—the highly sensitive area in Pakistan's Belt and Road hub of Gwadar—the group has sent a message of 'vulnerability' to China having ambitious plans for transport of Middle Eastern oil through Gwadar Port."[185]

With the rising number of anti-CPEC and anti-Chinese attacks, Chinese officials grew increasingly apprehensive about Pakistan's ability to protect the CPEC projects and their personnel. The Chinese government frequently pulled its workers out of high-risk areas and increased the pressure on Islamabad to strongly challenge the unrest and violence. China even periodically threatened to withdraw all of its workers from

Pakistan given the deteriorating security conditions.[186] Following an attack on Chinese workers in 2006, Chinese President Hu Jintao publicly stated that Pakistan needed to "catch the murderers, ensure safety of the Chinese there and properly handle the aftermath."[187] One Chinese diplomat stated that if the projects face security threats or other challenges related to security conditions in Balochistan, "it's easy: we stall them."[188] In 2011, with security worsening across Pakistan, China Kingho Group, one of China's largest private mining companies, pulled out of a $19 billion deal to build a coal mine and power and chemical plants over twenty years, which would have been Pakistan's largest foreign investment deal up to that point, citing concerns with its personnel's safety due to recent bombings in Pakistan's major cities.[189] Chinese officials stressed to their Pakistani counterparts that the ultimate success of CPEC hinged on the protection of Chinese workers and projects and the establishment of stability in the country more broadly, in particular in the difficult security environment in Balochistan.[190]

In response to the growing violence within Balochistan, China and Pakistan stepped up their security cooperation. China initially pushed for the Pakistan Army to be given a greater role in the implementation and protection of Chinese-led development projects.[191] With CPEC's route seen as a high-risk area, the army's involvement in the implementation of CPEC projects has acted as a guarantee of their success, contributing to an increase in the militarization of the province.[192] The Pakistani military, through the Frontier Works Organization (FWO), had already been playing a leading role in expanding infrastructure within Balochistan as private construction firms were often unable to function in many areas due to frequent attacks by Baloch militants, according to FWO's chief executive officer. The FWO, therefore, has held a "monopoly-like status" in bidding for CPEC projects in insecure areas within Balochistan.[193]

Even before a widespread insurgency erupted in the province, Musharraf had new military cantonments constructed in 2004 at Gwadar, Kohlu, and Sui to bolster the security of infrastructure projects in these regions, in the face of growing Baloch opposition and unrest. The director general of Inter-Services Public Relations justified the construction of the cantonments through a development lens. He argued that they would bring medical and educational facilities to these underdeveloped regions, help modernize the surrounding areas with increased transportation and energy infrastructure, provide new economic opportunities, and ultimately benefit the local Baloch communities.[194] Three years later, the Pakistani government set up a joint liaison committee between the Chinese embassy and the National Crisis Management Cell for the safety of Chinese workers in Pakistan, with security remaining Chinese officials' top priority.[195] As the number of Chinese nationals in Pakistan steadily increased, a senior police official in Lahore stated that associated security threats and challenges were only getting worse.[196] Gwadar, in particular, had been effectively turned into a militarized zone with the ubiquitous presence of security forces further stoking the anger of the local population. By 2016, the security arrangements put in place to protect Gwadar Port turned it into essentially a fortress with security checkpoints throughout the city. In 2020, the government began construction of a fence surrounding the twenty-four-square-kilometer city and port facilities as further protection against attacks, with only two entry points. There were media reports that the Chinese government pressured Pakistan to put into place these expanded security measures.[197]

Pakistan's heavy-handed approach to security was extended beyond Gwadar. By 2016, Balochistan's provincial home minister, Sarfraz Ahmed Bugti, stated, "We have tightened our security in those areas where the corridor is supposed to pass. We cannot allow Pakistan's economic backbone to be held hostage."[198] In July of the previous year, the chief of army staff, General Raheel Sharif, visited Balochistan's Makran Division to inspect an FWO-constructed stretch of road connecting Gwadar with the Indus Highway at Chaman, a distance of 870 kilometers. Within just over a year of the project's commencement, the FWO construction teams had experienced 136 security incidents causing 16 deaths (6 military personnel and 10 civilian workers). By September 2016, the number of CPEC workers killed in Balochistan, largely on road construction crews, had climbed to 44, with another 100 injured, necessitating that workers travel by armed convoy; in 2021, the Pakistan's Civil Aviation Authority provided an MCC subsidiary a license to operationalize the Juzzak Airport in Balochistan's Chagai District near the Saindak mines to run flights from Karachi for Chinese engineers working in the region, given the security challenges with moving Chinese workers by land through the province.[199] During his 2015 inspection of the road site, General Sharif stressed, "CPEC and Gwadar Port will be built and developed as one of the most strategic deep sea ports in the region at all costs."[200] A year later, he reiterated at a conference at General Headquarters in Rawalpindi that the army was aware of the continued hostilities against CPEC, and it was "ready to pay any price to turn this long cherished dream into reality."[201]

Additionally, the military, with the backing of the Chinese government, increasingly expanded its influence over the planning of CPEC, seeing this as an opportunity to strengthen both its own relations with China and its influence in Pakistani politics and the country's financial sector. In 2019, Prime Minister Khan established the National Development Council to guide the country's economic policy and included the chief of army staff at the time, General Qamar Javed Bajwa, as a member. One of the council's key functions was the planning and implementation of international infrastructure and development projects, such as CPEC.[202] That same year, the PTI government appointed former military spokesperson Lieutenant General Asim Saleem Bajwa as chairman of the newly established China–Pakistan Economic Corridor Authority (CPECA), a centralized governing body that provided the military a more formalized role in overseeing CPEC's development. The formation of CPECA was heavily criticized by Pakistan's political opposition, with Planning Ministry officials explaining that China had pushed for the formation of this body to give the military a greater role in CPEC's overall management given Chinese concerns with the slow pace of Pakistan's civilian government.[203] However, given continued concerns with the management of CPEC projects within the country and the increase in attacks against the projects and Chinese workers, Imran Khan replaced Bajwa with the Beijing favorite Khalid Mansoor in early August 2021. Mansoor had served as the president of the Overseas

Chamber of Commerce and Industry and had years of experience working directly with Chinese companies. One Pakistani official referred to him as "China's favorite man for the job."[204]

CPEC's master plan, a 231-page document published in the Pakistani press in 2017, highlighted security problems as the primary risk to China's investment in the economic corridor. "There are various factors affecting Pakistani politics, such as competing parties, religion, tribes, terrorists, and Western intervention," the document outlined. "The security situation is the worst in recent years." It further stated that the Chinese government will "strengthen the safety cooperation with countries, regions and international organizations, [and] jointly prevent and crack down on terrorist acts that endanger the safety of Chinese overseas enterprises and their staff."[205] Over security concerns, article 10 of the CPEC agreement between China and Pakistan stated that the Pakistani government "shall take the necessary measures to ensure the safety of Chinese personnel and projects."[206] CPEC's Long-Term Plan, agreed to by both governments in 2017, likewise recognized that "the mix of international, regional, national and extremist factors might cause disruptive activities, threatening the security of the CPEC." It therefore contained a provision for "a higher level of security assurance." The plan called for Pakistan to deploy

> security personnel from Army and other security forces to ensure the safety of projects' construction, operation and maintenance, employees and camps under the CPEC. In the Gwadar region a more rigorous safety precautions is [*sic*] built, especially in Gwadar Free Zone. Weapons are prohibited from entering the Free Zone. The management of Khunjerab Port is strengthened with 24-hour video surveillance along the section of China-Pakistan Highway between the border to the port and regulatory forces shall be increased if the workload of customs clearance requires so.[207]

Following a February 2022 meeting between President Xi and Prime Minister Khan, the Chinese and Pakistani governments released a joint statement affirming "their strong determination to safeguard CPEC from all threats and negative propaganda. Pakistan reaffirmed its commitment to the security of all Chinese personnel, projects and institutions in Pakistan and the Chinese side expressed its appreciation for the measures taken by Pakistan in this regard."[208] Following a March 2024 bombing in Khyber Pakhtunkhwa Province in which five Chinese nationals and one Pakistani were killed, China's Foreign Ministry again called for Pakistan "to take effective measures to protect the safety and security of Chinese nationals, institutions and projects in Pakistan," with reports that Pakistani security forces were increasing security for Chinese projects. By this time, there were even media reports that China was pushing for Pakistani permission to allow Chinese private security companies to guard its citizens and projects in Pakistan.[209]

In 2016, as CPEC's Long-Term Plan was being finalized, Pakistan's Ministry of Defense announced the formation of a 15,000-person Special Security Division (9,000 from the army and 6,000 from paramilitary forces) for the protection of Chinese workers and CPEC projects in Balochistan.[210] In August 2017, Pakistan's National Electric Power Regulatory Authority allowed power producers to pass these additional security costs for CPEC's nineteen power projects onto consumers through a 1 percent tariff on capital costs, which was expected to amount to $2.92 million annually.[211] The following month, the Chinese ambassador to Pakistan publicly praised Pakistani security arrangements to protect CPEC and Chinese workers and pledged his country's support to improve the capacity and capabilities of Pakistan's armed forces.[212]

This increasing militarization of CPEC further alienated many Baloch and exacerbated local opposition to the development projects. "CPEC has given us nothing," a young student in Gwadar stated. "We can't even walk freely in our own city." A local official also observed of the development of CPEC, "The plan seems to be to make life so miserable for the residents that they leave on their own."[213] The present khan of Kalat, Mir Suleman Dawood, argued that CPEC is a means of furthering Chinese expansionism within the region and an existential threat to the Baloch. He dubbed it a "Chinese military project," supported by the Pakistan Army's "illegal occupation" of Balochistan.[214] From the Baloch perspective, a Baloch journalist argued, "Enemy number one is Pakistan Army, enemy number two is China."[215]

Through the early 2020s, the BLA and other Baloch militant groups continued to target CPEC and the Chinese presence in Pakistan. On August 20, 2021, the BLA claimed responsibility for a suicide bombing targeting Chinese workers in a motorcade outside of Gwadar traveling to the Gwadar East Bay Expressway, a Chinese-backed project that began construction in November 2017. One Chinese worker and two local children were killed in the attack, with several others injured. After the bombing, the Chinese embassy in Islamabad called for Pakistan to increase security in the region to prevent future attacks.[216] In late April 2022, the BLA also claimed responsibility for a suicide attack at Karachi University's Confucius Institute, which it called a "symbol of Chinese economic, cultural, and political expansionism." The bombing targeted the Chinese staff at the Chinese-backed institute, killing three Chinese nationals along with their Pakistani driver. This also was the first instance of the BLA employing a female suicide bomber.[217] Following the attacks in Karachi, a masked BLA spokesperson warned President Xi Jinping in a video message, "The Baloch Liberation Army guarantees you that CPEC will fail miserably on Baloch land. . . . You still have time to quit Balochistan, or you will witness a retaliation from Baloch sons and daughters that you will never forget."[218] In April 2023, the BLF claimed responsibility for the destruction of several Chinese-owned mobile phone towers running along the CPEC route in Balochistan's Kech District; telecommunications businesses in Balochistan had reportedly received repeated warnings from Baloch militant groups "not to facilitate the expansionist aspirations of the imperialist powers (Pakistan and China)."[219]

Despite the repeated attacks, Pakistan and China continued to pursue the expansion of CPEC within Balochistan. In January 2021, with 199 development projects worth 6.1 billion rupees under construction in the western province, the Pakistani military's spokesperson announced, "Anti-state elements have been on the verge of destroying the peace in Balochistan. Therefore, security agencies are busy day and night to make this a failure. . . . All these projects are due to the security dividend for which we have offered sacrifices in the last two decades."[220] Despite this continued commitment, CPEC projects saw their progress hindered by various challenges, including Balochistan's difficult security environment, Pakistan's debt crisis, and the COVID-19 pandemic that emerged in early 2020, which contracted Pakistan's overall economy. In early 2020, projects within Balochistan had a completion rate of 24 percent, with several large-scale energy projects having already been shelved, compared to a nearly 50 percent completion rate for projects within the provinces of Sindh and Punjab.[221]

In an October 2022 meeting of the Joint Cooperation Committee on CPEC, the Chinese and Pakistani governments agreed to reinvigorate CPEC following the pandemic-related slowdown. Pakistani Minister for Planning and Development Ahsan Iqbal announced after the meeting that both sides had agreed to launch a $10 billion railway project connecting Karachi with Peshawar, move forward with several energy projects and explore potential opportunities in the mining sector to expand CPEC's portfolio, and increase business-to-business cooperation on CPEC projects.[222] Yet, even as the Pakistan government worked to launch CPEC 2.0 to "attract more Chinese companies and investment," CPEC projects continue to face a myriad of security-related challenges.[223]

Balochistan is not the only peripheral region in which Pakistan has faced challenges in expanding CPEC projects. The corridor follows a route that brings it through the sensitive northern region of Gilgit-Baltistan in Pakistan-administered Kashmir. Local residents raised objections to the growing government presence and the influence China brings to the region through the development of the CPEC route. During a series of protests against China and CPEC in 2016 and 2017, people in Gilgit-Baltistan expressed their fear that CPEC, which they referred to as the "Road of Gulami (Slavery)," would lead to the further exploitation of the region's water resources without financial benefit to local communities and an increase in the presence of heavy-handed security forces.[224]

Development efforts within Pakistan's periphery have historically faced numerous obstacles related to security, governance, and economics. Chinese officials themselves have even recognized that it is likely that

80 percent of the investment in Pakistan will be lost, with growing Chinese complaints over insecurity, corruption, procurement and licensing delays, and slow payments.[225] However, as analyst Jonathan Hillman has argued, "China is betting it can succeed where the United States and the international community have failed for decades."[226] As China and Pakistan continue to develop CPEC through increased investment in Balochistan and elsewhere in the country, even if new plans ultimately prove to be overblown, the difficult security environment limiting these projects' ultimate success cannot improve until the underlying drivers of conflict within the region, such as economic inequality, lack of opportunities for local communities, political underrepresentation, and lack of respect for human and civil rights, are meaningfully addressed. As the government further opens up Balochistan to outside investment from China and other countries, government officials should understand the extent to which intersecting international and domestic policies exacerbate tensions between center and periphery and the resulting restrictions on the ability to improve both domestic economic development and international cooperation.

CONCLUSION

Looking forward, one cannot fully understand the trajectory of regional politics within South Asia, and so many other regions around the world, without considering China's growing international role and influence, especially over the past two decades. South Asian leaders have made numerous foreign policy decisions in contexts increasingly created and shaped by the Chinese government. Looking backward, as this book demonstrates, this fact is no less true for domestic politics, particularly within strategic peripheries. In South Asia, China's actions at home and abroad, including securing control of its near periphery beginning in the 1950s, have helped to shape the context in which numerous political and economic decisions were made and government actions taken.

From 1947 onward, government officials in both India and Pakistan eyed their under-governed and underdeveloped peripheries with anxiety and saw the need to integrate the border regions into the newly independent states. While many officials would come to realize the potential risks that emanated from ignoring these regions, they also saw the economic and strategic opportunities that they offered. Through China's influence, whether as an adversary or an ally, efforts to expand government reach and increase development projects in the periphery quickened. Indian officials in the late 1940s, for instance, introduced plans for developing the northeastern frontier, but, in the face of divided priorities among different ministries and the plethora of challenges the government shouldered throughout the country with limited state resources, many senior officials felt that they could go slow in the Northeast as there was no immediate threat dictating a faster pace. It was after the newly established Communist government in Beijing invaded Tibet in 1950 and Chinese officials pushed their territorial claims in the broader region that New Delhi began to prioritize the expansion of government control in the border region. For India, the threat of Chinese expansionism pushed the central government to expedite the extension of government control within the northeastern periphery as a defensive measure against Chinese influence among the region's tribes and potential infiltration into the poorly administered territory to which China's Communist government lay claim. The bloody legacy of Partition inculcated in the minds of many within New Delhi that communalism and separatism were among India's leading threats, made all the more serious by external enemies who could take advantage of internal turmoil to further weaken the nation. However, India's push to consolidate government control into the northeastern frontier would soon contribute to the outbreak of antigovernment insurgencies in the region.

Similarly, for Pakistani officials, Balochistan posed some of the most pressing domestic security challenges to the state from the earliest days of independence. Yet, development remained stunted in many parts of the rural and sparsely populated province. In the decades after 1947, Pakistani officials consistently expressed interest in expanding access to Balochistan's natural resources and developing Gwadar as an international port, in addition to continuing to use development funds as a conflict resolution mechanism and means of generating political support. Yet, it was only after Chinese financing and interest in developing an economic corridor connecting western China with Balochistan's Arabian coast that the government pursued wide-scale and concerted infrastructure development within the province. Within Pakistan, China has long provided military and political support to Islamabad. Over the past two decades, this support manifested in an increasing number of development and infrastructure projects, culminating in the 2015 announcement of CPEC with the intention of connecting China with Pakistan's Gwadar Port. These efforts have helped to expand the Pakistani state's presence within underdeveloped Balochistan, further exacerbating tensions between center and periphery and resulting in the eruption of antistate and anti-Chinese violence in the early 2000s, which continues to plague the region to this day.

In both states, Chinese influence is necessary to understand the process of state expansion into the periphery as well as its timing. This study thus helps to demonstrate the fallacy of disconnecting international and domestic politics, which are linked to an extent too often ignored within traditional international relations studies, focused as they are on the politics of government-to-government interactions cloaked in the broader strategic interests of the state. The entangled nature of international and domestic politics is especially apparent within poorly administered frontier regions that frequently become spaces for regional cooperation and conflict. Both hostile and constructive interactions between states influence and condition the domestic state-building process in these areas and shape the complex and evolving tensions and conflicts between center and periphery inherent to so many postcolonial states. The problematic relationship between center and periphery, often a legacy of European colonial powers who left behind a "poisoned chalice" in their former colonies by haphazardly drawing borders irrespective of local cultures and communities, has produced some of the most pressing administrative, development, and security challenges for many governments around the world. These issues further produce inherent anxieties within central governments about the broader meaning of the state and its sovereignty.[1] The political analysis of India's and Pakistan's respective relationships with their peripheries points to the importance of considering the influence of international politics over these domestic political processes, especially as they relate to populations who often do not fit neatly into the clean political borders and identities created and propagated by central governments.

CHINA AND THE DOMESTIC POLITICS OF SOUTHEAST ASIA

China's international engagements have impacted the domestic politics not only of its South Asian neighbors but also in the Southeast Asian countries with which it shares a border, specifically Vietnam and Myanmar. A brief discussion of these two countries in this section is intended to signal the applicability of the book's argument to other cases in China's neighboring regions, where there are potentially similar center-periphery dynamics at play as in India and Pakistan, a consequence of China's rise that has not received the same attention as government-to-government engagements or economic cooperation.

Through the 1970s and 1980s, the increasingly adversarial relationship between China and Vietnam impacted how Vietnamese leaders perceived and acted toward minority communities in the periphery, with some parallels with the experience of India during the 1950s, 1960s, and 1970s given concerns with cultural links between these peripheral communities and communities across the border. After 1975 and the consolidation of Communist rule in a unified Vietnam, Vietnamese leaders were confronted with a deteriorating relationship with their key ally during the Vietnam War. They interpreted this newfound Chinese aggression as a response to "the birth of a peaceful, independent, unified and socialist Viet Nam," which Chinese officials saw as an "obstacle" to China's "expansionist design in South-East Asia," particularly in the context of the Soviet-China split.[2] In November 1978, Vietnam and the Soviet Union signed a "treaty of friendship and cooperation," which was accompanied by an increase in Soviet military support to its Southeast Asian ally.[3] During a February 1979 conversation with the secretary-general of the Organization of American States, Deng Xiaoping referred to Vietnam as "the Cuba of the East," now situated in Southeast Asia by the Soviet Union to constrain China.[4]

A key catalyst for worsening relations between China and Vietnam was the status of the ethnic Chinese people in Vietnam known as the Hoa. Beginning in the mid-1960s, Hanoi asserted that Beijing had "more and more feverishly used the question of Hoa people as a political card to interfere in the internal affairs of Viet Nam and to carry out a hostile policy towards Viet Nam . . . [as well as] a fifth column to exert pressure on their countries of residence and to carry out Chinese expansionist and hegemonistic design in the region."[5] In early 1977, in response to concerns about Chinese influence within Vietnam, the Vietnamese government sought to expel Chinese residents within its northern border region. By October 1978, Beijing complained that over 160,000 ethnic Chinese had been driven across the border into China from Vietnam.[6] Earlier that year, China had already canceled seventy-two aid projects to Vietnam due to these measures and withdrew all Chinese workers, with Deng Xiaoping privately explaining that this was done to avoid making Vietnam too powerful. Vietnam, on the other hand, claimed China intended to use the funds in support of members of the Hoa community expelled to China.[7] Throughout 1978, China and Vietnam exchanged a series of letters in which each blamed the other for causing the dispute, with Vietnam asserting that Chinese efforts to engage on the issue of the Hoa people amounted to "interference in Viet Nam's internal affairs."[8]

Tensions continued to mount between China and Vietnam over senior Chinese officials' concerns with the treatment of ethnic Chinese in Vietnam and with Vietnam's 1978 military invasion of Communist Cambodia (then known as Kampuchea under the control of Pol Pot's Khmer Rouge, which was closely aligned with China). In the early morning hours of February 17, 1979, China launched a punitive military invasion across the border into northern Vietnam in response to Vietnam's actions in Cambodia. Fighting only lasted a month before China unilaterally declared a ceasefire and Chinese troops withdrew.[9] However, through the 1970s and 1980s, the Chinese government also provided support to the United Front for the Liberation of Oppressed Races (Front Unifié de Lutte des Races Opprimées, or FULRO), a militant organization representing various ethnic minorities facing persecution by the Vietnamese government and fighting for political autonomy at the time. The group was hungry for international assistance, understanding that it needed external support to continue its fight, which had started in the mid-1960s. In 1975, FULRO even approached the

US embassy in Bangkok for US support, though, they were ultimately unsuccessful. Despite consisting of Christians, Buddhists, and other religions that were not an easy ideological fit with officially atheist Communist China, the group then approached representatives of the Chinese government for assistance given their mutual antagonism toward the Vietnamese government. Following negotiations, the Chinese government reportedly provided around five thousand rifles, along with other weapons and ammunition, to the FULRO forces.[10] After the 1979 Sino-Vietnamese war, senior Vietnamese officials continued to express concern about Chinese support to the country's ethnic minorities for the purpose of weakening Vietnam from within. In a December 1980 speech, Vietnam's deputy minister of interior, Tran Dong, stressed the connection between "our ethnic minority problem" and China's continued efforts to exploit these groups and their antigovernment struggle.[11] In 1991, following the collapse of the Soviet Union and Vietnam's withdrawal from Cambodia, China and Vietnam normalized their diplomatic relations. Despite normalizing their ties, both countries have continued to engage in a territorial dispute in the South China Sea.

Elsewhere in Southeast Asia, China's engagement with the Myanmar government also has had implications for Myanmar's peripheral regions in ways that mirror events in Pakistan.[12] China has increasingly engaged in several development projects in underdeveloped Rakhine State, on Myanmar's western border with Bangladesh. These efforts include a $1.3 billion special economic zone and major port at Kyaukphyu as well as a road, rail, and pipeline network to move energy resources from the Bay of Bengal to China's Yunnan Province, all part of the China–Myanmar Economic Corridor. Yet, these projects have been pursued alongside increasingly tense fighting between Myanmar's military and the Arakan Army, a group that emerged to fight for the rights of the Rakhine ethnic group, in addition to the latest military crackdown against Rohingya Muslims in the state, which the US Department of State determined in March 2022 to be an act of "genocide and crimes against humanity."[13] This peripheral region and its ethnic and religious minority groups have long been the target of discriminatory policies and violence at the hands of the central government, which has promoted a political identity based in the dominant Burman ethnicity and Buddhist faith.[14]

The Arakan Army, which has voiced general support for the expansion of development projects within Rakhine State, has nevertheless expressed its opposition to the way that the China-backed projects are being implemented, without input or benefit to local communities. Many within Rakhine State argue that these projects are being used to simply expand the military's presence and government control over the border region and its natural resources, thereby exacerbating tensions between the central government and its western periphery. Tun Kyi, a spokesperson for the Kyaukphyu Rural Development Association, explained, "Everything is controlled by the central government, and for a really huge project like this there is no law to protect ethnic minority people. The project will not bring profit to the Rakhine community and the Kyaukphyu community. The community will lose their rights."[15]

Chinese-led development could further intensify the violence within Rakhine State, especially with pressure from China potentially expanding Myanmar's military presence in the border region to provide increased security for Chinese-led projects.[16] Additionally, China has provided diplomatic cover to Myanmar in various international fora, including the United Nations, as its government faced increased international pressure and calls for sanctions for the violence perpetrated against the Rohingya. In 2018, for instance, after China voted against the move by the UN Human Rights Council to establish a body to investigate potential acts of genocide against the Rohingya by members of Myanmar's military forces. In the words of Myanmar's commander-in-chief, Senior General Min Aung Hlaing, "Myanmar is thankful for China as a good neighbor for its correct stance and standing against the international community over the Rakhine State issue." He added that Myanmar's military was ready to support the implementation of BRI-related projects.[17] Shortly after the early February 2021 coup d'état by Myanmar's military, which overthrew the civilian government led by Aung San Suu Kyi's National League for Democracy, China blocked a resolution introduced in the UN Security Council to condemn the action. Even though experts have claimed that China may not be happy with the actions of the military within Myanmar, the Chinese government has expressed skepticism of any international intervention within the region, and perhaps even signaled some tacit support for the steps taken by Myanmar's generals.[18] Such support, however, could have the effect of further emboldening Myanmar's military to continue and even expand violent atrocities within periphery and throughout the rest of the country, such as the use of air strikes against opposition groups in the country following the 2021 military coup.[19]

THE UNITED STATES' PIVOT TO ASIA

With the global rise of China and the economic growth of India over the past two decades, many have lauded the twenty-first century as the Asian century, signaling a key shift away from Europe and North America and toward Asian economies as the drivers of the next phase of globalization. In January 2021, as China celebrated the one-hundred-year anniversary of the Chinese Communist Party's formation, President Xi remarked, "The world is undergoing profound changes unseen in a century."[20] While the Chinese government exhibited a celebratory tone as it looked to the future, others around the world have watched with growing concern. In the words of noted British historian Peter Frankopan, "It is not always easy to remain sanguine if one seems to be standing in the wrong place at the wrong time. That is the case in the United States, where the rise of China seems not only to pose systemic questions about America's future but also to cast a shadow that makes yearning for the supposed golden years of the twentieth century understandable."[21]

To meet China's rise, the United States has increased its engagement across the Asian continent in recent years. Under President George W. Bush, the US government increased its economic outreach to the region, as demonstrated by the 2006 civil nuclear agreement with India. In April 2006, Assistant Secretary of State for South and Central Asian Affairs Richard Boucher told the House International Relations

Committee, "Our strategy rests on three integrated pillars: security cooperation; our commercial and energy interests; and political and economic reform. . . . Our goal is to revive ancient ties between South and Central Asia and to help create new links in the areas of trade, transport, democracy, energy and communications."[22] However, the Bush administration's efforts to strengthen its economic relationships within the region were ultimately hindered by its overarching focus on the war on terror and broader security issues.[23]

President Barack Obama renewed the US interest in Asia, billing himself as "America's first Pacific president," citing his experiences growing up in Hawaii and Indonesia.[24] With his administration's pivot to Asia to curb China's rapid growth, he voiced support for an increase in US engagements and alliances with Asian countries, both bilaterally and multilaterally, to support their prosperity and security. In a July 2011 speech in Chennai, India, foreshadowing the aims of China's BRI, Secretary of State Hillary Clinton stated,

> Historically, the nations of South and Central Asia were connected to each other and the rest of the continent by a sprawling trade network called the Silk Road. Let's work together to create a new Silk Road. Not a single thoroughfare like its namesake, but an international web and network of economic and transit connections. That means building more rail lines, highways, energy infrastructure . . . upgrading the facilities at border crossings . . . removing the bureaucratic barriers and other impediments to the free flow of goods and people . . . [and] casting aside the outdated trade policies.[25]

Within South Asia, these lofty goals failed to reach fruition at the time, especially in Pakistan, which was still reeling from contentious events earlier in the year, including the raid by US Navy SEALs against Osama bin Laden's compound in Abbottabad and CIA contractor Raymond Davis killing two men in Lahore. Moreover, unlike China's expansion of its economic links through the region, such sentiments on the part of the United States ultimately proved to be more rhetoric than substance as the US government continued to narrowly emphasize its security interests in South and Central Asia amid the troop surge in Afghanistan, despite the efforts of some US officials at the time to expand meaningful US engagement to include a broader spectrum of political and economic activities. Where the United States fell short, China continued to extend its reach, a political reality that US officials ignored at their own peril. Former US Ambassador to Pakistan Cameron Munter, who served in Islamabad from 2010 to 2012, argued that any improvement in relations between Pakistan the United States requires an understanding of the Pakistan-China relationship. "In the past, for 60 years or 70 years," he observed, "the Americans called the shots in a bilateral relationship. That's just not the case anymore. So number one is understand what the Chinese are doing because anything the Americans do is not going to be working in a vacuum. It's going to be working in the context set by the Chinese."[26]

After his election in 2016, President Donald Trump helped to crystallize the US position that China was Washington's primary geopolitical rivalry, consistently directing his ire toward China and its growing role within the international economy. "We can't continue to allow China to rape our country," he warned during the 2016 presidential campaign, "and that's what they're doing. It's the greatest theft in the history of the world."[27] On his first week in office, Trump withdrew the United States from the Trans-Pacific Partnership to pursue "bilateral trade negotiations to promote American industry, protect American workers, and raise American wages."[28] He also imposed new tariffs on Chinese imports, while senior US officials issued global warnings that the BRI was a vehicle for luring countries into debt traps.[29] Trump's approach to the region shifted more and more toward an expansion of its alliances with key regional countries involved in the Quadrilateral Security Dialogue, or "Quad," India, Japan, and Australia alongside the United States, in a bid to balance against China. In 2018, the Department of Defense even changed the name of the Pacific Command to the Indo-Pacific Command, a symbolic move emphasizing the important role that the United States' Indian Ocean allies and partners, in particular India, have as part of US engagement with the broader geographic region.[30]

In the first months of President Joe Biden's administration, the US-China relationship appeared to get off to a rocky start, as Secretary of State Antony Blinken and National Security Advisor Jake Sullivan held tense talks with senior Chinese officials in Anchorage, Alaska, on March 18–19, 2021. The US officials raised several points of concern for the United States, including Chinese human rights abuses in Xinjiang, Tibet, and Hong Kong, in addition to Chinese cyberattacks and mounting pressure on Taiwan. Secretary Blinken also highlighted the fact that the two countries had a number of intersecting interests as well, pointing to developments with North Korea and Afghanistan as well as the broader threat of climate change.[31] Yet, the talks yielded no significant diplomatic breakthroughs. Shortly after this meeting, the US government imposed new sanctions against Chinese officials over the treatment of the Uyghurs in Xinjiang.[32]

The Biden administration also continued US efforts to cultivate its alliances in the region as a counterweight to Chinese influence, informing NATO allies they would not "force allies into an 'us-or-them' choice with China."[33] During a March 2021 visit to India, Secretary of Defense Lloyd Austin stated in a press conference that in an effort to check Chinese aggression, the United States would work with "like minded countries who have shared interests" in supporting peace and stability in the Indo-Pacific region.[34] The White House's *National Security Strategy*, released in October 2022, further warned that China "harbors the intention and, increasingly, the capacity to reshape the international order in favor of one that tilts the global playing field to its benefit," with US competition with China "most pronounced in the Indo-Pacific." In balancing against and competing with China, the White House reiterated that, "As India is the world's largest democracy and a Major Defense Partner, the United States and India will work together, bilaterally and multilaterally, to support our shared vision of a free and open Indo-Pacific."[35] Following Donald Trump's reelection in November 2024, he signaled the same hawkish position on competition with China, including higher tariffs on Chinese imports and restrictions on Chinese ownership of US resources and infrastructure.[36]

As the United States has pivoted its financial tools and institutions to support economic development of key partners around the globe in a bid to compete with Beijing's growing influence, China's experience in Balochistan offers key lessons about the pitfalls and challenges of supporting development efforts in states' peripheries. International engagement in such regions that ignores the grievances of local communities carries the same risks of exacerbating tensions, and potentially violence, between the center and periphery. The BLA, for instance, has made it clear that its campaign of violence is directed not against Beijing specifically but against any international partner of the Pakistani government that supports an increased state presence in Balochistan. "This is a warning not only to China," an October 2024 BLA statement read, "but also to any nation or investor in the world who tries to set foot in Balochistan during Pakistan's occupation. Any foreign investor or government that attempts to occupy the resources of Balochistan in collaboration with Pakistan will face a severe reaction. We will not allow anyone to seize our resources and the future of our people until the Baloch nation is free. The international community must remember that the land of Balochistan and its resources belong solely to the Baloch nation, and we will protect our rights and liberation at any cost."[37] Any initiatives in these strategic regions that fail to meaningfully account for the underlying dynamics between center and periphery risk exacerbating the underlying drivers of conflict, as witnessed with China's experience over the past two decades.

However, as the US government works to find ways to strengthen existing bilateral and multilateral initiatives to counterbalance China, it is important to understand both the strengths and limits of China's growing international role. This book helps to demonstrate that China's influence and investments abroad have the potential to exacerbate domestic conflict and instability. Indeed, any serious effort to understand Chinese influence, not only in South Asia but in many other regions of the world, must be cognizant of this connection between international and domestic politics.

ACKNOWLEDGMENTS

Adversary and Ally is the third in a trilogy of books (alongside *The Terrorism Trap: How the War on Terror Escalates Violence in America's Partner States* and *Conquering the Maharajas: India's Princely States and the End of Empire, 1930–50*) examining indirect rule as a governing approach under British colonialism and its legacy in postcolonial states. I am grateful for the support and assistance I received from numerous individuals and institutions during the decade that I've worked on this series of projects. Over the years, I have benefited greatly from numerous discussions and guidance from Ambassador Akbar Ahmed, the Ibn Khaldun Chair of Islamic Studies at American University's School of International Service. During my time working as a researcher for Ambassador Ahmed, I learned from his vast experience as both an academic studying Pakistani tribal societies and an administrator of Pakistan's frontier areas, including in Balochistan. His unique insights into the structural challenges underpinning the conflict between center and periphery in postcolonial states helped to shape the ideas and arguments contained within *Adversary and Ally*. Similarly, I would like to thank Frankie Martin and James Smrikarov for the many discussions over the previous decade that contributed greatly to the development of this book and for their contributions in reviewing parts of the manuscript. I am also grateful for the unwavering support of my wife, Dr. Marina

Kozak, who's keen scientific insights helped to improve the book in numerous ways. At Columbia University Press, I would like to thank the two peer reviewers whose comments helped to improve the final manuscript greatly as well as Caelyn Cobb, senior editor in global history and politics, who masterfully guided the manuscript through the review and production process. In addition, I am grateful to Dr. Emily Simon, Columbia University Press's assistant editor, production editor Marisa Lastres, and Ryan Perks, the book's copy editor, for their work in finalizing and improving the text. I would also like to again thank my parents, Darrell and Deborah Akins, for their constant support for my academic endeavors over the years, which did not always follow a clear path.

I would be remiss if I did not recognize that scholarship is inherently a cumulative exercise, with my work building on and in conversation with the tireless efforts of the many researchers before me who have dedicated themselves to providing a clearer and more nuanced understanding of the broad topic of this book. So, I would like to express my gratitude to the countless scholars who have unknowingly inspired me with their own research and writing. Of course, all views expressed and any errors in this book are mine alone. Finally, *Adversary and Ally* has undergone prepublication security review according to US Department of State guidelines for personal capacity publications. All statements and opinions in the book represent the author's personal views alone and do not constitute an expression of any official position or policy of the US Department of State or the US government.

NOTES

1. ADVERSARY AND ALLY

1. "India and China Troops Clash on Arunachal Pradesh Mountain Border," *BBC News*, December 13, 2022, https://www.bbc.com/news/world-asia-63953400#:~:text=India%20and%20China%20troops%20clash%20on%20Arunachal%20Pradesh%20mountain%20border,-13%20December%202022&text=India%20says%20its%20forces%20have,least%2024%20troops%20in%202020; Shusant Singh, "India and China's Latest Border Clash Is Not a One-Off," *Foreign Policy*, December 23, 2022, https://foreignpolicy.com/2022/12/23/india-china-border-clash-arunachal-pradesh-deterrence/.
2. Soutik Biswas, "India-China Clash: An Extraordinary Escalation 'with Rocks and Clubs,'" *BBC News*, June 16, 2020, https://www.bbc.com/news/world-asia-india-53071913; Michael Safi et al., "Soldiers Fell to Their Deaths as India and China's Troops Fought with Rocks," *Guardian*, June 17, 2020, https://www.theguardian.com/world/2020/jun/17/shock-and-anger-in-india-after-worst-attack-on-china-border-in-decades.
3. "Chinese and Pakistani Border Guards Hold Hands at Khunjerab Pass," *Huffington Post*, June 24, 2013, https://www.huffpost.com/entry/china-pakistan-guards-hold-hands_n_3491642.
4. Harrison Akins, "Between Allies and Enemies: Explaining the Volatility of the U.S.-Pakistan Relationship, 1947–2018," Policy Brief 7:18 (Howard H. Baker Jr. Center for Public Policy, March 2018); Harrison Akins, "Trump, China, and Pakistan's Search for an All-Weather Ally," *Los Angeles Review of Books*, July 7, 2019, https://lareviewofbooks.org/blog/essays/trump-china-pakistans-search-weather-ally/; T. V. Paul, "Why Has the India-Pakistan Rivalry Been so Enduring? Power Asymmetry and an Intractable Conflict," *Security Studies* 15, no. 4 (2006): 600–630.

5. Howard French, *Everything Under the Heavens: How the Past Helps Shape China's Push for Global Power* (Vintage Books, 2017), 11.
6. "President Xi Jinping Delivers Important Speech and Proposes to Build a Silk Road Economic Belt with Central Asian Countries," Consulate-General of the People's Republic of China in Toronto, September 7, 2013, http://toronto.china-consulate.gov.cn/eng/zgxw/201309/t20130913_7095490.htm.
7. Wu Jiao and Zhang Yunbi, "Xi in Call for Building of New 'Maritime Silk Road,'" *China Daily*, October 4, 2013, https://usa.chinadaily.com.cn/china/2013-10/04/content_17008940.htm.
8. Peter Frankopan, *The New Silk Roads: The Present and Future of the World* (Bloomsbury Publishing, 2018); Jonathan E. Hillman, *The Emperor's New Road: China and the Project of the Century* (Yale University Press, 2020).
9. Peter Koenig, "China—The Belt and Road Initiative—The Bridge That Spans the World," Global Research, November 24, 2019, https://www.globalresearch.ca/china-belt-road-initiative-bridge-spans-world/5695727; Michael Clarke, "Beijing's Pivot West: The Convergence of *Innenpolitik* and *Aussenpolitik* on China's 'Belt and Road?,'" *Journal of Contemporary China* 29, no. 123 (2020): 336–353; Romi Jain, "Pitfalls or Windfalls in China's Belt and Road Economic Outreach?," *Asian Survey* 60, no. 4 (2020): 686; Ray Silvius, "China's Belt and Road Initiative as Nascent World Order Structure and Concept? Between Sino-Centering and Sino-Deflecting," *Journal of Contemporary China* 30, no. 121 (2021): 314–329; Jared McKinney, "How Stalled Global Reform Is Fueling Regionalism: China's Engagement with the G20," *Third World Quarterly* 39, no. 4 (2018): 709–726.
10. Andrew Chatzky and James McBride, "Backgrounder: China's Massive Belt and Road Initiative," Council on Foreign Relations, February 2, 2023, https://www.cfr.org/backgrounder/chinas-massive-belt-and-road-initiative.
11. Daniel S. Markey, *China's Western Horizon: Beijing and the New Geopolitics of Eurasia* (Oxford University Press, 2020).
12. Jarrett Renshaw et al., "Biden Says China Will Not Surpass U.S. as Global Leader on His Watch," Reuters, March 25, 2021, https://www.reuters.com/article/world/biden-says-china-will-not-surpass-us-as-global-leader-on-his-watch-idUSKBN2BH32Z/.
13. *National Security Strategy*, Executive Office of the President, White House, October 12, 2022, https://bidenwhitehouse.archives.gov/wp-content/uploads/2022/10/Biden-Harris-Administrations-National-Security-Strategy-10.2022.pdf.
14. "China GDP Surpasses Japan, Capping Three-Decade Rise," *Bloomberg News*, August 16, 2010, https://www.bloomberg.com/news/articles/2010-08-16/china-economy-passes-japan-s-in-second-quarter-capping-three-decade-rise.
15. Written testimony of Geoffrey R. Pyatt, "Assessing U.S. Efforts to Counter China's Coercive Belt and Road Diplomacy," US Department of State, June 14, 2023, https://2021-2025.state.gov/assessing-u-s-efforts-to-counter-chinas-coercive-belt-and-road-diplomacy/.
16. Ryan Hass, "The Trajectory of Chinese Foreign Policy: From Reactive Assertiveness to Opportunistic Activism," John L. Thornton China Center, Center for East Asia

Policy Studies, Brookings Institution, March 2018, https://www.brookings.edu/wp-content/uploads/2018/03/fp_20171104_hass_the_trajectory_of_chinese_foreign_policy.pdf; Michael H. Hunt, *The Genesis of Chinese Communist Foreign Policy* (Columbia University Press, 1996).

17. Mohan Malik, *China and India: Great Power Rivals* (First Forum, 2011); Harsh V. Pant, "Rising China in India's Vicinity: A Rivalry Takes Shape in Asia," *Cambridge Review of International Affairs* 25, no. 3 (2013): 1–18; T. V. Paul, ed., *The China-India Rivalry in the Globalization Era* (Georgetown University Press, 2018).

18. Hass, "The Trajectory of Chinese Foreign Policy"; Ronald C. Keith, *Deng Xiaoping and China's Foreign Policy* (Routledge, 2018).

19. Markey, *China's Western Horizon*, 15–19.

20. The term "periphery" has been used by scholars in varying ways. Within Immanuel Wallerstein's world systems theory, for example, "periphery countries" are those smaller or weaker countries that are dominated by either core or semi-periphery countries within the global economic system, usually for cheap labor and raw materials as inputs to core countries' economic production. However, within this book, I use "periphery" to describe rural frontier regions physically on the edges of a state's territory whose inhabitants often possess different cultures and political identities from groups dominating government and economic institutions in the centers of power and have a history of resistance to state authority, as outlined in this section. See Akbar Ahmed, *The Thistle and the Drone: How America's War on Terror Became a Global War on Tribal Islam* (Brookings Institution Press, 2013), 11–34.

21. James C. Scott, *The Art of Not Being Governed: An Anarchist History of Southeast Asia* (Yale University Press, 2009), 26–32; James C. Scott, *Against the Grain: A Deep History of the Earliest States* (Yale University Press, 2017), 33.

22. Clifford Geertz, *The Interpretation of Cultures* (Basic Books, 1973), 297.

23. Lord Curzon of Kedleston, *The Romanes Lecture 1907: Frontiers* (Clarendon Press, 1907), 40.

24. Curzon, 6, 7.

25. Peter Fleming, *Bayonets to Lhasa: The British Invasion of Tibet* (Harper, 1961), 23.

26. Mark Condos, "'Fanaticism' and the Politics of Resistance along the North-West Frontier of British India," *Comparative Studies in Society and History* 58, no. 3 (2016): 717–745.

27. K. Sivaramakrishnan, *Modern Forests: Statemaking and Environmental Change in Colonial Eastern India* (Stanford University Press, 1999), 38.

28. *Lord Curzon in India: Being a Selection from His Speeches as Viceroy & Governor-General of India, 1898–1905* (Macmillan and Co., 1906), 37.

29. Harrison Akins, "Mashar Versus Kashar in Pakistan's FATA: Intra-Tribal Conflict and the Obstacles of Reform," *Asian Survey* 58, no. 6 (2018): 1136–1159; Lauren Benton, "Colonial Law and Cultural Differences: Jurisdictional Politics and the Formation of the Colonial State," *Comparative Studies in Society and History* 41, no. 3 (1999): 563–588; Benjamin D. Hopkins, *Ruling the Savage Periphery: Frontier Governance and the Making of the Modern State* (Harvard University Press, 2020); Adnan

Naseemullah and Paul Staniland, "Indirect Rule and Varieties of Governance," *Governance* 29, no. 1 (2016): 13–30.

30. Hopkins, *Ruling the Savage Periphery*, 7.
31. Christian Tripodi, "'Good for One but Not the Other': The 'Sandeman System' of Pacification as Applied to Baluchistan and the North-West Frontier, 1877–1947," *Journal of Military History* 73, no. 3 (2009): 769.
32. Simpson, *The Frontier in British India*, 250–251; Christian Tripodi, *Edge of Empire: The British Political Officer and Tribal Administration on the North-West Frontier, 1877–1947* (Ashgate, 2011), 54–63.
33. Richard Bruce, *The Forward Policy and Its Results, or Thirty-Five Years' Work Amongst the Tribes on Our North-Western Frontier of India* (Longmans, Green, and Co., 1900), 66, 110.
34. Hopkins, *Ruling the Savage Periphery*; Elisabeth Leake, "At the Nation-State's Edge: Centre-Periphery Relations in Post-1947 South Asia," *Historical Journal* 29, no. 2 (2016): 509–539; Thomas Simpson, *The Frontier in British India: Space, Science, and Power in the Nineteenth Century* (Cambridge University Press, 2021), 224–258; Thomas Simpson, "Bordering and Frontier-Making in Nineteenth-Century British India," *Historical Journal* 58, no. 2 (2015): 513–542; Tripodi, "'Good for One but Not the Other.'"
35. Jangkhomang Guite, "Colonialism and Its Unruly?—The Colonial State and Kuki Raids in Nineteenth Century Northeast India," *Modern Asian Studies* 48, no. 5 (2014): 1188–1232.
36. Simpson, "Bordering and Frontier-Making in Nineteenth-Century British India," 513.
37. Adnan Naseemullah, *Patchwork States: The Historical Roots of Subnational Conflict and Competition in South Asia* (Cambridge University Press, 2022), 6.
38. Thomas Blom Hansen and Finn Stepputat, eds., *Sovereign Bodies: Citizens, Migrants, and States in the Postcolonial World* (Princeton University Press, 2005), 4.
39. Kyle J. Gardner, *The Frontier Complex: Geopolitics and the Making of the India-China Border, 1846–1962* (Cambridge University Press, 2021), 3.
40. Hopkins, *Ruling the Savage Periphery*; Leake, "At the Nation-State's Edge"; Simpson, "Bordering and Frontier-Making in Nineteenth-Century British India."
41. Ahmed, *The Thistle and the Drone*, 134–254.
42. See, for instance, Arkotong Longkumer, *The Greater India Experiment: Hindutva and the Northeast* (Stanford University Press, 2021).
43. Sanjib Baruah, *In the Name of the Nation: India and Its Northeast* (Stanford University Press, 2020), 12.
44. Anil Yadav, *Is That Even a Country, Sir!: Journeys in Northeast India by Train, Bus and Tractor*, trans. Anurag Basnet (Speaking Tiger, 2017), 1.
45. B. K. Nehru, foreword to *Sentinels of the North-East: The Assam Rifles*, by Major General D. K. Palit (Palit and Palit, 1984), 5.
46. Karishma Kuenzang, "Poetry: Poems from Nagaland," *Hindustan Times*, October 9, 2021, https://www.hindustantimes.com/lifestyle/brunch/poetry-poems-from-nagaland-101633795664615.html.

47. Ahmed, *The Thistle and the Drone*, 64.
48. Bruce Bueno de Mesquita and Randolph M. Siverson, "War and the Survival of Political Leaders: A Comparative Study of Regime Types and Political Accountability," *American Political Science Review* 89, no. 4 (1995): 841–855; James D. Fearon, "Domestic Political Audiences and the Escalation of International Disputes," *American Political Science Review* 88, no. 3 (1994): 577–592; Robert D. Putnam, "Diplomacy and Domestic Politics: The Logic of Two-Level Games," *International Organizations* 42, no. 3 (1988): 427–460.
49. Peter Gourevitch, "The Second Image Reversed: The International Sources of Domestic Politics," *International Organization* 32, no. 4 (1978): 881–912; Kenneth N. Waltz, *Man, State, and War: A Theoretical Analysis* (Columbia University Press, 1954).
50. Harrison Akins, "Violence on the Home Front: Interstate Rivalry and Pro-Government Militias," *Terrorism and Political Violence* 33, no. 3 (2021): 466–488; Sabine C. Carey et al., "Governments, Informal Links to Militias, and Accountability," *Journal of Conflict Resolution* 59, no. 5 (2015): 850–876; Gourevitch, "The Second Image Reversed"; Mark Toukan, "International politics by Other Means: External Sources of Civil War," *Journal of Peace Research* 56, no. 6 (2019): 812–826; Gary Uzonyi, "Interstate Rivalry, Genocide, and Politicide," *Journal of Peace Research* 55, no. 4 (2018): 476–490.
51. Christophe Jaffrelot, *The Pakistan Paradox: Instability and Resilience*, trans. Cynthia Scoch (Hurst & Co., 2015), 439–507; Zia ur-Rehman, "In a Region of Majestic Beauty, Sunnis and Shiites Wage Bloody War," *New York Times*, October 25, 2024, https://www.nytimes.com/2024/10/25/world/asia/pakistan-kurram-sunni-shiite.html.
52. Harrison Akins, *The Terrorism Trap: How the War on Terror Escalates Violence in America's Partner States* (Columbia University Press, 2023), 91–146.
53. The focus on political elites in this study centers on those who make up the "official mind" within the government decision-making process, rather than a broader category of elites that includes nongovernment figures such as businessmen or other economic actors. This conception of government officialdom underlying the decision-making process not only includes senior officials at the upper echelons of the state bureaucracy making the final decision on matters of policy but also mid-level bureaucrats, diplomats, military officials, intelligence officers, and administrators in the field whose work, analysis, and reporting feeds into the policy process and influences senior officials' views and decisions. Additionally, I include in the analysis the arguments and actions of leading politicians, including key opposition figures, whose public critiques and political pressure similarly play a role in shaping government policy and actions.
54. Robert Jervis, *Perception and Misperception in International Politics* (Princeton University Press, 1976).
55. Christopher Clary, *The Difficult Politics of Peace: Rivalry in Modern South Asia* (Oxford University Press, 2022), 32–5.
56. Clary, 295.
57. Jervis, *Perception and Misperception in International Politics*, 158.

58. Idean Salehyan, "Transnational Rebels: Neighboring States as Sanctuary for Rebel Groups," *World Politics* 59, no. 2 (2007): 217–242; Idean Salehyan, "The Delegation of War to Rebel Organizations," *Journal of Conflict Resolution* 54, no. 3 (2010): 493–515; Idean Salehyan et al., "Explaining External Support for Insurgent Groups," *International Organization* 65 (2011): 709–744; Milos Popovic, "Fragile Proxies: Explaining Rebel Defection Against Their State Sponsors," *Terrorism and Political Violence* 29, no. 5 (2017): 922–942; Mark Toukan, "International Politics by Other Means: External Sources of Civil War," *Journal of Peace Research* 56, no. 6 (2019): 812–826.
59. William Sewell, "Three Temporalities: Toward an Eventful Sociology," in *The Historic Turn in the Human Sciences*, ed. Terrence J. McDonald (University of Michigan Press, 1996), 254–280.
60. James Mahoney, "Strategies of Causal Assessment in Comparative Historical Analysis," in *Comparative Historical Analysis in the Social Sciences*, ed. James Mahoney and Dietrich Rueschemeyer (Cambridge University Press, 2003), 265.
61. See Simpson, "Bordering and Frontier-Making in Nineteenth-Century British India"; Simpson, *The Frontier in British India.*
62. Leake, "At the Nation-State's Edge," 512.
63. Hillman, *The Emperor's New Road.*
64. Markey, *China's Western Horizon.*
65. Andrew Small, *The China–Pakistan Axis: Asia's New Geopolitics* (Oxford University Press, 2020), 77.
66. Deborah Brautigam, *The Dragon's Gift: The Real Story of China in Africa* (Oxford University Press, 2009); Philippe Le Corre and Alain Sepulchre, *China's Offensive in Europe* (Brookings Institution Press, 2016); Jonathan Fulton, "Domestic Politics as Fuel for China's Maritime Silk Road Initiative: The Case of the Gulf Monarchies," *Journal of Contemporary China* 29, no. 122 (2020): 175–190; James Reardon-Anderson, ed., *The Red Star and the Crescent: China and the Middle East* (Oxford University Press, 2018); David H. Shinn and Joshua Eisenman, *China and Africa: A Century of Engagement* (University of Pennsylvania Press, 2012); Laurids S. Lauridsen, "Drivers of China's Regional Infrastructure Diplomacy: The Case of the Sino-Thai Railway Project," *Journal of Contemporary Asia* 50, no. 3 (2020): 380–406; David H. Shinn and Joshua Eisenman, *China's Relations with Africa: A New Era of Strategic Engagement* (Columbia University Press, 2023); Sebastian Strangio, *In the Dragon's Shadow: Southeast Asia in the Chinese Century* (Yale University Press, 2020); David Styan, "China's Maritime Silk Road and Small States: Lessons from the Case of Djibouti," *Journal of Contemporary China* 29, no. 122 (2020): 191–206; Suisheng Zhao, "A Neo-Colonialist Predator or Development Partner? China's Engagement and Rebalance in Africa," *Journal of Contemporary China* 23, no. 90 (2014): 1033–1052; Yizheng Zou and Lee Jones, "China's Response to Threats to Its Overseas Economic Interests: Softening Non-Interference and Cultivating Hegemony," *Journal of Contemporary China* 29, no. 121 (2021): 92–108.
67. Berenice Guyot-Rechard, *Shadow States: India, China and the Himalayas, 1910–1962* (Cambridge University Press, 2017).

68. Bertil Lintner, *Great Game East: India, China, and the Struggle for Asia's Most Volatile Frontier* (Yale University Press, 2015), 82.
69. Manoj Joshi, *Understanding the India-China Border: The Enduring Threat of War in High Himalaya* (Oxford University Press, 2022).

2. "ANOTHER GREAT GAME"

1. See, for example, Kallol Bhattacherjee, *The Great Game in Afghanistan: Rajiv Gandhi, General Zia and the Unending War* (HarperCollins, 2017); Thomas Fingar, *The New Great Game: China and South and Central Asia in the Era of Reform* (Stanford University Press, 2016); Marlene Laruelle et al., eds., *China and India in Central Asia: A New "Great Game"?* (Palgrave Macmillan, 2010); Djoomart Otorbaev, *Central Asia's Economic Rebirth in the Shadow of the New Great Game* (Routledge, 2023); Ahmed Rashid, *Taliban: Islam, Oil and the New Great Game in Central Asia* (I. B. Tauris, 2002).
2. Lintner, *Great Game East*, 1–2.
3. Ankit Panda, "Geography's Curse: India's Vulnerable 'Chicken Neck,'" *Diplomat*, November 8, 2013.
4. Fleming, *Bayonets to Lhasa*, 12.
5. Fleming, 11.
6. Fleming, 230.
7. National Archives of India, New Delhi (henceforth cited as NAI), File No. 156–134, PR_000005003135, Affairs on the North-East Frontier, Foreign and Political Department, Government of India, December 1914; Guyot-Rechard, *Shadow States*, 33.
8. Guyot-Rechard, *Shadow States*, 25.
9. Guyot-Rechard, 29.
10. Hsaio-ting Lin, *Tibet and Nationalist China's Frontier: Intrigues and Ethnopolitics, 1928–1949* (University of British Columbia Press, 2006).
11. "Convention Between Great Britain and Russia, 1907," Tibet Justice Center, accessed July 8, 2025, https://www.tibetjustice.org/materials/treaties/treaties12.html.
12. B. R. Ambedkar, *History of the Frontier Areas Bordering on Assam* (Assam Government Press, 1942), 221–222.
13. Simpson, *The Frontier in British India*, 64.
14. Debojyoti Das, "Understanding Margins, State Power, Space and Territoriality in the Naga Hills," *Journal of Borderland Studies* 29, no. 1 (2014): 63–80; Simpson, *The Frontier in British India*, 183–184.
15. NAI, File No. 146/51, PR_000004010255, Lieutenant Woodthorpe's report on the Survey operations in the Naga Hills during 1875–1876, Foreign Department, Government of India, January 1877.
16. NAI, File No. 146/51, PR_000004010255, Lieutenant Woodthorpe's report on the Survey operations in the Naga Hills during 1875–1876, Foreign Department, Government of India, January 1877.

17. NAI, File No. 331/395D, PR_ 000004010094, Naga Affairs—Attack on Baladhan Tea Garden. Assistance rendered by the Maharaja of Manipur. Services Performed by British Officers, Foreign Department, Government of India, March 1880.
18. NAI, File No. 133–177, PR_000004010254, Naga Hills, Foreign Department, Government of India, August 1877.
19. Lipokmar Dzuvichu, "Roads and the Raj: The Politics of Road Building in Colonial Naga Hills, 1860s–1910s," *Indian Economic and Social History Review* 50, no. 4 (2013): 474; Alexander Mackenzie, *History of the Relations of the Government with the Hill Tribes of the North-East Frontier of Bengal* (Home Department Press, 1884), 470; NAI, File No. 133–177, PR_000004010254, Naga Hills, Foreign Department, Government of India, August 1877; Simpson, *The Frontier in British India*, 35–36, 237–49; NAI, File No. 331/395D, PR_ 000004010094, Naga Affairs—Attack on Baladhan Tea Garden. Assistance rendered by the Maharaja of Manipur. Services Performed by British Officers, Foreign Department, Government of India, March 1880.
20. NAI, File No. 616–640, PR_000004010095, Naga Hills Affairs, Foreign Department, Government of India, August 1881.
21. Simpson, *The Frontier in British India*, 55.
22. NAI, File No. 14–25, PR_000004008149, Policy to Be Pursued in Dealing with Transfrontier Naga Tribes, Foreign Department, Government of India, March 1886.
23. Robert Reid, *History of the Frontier Areas Bordering on Assam from 1883–1941* (Assam Government Press, 1942), 99–100, 132–133.
24. Hopkins, *Ruling the Savage Periphery*, 198–210; Mackenzie, *History of the Relations of the Government with the Hill Tribes of the North-East Frontier of Bengal*, 369; Jangkhomang Guite, "Colonial Violence and Its 'Small Wars': Fighting the Kuki 'Guerillas' During the Great War in Northeast India, 1917–1919," *Small Wars & Insurgencies* 30, no. 2 (2019): 447–478; Jangkhomang Guite and Thongkholal Haokip, eds., *The Anglo-Kuki War, 1917–1919: A Frontier Uprising Against Imperialism During the First World War* (Routledge, 2019).
25. Hopkins, *Ruling the Savage Periphery*, 56–57.
26. Richard M. Eaton, "Conversion to Christianity Among the Nagas, 1876–1971," *Indian Economic and Social History Review* 21, no. 1 (1984): 1–4.
27. NAI, File No. 134, PR_000005003163, Rival Missionary enterprise in the Manipur State. Question of the withdrawal of the recognition of Mr. Watkin Roberts as a Missionary in India, Foreign and Political Department, Government of India, 1930.
28. Simpson, *The Frontier in British India*, 70–115.
29. Shakespear, *History of the Assam Rifles*, 126.
30. NAI, File No. 76–83, PR_000005001774, Reports on an exploration on the North-East Frontier, 1913, by Captains F. M. Bailey, I. A. and H. T. Morshead, R. E., Foreign and Political Department, Government of India, October 1916.
31. NAI, File No. 76–83, PR_000005001774, Reports on an exploration on the North-East Frontier, 1913, by Captains F. M. Bailey, I. A. and H. T. Morshead.
32. Bertil Lintner, *China's India War: Collision Course on the Roof of the World* (Oxford University Press, 2018), 40–44.

33. NAI, File No. 156–134, PR_000005003135, Affairs on the North-East Frontier, Foreign and Political Department, Government of India, December 1914.
34. Sonika Gupta, "Frontiers in Flux: Indo-Tibetan Border: 1946–1948," *India Quarterly* 77, no. 1 (2021): 42–58.
35. Guyot-Rechard, *Shadow States*, 223.
36. Palit, *Sentinels of the North-East*, 96–97.
37. Guyot-Rechard, *Shadow States*, 69.
38. Melvyn C. Goldstein, *A History of Modern Tibet, 1913–1951: The Demise of the Lamaist State* (University of California Press, 1989), 401.
39. Guyot-Rechard, *Shadow States*, 89.
40. National Archives, London, UK, FO/371/63533, Situation in India—preparations for the transfer of power (Folder 6), March–May 1947.
41. Ramachandra Guha, *India After Gandhi: The History of the World's Largest Democracy* (Ecco, 2008), 273.
42. NAI, File No. 67/48-P.S., PP_000000005874, Memorandum of statement of the case of hill tribes of Assam 1948, Private Papers of Sardar Patel, 1948.
43. Lintner, *Great Game East*, 61.
44. See "Naga-Akbar Hydari Accord (Nine Point Agreement), Kohima, 26–28 June 1947," UN Peacemaker, accessed July 25, 2025, https://peacemaker.un.org/sites/default/files/document/files/2024/05/in470628naga-akbar20hydari20accord.pdf.
45. Guha, *India After Gandhi*, 269.
46. Ramachandra Guha, *Savaging the Civilized: Verrier Elwin, His Tribals, and India* (Penguin Press, 2014), 155.
47. Guha, 157–158, 168–169.
48. "The Agreement of the Central People's Government and the Local Government of Tibet on Measures for the Peaceful Liberation of Tibet, 23 May, 1951," Tibet Justice Center, accessed July 8, 2025, https://www.tibetjustice.org/materials/china/china3.html.
49. *Selected Works of Jawaharlal Nehru*, 2nd ser., vol. 25, ed. S. Gopal (Jawaharlal Nehru Memorial Fund, 1999), 328.
50. Guha, *India After Gandhi*, 176–177.
51. Subir Bhaumak, *Insurgent Crossfire: North-East India* (Lancer Publishers, 1996), 25.
52. Wilson Center Digital Archive, Cable from the Chinese Foreign Ministry, "Report on Negotiations regarding the Tibet issue between China and India," November 24, 1950, History and Public Policy Program Digital Archive, PRC FMA 105-00011-02, 42–44, obtained by Dai Chaowu and translated by 7Brands, http://digitalarchive.wilsoncenter.org/document/114749.
53. Jawaharlal Nehru, *Letters for a Nation: From Jawaharlal Nehru to His Chief Ministers, 1947–1963*, ed. Madhav Khosla (Penguin Books, 2014), 285, 287.
54. Nehru, 287.
55. NAI, File No. 2/439, PP_000000006136, China & Tibet, Private Papers of Sardar Patel, 1950.
56. NAI, File No. 2/439, PP_000000006136, China & Tibet.

57. National Archives, UK, DO/133/28, China—relations with India and other states, treatment of foreign nationals, internal developments, 1951–1952.
58. NAI, File No. 2/439, PP_000000006136, China & Tibet.
59. NAI, File No. 80-R&I/51, PR_000005002318, Sikkim & Tibet (Reports), Indian Ministry of External Affairs, 1951.
60. NAI, File No. 80-R&I/51, PR_000005002318, Sikkim & Tibet (Reports).
61. NAI, File No. 7 (1)P/52, PR_000005002060, Tibet Policy: Top Secret notes on India & China on Tibet, Indian Ministry of External Affairs, 1952.
62. NAI, File No. 2/439, PP_000000006136, China & Tibet.
63. NAI, File No. 2/439, PP_000000006136, China & Tibet.
64. Bhaumak, *Insurgent Crossfire*, 14.
65. Marguerite Higgins, "Recognition of China, Way to End Cold War, Nehru's Advice to American," *Hindu*, October 31, 1952.
66. CIA Reading Room, Nehru's China Trip, NSC Briefing, Central Intelligence Agency, November 8, 1954, declassified and approved for release May 17, 2001.
67. Wilson Center Digital Archive, Agreement between the Republic of India and the People's Republic of China on Trade and Intercourse Between the Tibet Region of China and India, April 29, 1954, History and Public Policy Program Digital Archive, *Renmin ribao* [People's Daily], April 30, 1954, http://digitalarchive.wilsoncenter.org/document/121558.
68. Wilson Center Digital Archive, Summary of the Talks Between Premier Zhou and Nehru and U Nu, April 16, 1955, History and Public Policy Program Digital Archive, PRC FMA 207-00015-01, 1–10, obtained by Amitav Acharya and translated by Yang Shanhou, http://digitalarchive.wilsoncenter.org/document/114671.
69. Lintner, *China's India War*, 22.
70. Nehru, *Letters for a Nation*, 221.
71. Arunabh Ghosh, "Before 1962: The Case for 1950s China-India History," *Journal of Asian Studies* 76, no. 3 (2017): 697–727.
72. NAI, File No. 80-R&I/51, PR_000005002318, Sikkim & Tibet (Reports).
73. NAI, File No. 80-R&I/51, PR_000005002318, Sikkim & Tibet (Reports).
74. NAI, File No. 80-R&I/51, PR_000005002318, Sikkim & Tibet (Reports).
75. Guyot-Rechard, *Shadow States*, 18, 208–212.
76. NAI, File No. 7 (1)P/52, PR_000005002060, Tibet Policy: Top Secret notes on India & China on Tibet.
77. NAI, File No. 26(28)-EI/53, PR_000004001363, Fourteen of a set of fresh rules . . . the terms of service condition of the agency service NEF Agency, Indian Ministry of External Affairs, 1955.
78. NAI, File No. 26(28)-EI/53, PR_000004001363, Fourteen of a set of fresh rules . . . the terms of service condition of the agency service NEF Agency.
79. NAI, File No. 2/439, PP_000000006136, China & Tibet; CIA Reading Room, Reports of Chinese Communist Plans to Attack India, Information from Foreign Documents or Radio Broadcasts, Central Intelligence Agency, September 22, 1952, sanitized copy approved for release September 14, 2011.

80. NAI, File No. 3/6, PP_000000005350, Assam Ministerial Sep–Dec 1950, Private Papers of Sardar Patel, 1950.
81. NAI, File No. 3/6, PP_000000005350, Assam Ministerial Sep–Dec 1950.
82. NAI, File No. 3/6, PP_000000005350, Assam Ministerial Sep–Dec 1950.
83. National Archives, UK, DO/133/26, China—propaganda, relations with India, Chinese in India, foreign missionaries in China, internal developments, February–May 1951.
84. Palit, *Sentinels of the North-East*, 193.
85. Guha, *India After Gandhi*, 181.
86. CIA Reading Room, The China-India Border Dispute, Geographic Intelligence Memorandum, Office of Research and Reports, Central Intelligence Agency, November 20, 1959, declassified and approved for release May 11, 2000.
87. Harrison Akins, "The Assam Rifles and India's North-East Frontier Policy," *Small Wars & Insurgencies* 31, no. 6 (2020): 1385; "MoD Can't Locate Five Key Reports on Military Reforms," *Times of India*, October 14, 2011; Claude Arpi, "1962 War: 'Secret Reports' Lost Forever?," *Indian Defence Review*, August 12, 2020, http://www.indiandefencereview.com/1962-war-secret-reports-lost-forever/. The report of the Himmatsinhji Committee reportedly remains "lost." In October 2011, *The Times of India* reported that the Defense Ministry was unable to locate the report within the ministry, along with four other reports that were sought by a military researcher through a right to information request.
88. NAI, File No. 2/439, PP_000000006136, China & Tibet.
89. NAI, File No. 2/439, PP_000000006136, China & Tibet.
90. NAI, File No. 2/439, PP_000000006136, China & Tibet.
91. Nehru, *Letters for a Nation*, 220.
92. Nehru, 220–221.
93. NAI, File No. 71_NEF/47, PR_000005003232, Extension of regular administration to the Naga Hills Tribal Area. Four-year plan for that area, Indian Ministry of External Affairs & Commonwealth Relations, 1947.
94. NAI, File No. 15(11)-NEF/47, PR_000005003230, Summary for Cabinet: Development of the North East Tribal Areas, Indian Ministry of External Affairs, 25 April 1947.
95. *Selected Works of Jawaharlal Nehru*, 183; Nehru, *Letters for a Nation*, 59.
96. *Selected Works of Jawaharlal Nehru*, 183–184.
97. Baruah, *In the Name of the Nation*, 31.
98. Verrier Elwin, *Nagaland* (Assam Government Research Department, Adviser's Secretariat, 1961), 44; Hopkins, *Ruling the Savage Periphery*.
99. NAI, File No. 71_NEF/47, PR_000005003232, Extension of regular administration to the Naga Hills Tribal Area. Four-year plan for that area, Indian Ministry of External Affairs & Commonwealth Relations, 1947.
100. NAI, File No. 15(11)-NEF/47, PR_000005003230, Summary for Cabinet: Development of the North East Tribal Areas, Indian Ministry of External Affairs, April 25, 1947.
101. NAI, File No. 15(11)-NEF/47, PR_000005003230, Summary for Cabinet: Development of the North East Tribal Areas.

102. NAI, File No. 15(11)-NEF/47, PR_000005003230, Summary for Cabinet: Development of the North East Tribal Areas.
103. Palit, *Sentinels of the North-East,* 5.
104. NAI, File No. 71_NEF/47, PR_000005003232, Extension of regular administration to the Naga Hills Tribal Area. Four-year plan for that area, Indian Ministry of External Affairs & Commonwealth Relations, 1947.
105. NAI, File No. 71_NEF/47, PR_000005003232, Extension of regular administration to the Naga Hills Tribal Area. Four-year plan for that area.
106. Guyot-Rechard, *Shadow States*, 80–81.
107. Boaz Atzili and Min Jung Kim, "Buffer Zones and International Rivalry: Internal and External Geographic Separation Mechanisms," *International Affairs* 99, no. 2 (2023): 645–665.
108. Palit, *Sentinels of the North-East*, 197.
109. B. K. Nehru, *Nice Guys Finish Second: Memoirs* (Penguin India, 2000), 477.
110. Nari Rustomji, *Imperilled Frontiers: India's North-Eastern Borderlands* (Oxford University Press, 1983), 97.
111. NAI, File No. 3/6, PP_000000005346, Assam Ministerial, Private Papers of Sardar Patel, 1948–1950.
112. Guyot-Rechard, *Shadow States*, 107.
113. Palit, *Sentinels of the North-East*, 197.
114. Guyot-Rechard, *Shadow States*, 106.
115. Guyot-Rechard, 106
116. Guyot-Rechard, 131–133.
117. Jyotirindra Dasgupta, "Community, Authenticity, and Autonomy: Insurgence and Institutional Development in India's Northeast," *Journal of Asian Studies* 56, no. 2 (1997): 364.
118. The actual perpetrators and ultimate goal of the massacre have been subject to some debate. See Guyot-Rechard, *Shadow States*, 123–124.
119. Guha, *Savaging the Civilized*, 224–225.
120. Guha, 231.
121. Nehru, *Letters for a Nation*, 58.
122. Guha, *Savaging the Civilized*, 258.
123. Verrier Elwin, *A Philosophy for NEFA* (North-East Frontier Agency, 1957), 46, 53–54, 59.
124. Guha, *Savaging the Civilized*, 257.
125. Guha, 265–266.
126. NAI, File No. 4 (5)-NEFA/56, PR_000005003519, Dr. Elwin Notes on His Visit to Bomdila and Tawang, Ministry of External Affairs, Government of India, 1956.
127. NAI, File No. 4 (5)-NEFA/56, PR_000005003519, Dr. Elwin Notes on His Visit to Bomdila and Tawang.
128. NAI, File No. 4 (5)-NEFA/56, PR_000005003519, Dr. Elwin Notes on His Visit to Bomdila and Tawang.
129. Guyot-Rechard, *Shadow States*, 219, 228–229.
130. Lintner, *Great Game East*, 64.

131. Lintner, 64–65.
132. Guha, *India After Gandhi*, 276–277.
133. Lintner, *Great Game East*, 66.
134. Lintner, 282–283.
135. Lintner, 283.
136. *Selected Works of Jawaharlal Nehru*, 210.
137. B. N. Mullik, *My Years with Nehru, 1948–1964* (Allied Publishers, 1972), 310–311.
138. Lintner, *Great Game East*, 66.
139. Guha, *India After Gandhi*, 278.
140. Guha, 279–280.
141. Guha, 280.
142. Lintner, *Great Game East*, 66.
143. Mullik, *My Years with Nehru*, 313–314.
144. NAI, File No. 4/17/57-Poll.II, PR_000004009656, Reports & Returns: Fortnightly Reports from the Government of Assam for 1957, Indian Ministry of Home Affairs, 1957.
145. NAI, File No. 4/17/57-Poll.II, PR_000004009656, Reports & Returns: Fortnightly Reports from the Government of Assam for 1957.
146. NAI, File No. 4/17/57-Poll.II, PR_000004009656, Reports & Returns: Fortnightly Reports from the Government of Assam for 1957.
147. NAI, File No. 1 (29)/ NEFA/59, PR_000004008699, The Armed Forces (Special Powers) Regulation, 1958, Appendix A, Indian Ministry of External Affairs, 1958.
148. As of April 2023, under new guidance introduced by the Home Ministry, the AFSPA was still in effect in areas of forty-one districts across the northeastern states of Assam, Manipur, Nagaland, and Arunachal Pradesh. See Rokibuz Zaman, "'Historic' Decision by Centre Reduces AFSPA's Footprint? Not By Much," *Scroll.in*, March 27, 2023, https://scroll.in/article/1046309/historic-decision-by-centre-reduces-afspas-footprint-not-by-much.
149. Ananya Vajpeyi, "Resenting the Indian State: For a New Political Practice in the Northeast," in *Beyond Counterinsurgency: Breaking the Impasse in Northeast India*, ed. Sanjib Baruah (Oxford University Press, 2009), 36.
150. National Archives, UK, DO/133/192, Nagaland—political situation (reported by Deputy High Commission, Calcutta), 1970.
151. Ved Mehta, *Portrait of India* (Yale University Press, 1993), 213.
152. NAI, File No. CG/133/61, PR_000004001769, Naga-Phizo, Indian Ministry of External Affairs, 1961, pp. 3, 8.
153. Desmond Doig, "Aspects of Lingering Strife in Nagaland, Difficulties of Terrain and Human Element," *Statesman*, May 22, 1962.
154. Desmond Doig, "Recent Progress in Nagaland and After, Shilu Ao on Role of Church Leaders," *Statesman*, May 19, 1962.
155. Doig, "Aspects of Lingering Strife in Nagaland, Difficulties of Terrain and Human Element."
156. Doig, "Recent Progress in Nagaland and After, Shilu Ao on Role of Church Leaders."

157. NAI, File No. CG/133/61, PR_000004001769, Naga-Phizo.
158. NAI, File No. 4/17/57-Poll.II, PR_000004009656, Reports & Returns: Fortnightly Reports from the Government of Assam for 1957.
159. NAI, File No. 4/17/57-Poll.II, PR_000004009656, Reports & Returns: Fortnightly Reports from the Government of Assam for 1957.
160. Lintner, *Great Game East*, 68; Mehta, *Portrait of India*, 211–213.
161. Guha, *India After Gandhi*, 327–328.
162. NAI, File No. CG/133/61, PR_000004001769, Naga-Phizo.
163. NAI, File No. NII/102(5)/63, PR_000004008707, Amnesty Declared for Naga Hostiles, Indian Ministry of Home Affairs, 1963.
164. NAI, File No. NII/102(5)/63, PR_000004008707, Amnesty Declared for Naga Hostiles.
165. Palit, *Sentinels of the North-East*, 248.
166. NAI, File No. CG/133/61, PR_000004001769, Naga-Phizo.
167. NAI, File No. CG/133/61, PR_000004001769, Naga-Phizo.

3. THE CHINA-INDIA WAR AND THE NORTHEASTERN INSURGENCIES

1. NAI, File No. 30(3)-NEF/55, PR_000004001365, Political situation reports on Sikkim from the political officer in Sikkim Gangtok, Indian Ministry of External Affairs, 1955; CIA Reading Room, Resistance in Tibet, Geographic Intelligence Memorandum, Office of Research and Reports, Central Intelligence Agency, July 21, 1958, declassified and approved for release May 11, 2000.
2. NAI, File No. 30(3)-NEF/55, PR_000004001365, Political situation reports on Sikkim from the political officer in Sikkim Gangtok, Indian Ministry of External Affairs, 1955.
3. Bhaumak, *Insurgent Crossfire*, 25.
4. Memorandum for the Special Group, January 9, 1964, Document 337, *Foreign Relations of the United States* [hereafter cited as *FRUS*], *1964–1968*, vol. 30, *China* (US Government Printing Office, 1998); Mike Dunham, *Buddha's Warrior: The Story of the CIA-Backed Tibetan Freedom Fighters, the Chinese Invasion, and the Ultimate Fall of Tibet* (Penguin, 2004); Lintner, *Great Game East*, 26–36.
5. CIA Reading Room, Resistance in Tibet, Geographic Intelligence Memorandum, Office of Research and Reports, Central Intelligence Agency, July 21, 1958, declassified and approved for release May 11, 2000; Wang Gungwu and Zheng Yongnian, *China and the New International Order* (Routledge, 2008), 5.
6. NAI, File No. 52-R&I/56, PR_000005014121, Reports on Sikkim (Gangtok), Indian Ministry of External Affairs, 1956.
7. NAI, File No. 6(33)/58, PR_000005002784, Sikkim (Gangtok) Reports (Other than Annual) from 1958, Indian Ministry of External Affairs, 1958.
8. Bhaumak, *Insurgent Crossfire*, 29.

9. Wilson Center Digital Archive, Discussion between N. S. Khrushchev and Mao Zedong, October 2, 1959, History and Public Policy Program Digital Archive, Archive of the President of the Russian Federation (APRF), f. 52, op. 1, d. 499, ll. 1–33, copy in Volkogonov Collection, Manuscript Division, Library of Congress, Washington, DC, translated by Vladislav M. Zubok, http://digitalarchive.wilsoncenter.org/document/112088.
10. Wilson Center Digital Archive, Report from the PLA General Staff Department, "Behind India's Second Anti-China Wave," October 29, 1959, History and Public Policy Program Digital Archive, PRC FMA 105-00944-07, 84–90, translated by 7Brands, http://digitalarchive.wilsoncenter.org/document/114758.
11. Wilson Center Digital Archive, Report from the PLA General Staff Department, "Behind India's Second Anti-China Wave."
12. Wilson Center Digital Archive, Pakistani Ambassador Raza Pays Formal Visit to Chinese Premier Zhou, September 5, 1962, History and Public Policy Program Digital Archive, PRC FMA 105-01802-03, 41–46, obtained by Sulmaan Khan and translated by Anna Beth Keim, http://digitalarchive.wilsoncenter.org/document/112750.
13. Wilson Center Digital Archive, Pakistani Ambassador Raza Pays Formal Visit to Chinese Premier Zhou.
14. Lintner, *China's India War*, 123.
15. Wilson Center Digital Archive, Record of Conversation Between Zhou Enlai and Vice-President Sarvepalli Radhakrishnan, April 21, 1960, History and Public Policy Program Digital Archive, Nehru Memorial Museum and Library, P. N. Haksar Papers (I-II Installment), Subject File #26, 86–92, http://digitalarchive.wilsoncenter.org/document/175921.
16. Wilson Center Digital Archive, Notes on the Conversation Held Between Sardar Swaran Singh and Marshal Chen Yi, April 22, 1960, History and Public Policy Program Digital Archive, Nehru Memorial Museum and Library, P. N. Haksar Papers (I-II Installment), Subject File #26, 93–109, http://digitalarchive.wilsoncenter.org/document/175922.
17. Wilson Center Digital Archive, Record of Talks between P.M. [Jawaharlal Nehru] and Premier Chou En Lai [Zhou Enlai] held on 22nd April, 1960 from 10 a.m. to 1.10 p.m., April 22, 1960, History and Public Policy Program Digital Archive, Nehru Memorial Museum and Library, P. N. Haksar Papers (I-II Installment), Subject File #24, 40–53, http://digitalarchive.wilsoncenter.org/document/175916.
18. Wilson Center Digital Archive, Record of Conversation between R. K. Nehru and Zhou Enlai, April 21, 1960, History and Public Policy Program Digital Archive, Nehru Memorial Museum and Library, P. N. Haksar Papers (I-II Installment), Subject File #26, 110–121, http://digitalarchive.wilsoncenter.org/document/175923.
19. Steven A. Hoffman, *India and the China Crisis* (University of California Press, 1990), 80.
20. Wilson Center Digital Archive, Record of Talks between P.M. [Jawaharlal Nehru] and Premier Chou En Lai [Zhou Enlai] held on 24th April, 1960, from 10.30 a.m. to 1.45 p.m., April 24, 1960, History and Public Policy Program Digital Archive,

Nehru Memorial Museum and Library, P. N. Haksar Papers (I-II Installment), Subject File #24, 69–85, http://digitalarchive.wilsoncenter.org/document/121124.

21. Wilson Center Digital Archive, Record of Talks between P.M. [Jawaharlal Nehru] and Premier Chou En Lai [Zhou Enlai] held on 24th April, 1960, from 10.30 a.m. to 1.45 p.m.
22. Wilson Center Digital Archive, Record of Talks between P.M. [Jawaharlal Nehru] and Premier Chou En Lai [Zhou Enlai] held on 24th April, 1960, from 10.30 a.m. to 1.45 p.m.
23. NAI, File No. 6(14) R & I/58, PR_000004009221, China—Reports (Other than Annual) from Peking, Indian Ministry of External Affairs, 1958; NAI, File No. 6(14) R & I/60, PR_000004009361, Reports (Other than Annual) from Peking (China), Indian Ministry of External Affairs, 1960.
24. NAI, File No. 6(14) R & I/60, PR_000004009361, Reports (Other than Annual) from Peking (China), Indian Ministry of External Affairs, 1960.
25. Wilson Center Digital Archive, Record of Conversation between R. K. Nehru and Zhou Enlai, April 21, 1960, History and Public Policy Program Digital Archive, Nehru Memorial Museum and Library, P. N. Haksar Papers (I-II Installment), Subject File #26, 110–121, http://digitalarchive.wilsoncenter.org/document/175923.
26. Wilson Center Digital Archive, Cable from the Chinese Embassy in India, "Overview of India's Foreign Relations in 1961," January 1, 1962, History and Public Policy Program Digital Archive, PRC FMA 105-01519-01, 1–14, translated by Anna Beth Keim, http://digitalarchive.wilsoncenter.org/document/116482.
27. NAI, File No. 6(33)R&I/60, PR_000005002789, Reports (Other than Annual) from Gangtok (Sikkim), Indian Ministry of External Affairs, 1960.
28. CIA Reading Room, The Sino-Indian Border Dispute in the North East Frontier Agency, Geographic Intelligence Memorandum, Office of Research and Reports, Central Intelligence Agency, November 1962, declassified and approved for release May 11, 2000.
29. CIA Reading Room, Likely Developments in the Sino-Indian Border Dispute, Memorandum for the Director, Office of National Estimates, Central Intelligence Agency, May 7, 1962, declassified and approved for release November 29, 2005.
30. NAI, File No. 6(33)R&I/60, PR_000005002789, Reports (Other than Annual) from Gangtok (Sikkim).
31. NAI, File No. 6(33)R&I/60, PR_000005002789, Reports (Other than Annual) from Gangtok (Sikkim).
32. NAI, File No. 6(33)R&I/60, PR_000005002789, Reports (Other than Annual) from Gangtok (Sikkim).
33. Guha, *India After Gandhi*, 307.
34. Guyot-Rechard, *Shadow States*, 189.
35. CIA Reading Room, The Sino-Indian Border Dispute in the North East Frontier Agency, Geographic Intelligence Memorandum, Office of Research and Reports, Central Intelligence Agency, November 1962, declassified and approved for release May 11, 2000.

36. Guyot-Rechard, *Shadow States*, 193.
37. Guyot-Rechard, 200.
38. Palit, *Sentinels of the North-East*, 233–234.
39. CIA Reading Room, Sino-Indian Border Dispute, NSC Briefing Memorandum, Central Intelligence Agency, November 10, 1959, declassified and approved for release August 12, 2002.
40. Lintner, *China's India War*, 98–99.
41. Wilson Center Digital Archive, Chinese Foreign Ministry, Presentation of Diplomatic Note to India Concerning Indian Military Personnel's Encroachment on Chinese Territory, April 21, 1962, History and Public Policy Program Digital Archive, PRC FMA 106-01397-03, 10–11, translated by Anna Beth Keim, https://digitalarchive.wilsoncenter.org/document/114498.
42. Guha, *India After Gandhi*, 334.
43. Telegram From the Embassy in India to the Department of State, October 18, 1962, Document 177, *FRUS, 1961–1963*, vol. 19, *South Asia* (US Government Printing Office, 1996); Telegram from the Embassy in India to the Department of State, October 25, 1962, Document 180, *FRUS, 1961–1963*, vol. 19.
44. Khosla, *Letters for a Nation*, 245–246.
45. Khosla, 250–251.
46. CIA Reading Room, Logistic Requirements and Capabilities of Communist China to Conduct Military Campaigns Against India, Office of Research and Reports, Central Intelligence Agency, November 18, 1962, declassified and approved for release December 3, 2003; CIA Reading Room, The Sino-Indian Border Dispute in the North East Frontier Agency, Geographic Intelligence Memorandum, Office of Research and Reports, Central Intelligence Agency, November 1962, declassified and approved for release May 11, 2000.
47. Telegram from the Embassy in India to the Department of State, November 23, 1962, Document 214, *FRUS, 1961–1963*, vol. 19.
48. Guha, *India After Gandhi*, 337.
49. Guha, 336–337.
50. P. K. Balachandran, "1962 Flashback: When a Non Aligned Team Tried to Help India-China Negotiate Peace," *Citizen*, June 25, 2020, https://www.thecitizen.in/index.php/en/NewsDetail/index/6/18948/1962-Flashback:-When-a-Non-Aligned-Team-Tried-to-Help-India-China-Negotiate-Peace--.
51. Hoffman, *India and the China Crisis*, 225–228.
52. NAI, Secret File No. C/125(106)CH/63, PR_000004008697, Lok Sabha starred Question D. no. 1414 26 Chinese Civilian posts along Sino-India frontier, China Division, Indian Ministry of External Affairs, August 19, 1963.
53. Wilson Center Digital Archive, Premier Chou En-Lai's [Zhou Enlai's] Letter to the Leaders of Asian and African Countries on the Sino-Indian Boundary Question, November 15, 1962, History and Public Policy Program Digital Archive, Peking: Foreign Languages Press, 1973, http://digitalarchive.wilsoncenter.org/document/175946; NAI, File No. C/125/124/CH63, PR_000004008698, Rajya Sabha starred Question

no. 1184 Re; A book entitled "A brief history of Modern China" by Liu Pei containing a map claiming all Asian continent as part of China, Indian Ministry of External Affairs, August 1963.

54. NAI, File No. C/125(61)CH/63, PR_000004010147, Reports on debates by our officers attending Parliament—Re Sino-Indian conflict, Indian Ministry of External Affairs, September 16, 1963.
55. Memorandum of Conversation, November 28, 1962, Document 212, *FRUS, 1961–1963*, vol. 19.
56. NAI, File No. HI/1012(14)/64, PR_000005002084, Political Reports (Other than Annual Reports) from Peking, Indian Ministry of External Affairs, 1964.
57. NAI, File No. HI/1012(14)/64, PR_000005002083, Political Reports from Peking, Indian Ministry of External Affairs, 1964.
58. NAI, File No. HI/1012(14)/64, PR_000005002083, Political Reports from Peking.
59. NAI, File No. HI/1012(14)/64, PR_000005002083, Political Reports from Peking.
60. NAI, File No. HI/1012(14)/64, PR_000005002084, Political Reports (Other than Annual Reports) from Peking, Indian Ministry of External Affairs, 1964.
61. NAI, File No. C/125 (97)/65/ CH/63, PR_000004002226.Lok Sabha Starred Question D. No. 877 dated 29 X 65 for 15 XI 65 by Smt. Tarheswari Sinha regarding remilitarization of the 20 demilitarised Zone by China, Indian Ministry of External Affairs, 1965.
62. CIA Reading Room, The President's Daily Brief, Central Intelligence Agency, September 16, 1965, sanitized copy approved for release July 24, 2015.
63. CIA Reading Room, U-2 Coverage of the Sino-Indian Border, Memorandum for the Chairman of the United States Intelligence Board, Central Intelligence Agency, September 23, 1965, sanitized copy approved for release February 28, 2012.
64. Palit, *Sentinels of the North-East*, 251–252.
65. Lintner, *China's India War*, 167.
66. CIA Reading Room, Ten Years of Chinese Communist Foreign Policy, Section II: South and Southeast Asia, Intelligence Report, Directorate of Intelligence, Central Intelligence Agency, April 4, 1968, sanitized copy approved for release December 3, 2009.
67. National Archives, UK, FCO/37/68, India—Political relations with China (Folder 2), 1967.
68. CIA Reading Room, Expansion of Hasimara Airfield, India, Photographic Interpretation Report, National Photographic Interpretation Center, January 1970, declassified and approved for release June 18, 2002.
69. National Archives, UK, FCO/37/647, Report on tour of Assam and North-Eastern India, 1970.
70. NAI, File No. WII/102(43)/65, PR_000005003268, Discussion of Indian ambassador in Washington with Mr. Talbot and Mr. Dean Rusk on 14.6.65, Indian Ministry of External Affairs, June 14, 1965.
71. NAI, File No. WII/125/55/66, PR_000005014048, Starred Q. No. 4810 by Shri Bibhuti Mishra for answer in the Lok Sabha on 29.8.66 regarding US pressure on India to limit her defence cost, Indian Ministry of External Affairs, 1966.

72. NAI, File No. HI/1012(14)/64, PR_000005002083, Political Reports from Peking.
73. NAI, File No. 303/CJK, PR_000005002299, Sino-Soviet Pact on Sinkiang, certain developments in Sinkiang, Indian Ministry of External Affairs, 1949.
74. Bhaumak, *Insurgent Crossfire*, 24.
75. NAI, PP_000000005351, Assam Co-Operative Cottage Industries Association, Private Papers of Sardar Patel, 1948.
76. NAI, PP_000000005346, Assam Ministerial, Private Papers of Sardar Patel, 1948–1950.
77. NAI, PP_000000005346, Assam Ministerial.
78. NAI, File No. 147-NEF/49, PR_000005003235, Burmese goodwill mission to Assam-Lushai delegation of U.M.F.O., Indian Ministry of External Affairs, 1949.
79. NAI, File No. 147-NEF/49, PR_000005003235, Burmese goodwill mission to Assam-Lushai delegation of U.M.F.O.
80. NAI, File No. 147-NEF/49, PR_000005003235, Burmese goodwill mission to Assam-Lushai delegation of U.M.F.O.
81. Major Sitaram Johri, *Where India, China, and Burma Meet* (Thacker Spink and Co.: 1963), 111, 163.
82. Suchitra Vijayan, *Midnight's Borders: A People's History of Modern India* (Melville House, 2021), 99.
83. National Archives, UK, FCO/37/518, Assam, 1969.
84. CIA Reading Room, India's Revamped Defense Posture, Special Report, Office of Current Intelligence, Central Intelligence Agency, November 20, 1964, declassified and approved for release November 13, 2006; Guyot-Rechard, *Shadow States*, 263.
85. Guha, *Savaging the Civilized*, 295, 301.
86. NAI, Secret File No. NII/102(33)/72, PR_000004010113, Foreign involvement in insurgency in North Eastern India—Preparation of white paper on the subject by the Ministry of Defence, Indian Ministry of Home Affairs, 1972.
87. National Archives, UK, FCO/37/263, Brief for Commonwealth Secretary on Nagaland (Folder 2), 1967–1968.
88. National Archives, UK, FCO/37/263, Brief for Commonwealth Secretary on Nagaland (Folder 2), 1967–1968.
89. Lintner, *Great Game East*, 42.
90. Bhaumik, *Insurgent Crossfire*, 45.
91. "Indian Army Halts Nagaland Fighting," *New York Times*, June 26, 1964; Guha, *India After Gandhi*, 409.
92. National Archives, UK, FCO/37/263, Brief for Commonwealth Secretary on Nagaland (Folder 2), 1967–1968.
93. National Archives, UK, DO/133/185, Nagaland—political situation, 1964–1965.
94. National Archives, UK, FCO/37/264, Brief for Commonwealth Secretary on Nagaland (Folder 3), 1968.
95. Lintner, *Great Game East*, 42–43.
96. Lintner, *China's India War*, 138; National Archives, UK, FCO/37/264, Brief for Commonwealth Secretary on Nagaland (Folder 3), 1968.

97. NAI, File No. 14015/4/75-NE, PR_000004010321, Declaration of Naga National Council Federal Govt. of Nagaland and Naga Army etc. as unlawful—Original documents (Exhibits) returned by the tribunal, Indian Ministry of Home Affairs, 1975.
98. NAI, Secret File No. NII/102(33)/72, PR_000004010113, Foreign involvement in insurgency in North Eastern India—Preparation of white paper on the subject by the Ministry of Defence.
99. NAI, Secret File No. NII/102(33)/72, PR_000004010113, Foreign involvement in insurgency in North Eastern India—Preparation of white paper on the subject by the Ministry of Defence.
100. National Archives, UK, FCO/37/264, Brief for Commonwealth Secretary on Nagaland (Folder 3), 1968.
101. NAI, Secret File No. NII/102(33)/72, PR_000004010113, Foreign involvement in insurgency in North Eastern India—Preparation of white paper on the subject by the Ministry of Defence.
102. NAI, File No. 108/68, PR_000005002409, Note—Memoranda and letter exchanged between India and China, Indian Ministry of External Affairs, 1968.
103. Lintner, *Great Game East*, 76.
104. CIA Reading Room, India's Troubled Eastern Region, Weekly Summary Special Report, Directorate of Intelligence, Central Intelligence Agency, July 26, 1968, declassified and approved for release October 12, 2006.
105. National Archives, UK, FCO/37/264, Brief for Commonwealth Secretary on Nagaland (Folder 3), 1968.
106. National Archives, UK, FCO/37/263, Brief for Commonwealth Secretary on Nagaland (Folder 2), 1967–1968.
107. National Archives, UK, FCO/37/69, India—Political relations with China (Folder 3), 1967–1968.
108. National Archives, UK, FCO/37/263, Brief for Commonwealth Secretary on Nagaland (Folder 2), 1967–1968; National Archives, UK, FCO/37/264, Brief for Commonwealth Secretary on Nagaland (Folder 3), 1968.
109. National Archives, UK, FCO/37/264, Brief for Commonwealth Secretary on Nagaland (Folder 3), 1968.
110. NAI, Secret File No. NII/102(33)/72, PR_000004010113, Foreign involvement in insurgency in North Eastern India—Preparation of white paper on the subject by the Ministry of Defence; NAI, File No. 108/68, PR_000005002409, Note—Memoranda and letter exchanged between India and China, Indian Ministry of External Affairs, 1968.
111. Bhaumik, *Insurgent Crossfire*, 47.
112. Wilson Center Digital Archive, K. R. Narayanan, "India and the Chinese Bomb," December 24, 1964, History and Public Policy Program Digital Archive, National Archives of India, Ministry of External Affairs, File No. HI/1012(14)/64-I & II, "Monthly Political Report from Peking," obtained by Vivek Prahladan, http://digitalarchive.wilsoncenter.org/document/165245.

113. Wilson Center Digital Archive, Note, P. S. Ratnam, "Starred Question No. 8196 for 30-8-1965 in Lok Sabha," August 30, 1965, History and Public Policy Program Digital Archive, National Archives of India, Ministry of External Affairs, 1965, Disarmament Unit, File No. U-IV/125/62/65, obtained by Vivek Prahladan, https://digitalarchive.wilsoncenter.org/document/165241.
114. Wilson Center Digital Archive, K. R. Narayanan, "India and the Chinese Bomb," December 24, 1964, History and Public Policy Program Digital Archive, National Archives of India, Ministry of External Affairs, File No. HI/1012(14)/64-I & II, "Monthly Political Report from Peking," obtained by Vivek Prahladan, http://digitalarchive.wilsoncenter.org/document/165245.
115. National Archives, UK, FCO/37/264, Brief for Commonwealth Secretary on Nagaland (Folder 3), 1968; NAI, Secret File No. NII/102(33)/72, PR_000004010113, Foreign involvement in insurgency in North Eastern India—Preparation of white paper on the subject by the Ministry of Defence.
116. NAI, Secret File No. NII/102(33)/72, PR_000004010113, Foreign involvement in insurgency in North Eastern India—Preparation of white paper on the subject by the Ministry of Defence.
117. NAI, Secret File No. NII/102(33)/72, PR_000004010113, Foreign involvement in insurgency in North Eastern India—Preparation of white paper on the subject by the Ministry of Defence.
118. NAI, File No. PP(JS)3(3)/74, PR_000005002415, China's Foreign Policy, Indian Ministry of External Affairs, 1974.
119. NAI, File No. 14015/4/75-NE, PR_000004010321, Declaration of Naga National Council Federal Govt. of Nagaland and Naga Army etc. as unlawful—Original documents (Exhibits) returned by the tribunal, Indian Ministry of Home Affairs, 1975.
120. NAI, File No. 14015/4/75-NE, PR_000004010321, Declaration of Naga National Council Federal Govt. of Nagaland and Naga Army etc. as unlawful—Original documents (Exhibits) returned by the tribunal.
121. NAI, File No. 14015/4/75-NE, PR_000004010321, Declaration of Naga National Council Federal Govt. of Nagaland and Naga Army etc. as unlawful—Original documents (Exhibits) returned by the tribunal.
122. Lintner, *Great Game East*, 78.
123. Guha, *India After Gandhi*, 548.
124. Lintner, *Great Game East*, 87.
125. Bhaumik, *Insurgent Crossfire*, 143.
126. Bhaumik, 145.
127. Bhaumik, 144.
128. Bhaumik, 144.
129. Lintner, *Great Game East*, 91.
130. Lintner, 93.
131. Lintner, 93.

132. CIA Reading Room, India's Troubled Eastern Region, Weekly Summary Special Report, Directorate of Intelligence, Central Intelligence Agency, July 26, 1968, declassified and approved for release October 12, 2006.
133. NAI, Secret File No. NII/102(33)/72, PR_000004010113, Foreign involvement in insurgency in North Eastern India—Preparation of white paper on the subject by the Ministry of Defence.
134. National Archives, UK, FCO/37/740, Political and administrative affairs in Nagaland, 1970.
135. Lintner, *Great Game East*, 92, 97.
136. NAI, Secret File No. NII/102(33)/72, PR_000004010113, Foreign involvement in insurgency in North Eastern India—Preparation of white paper on the subject by the Ministry of Defence.
137. National Archives, UK, FCO/37/735, Political and administrative affairs in Mizos' area, Calcutta, 1970.
138. Lintner, *Great Game East*, 117.
139. NAI, File. No. 10(31)/70, PR_000005001964, Statehood for Manipur, Tripura and Meghalaya and connected problems of North-Eastern Region, Indian Ministry of Home Affairs, 1970.
140. NAI, File. No. 10(31)/70, PR_000005001964, Statehood for Manipur, Tripura and Meghalaya and connected problems of North-Eastern Region.
141. NAI, File. No. 10(31)/70, PR_000005001964, Statehood for Manipur, Tripura and Meghalaya and connected problems of North-Eastern Region.
142. Lintner, *Great Game East*, 118.
143. Yadav, *Is That Even a Country, Sir!*, 209.
144. Lintner, *Great Game East*, 133–134.
145. NAI, File No. WII/ 101/45/70, PR_000005002943, A Review of India's Foreign Policy, Indian Ministry of External Affairs, 1970.
146. NAI, File No. UI/221.1/24/75, PR_000005003295, China questioning our sovereignty over Arunachal Pradesh at the I.T.C. Administrative Radio conference on LF/MF Broadcasting, Indian Ministry of External Affairs, 1975.
147. NAI, File No. PP(JS)3(9)/75, PR_000005003294, China–General and Sino-Indian Relations, Indian Ministry of External Affairs, 1975.
148. NAI, File No. PP(JS)3(9)/75, PR_000005003294, China—General and Sino-Indian Relations.
149. NAI, File No. PP(JS)3(9)/75, PR_000005003294, China—General and Sino-Indian Relations, Indian Ministry of External Affairs, 1975.
150. NAI, File No. HI/1011(5)/78, PR_000005002394, Annual Reports Etc—1977 Reco from Peking.
151. NAI, File No. III/103/9/82, PR_000004009425, Visit of Foreign Minister of India to China from 12 to 19 February 1979, Indian Ministry of External Affairs, 1979.
152. NAI, File No. III/103/9/82, PR_000004009425, Visit of Foreign Minister of India to China from 12 to 19 February 1979.

153. State Department Reading Room, C05342374, Indian Foreign Minister's Visit to China, Diplomatic Cable, US Department of State, February 22, 1979, declassified and approved for release May 13, 2013, p. 4.
154. Lintner, *Great Game East*, 344–345; Small, *The China-Pakistan Axis*, 77.
155. State Department Reading Room, C05274663, MEA Readout on Chinese FM's Visit, Diplomatic Cable, US Department of State, April 6, 1990, declassified and approved for release May 10, 2013.
156. State Department Reading Room, 702086, India: Border Dispute with China, INR Brief, Bureau of Intelligence and Research, US Department of State, December 28, 1992, declassified and approved for release October 3, 1997.
157. Guha, *India After Gandhi*, 704.
158. "Spurious Goods-Maker Fake Claim," *Economic Times*, October 14, 2009.
159. Zeba Siddiqui and Fayaz Bukhari, "India, China Clash Over Kashmir as It Loses Its Special Status and Is Divided," Reuters, October 31, 2019, https://www.reuters.com/article/us-india-kashmir/india-china-clash-over-kashmir-as-it-loses-special-status-and-is-divided-idUSKBN1XA0M9.
160. Joshi, *Understanding the India-China Border.*
161. "China Regains Slot as India's Top Trade Partner Despite Tensions," *BBC News*, February 23, 2021, https://www.bbc.com/news/business-56164154.
162. Sanjeev Miglani, "India Tells China Border Troop Pullback Needed for Better Ties," Reuters, September 17, 2021, https://www.reuters.com/world/india/india-tells-china-border-troop-pullback-needed-better-ties-2021-09-17/.
163. Shivshankar Menon, "India-China Ties: The Future Holds 'Antagonistic Cooperation,' Not War," *Wire*, December 7, 2020, https://m.thewire.in/article/external-affairs/india-china-ties-expect-antagonistic-cooperation-future-not-war.

4. "ALL-WEATHER ALLIES"

1. Edward F. Knight, *Where Three Empires Meet: A Narrative of Recent Travel in Kashmir, Western Tibet, Gilgit, and the Adjoining Countries* (Longmans, Green, and Co., 1893), 349–352.
2. Small, *The China-Pakistan Axis*, 21.
3. Pervaiz Iqbal Cheema, *Pakistan's Defense Policy, 1947–58* (St. Martin's Press, 1990), 77.
4. Cheema, 32, 87, 125.
5. The Ambassador in Pakistan (Hildreth) to the Department of State, December 8, 1953, Document 1144, *FRUS, 1952–1954*, vol. 11, pt. 2, *Africa and South Asia* (US Government Printing Office, 1983).
6. Wilson Center Digital Archive, Cable from the Chinese Embassy in Pakistan, "Pakistani President's Exclusive Conversation with American Reporters," May 17, 1956, History and Public Policy Program Digital Archive, PRC FMA 105-00779-04, 12–13,

obtained by Sulmaan Khan and translated by Anna Beth Keim, http://digitalarchive.wilsoncenter.org/document/114882.

7. Wilson Center Digital Archive, Cable from the Chinese Embassy in Pakistan, "The Main Themes of Pakistan's Diplomatic Activities," June 30, 1956, History and Public Policy Program Digital Archive, PRC FMA 105-0779-04, 14–17, obtained by Sulmaan Khan and translated by Anna Beth Keim, http://digitalarchive.wilsoncenter.org/document/114883.
8. National Archives, UK, FCO/37/193, Pakistan—Political relations with China (Folder 1), 1967.
9. National Archives, UK, FCO/37/193, Pakistan—Political relations with China (Folder 1), 1967.
10. National Archives, UK, FCO/37/693, Pakistan—Political relations with China, 1970.
11. Wilson Center Digital Archive, Abstract of Conversation Between Chinese Premier Zhou Enlai and Pakistani Ambassador to China Sultanuddin Ahmad, January 4, 1956, History and Public Policy Program Digital Archive, PRC FMA 105-00351-01, 1–9, obtained by Sulmaan Khan and translated by Anna Beth Keim, http://digitalarchive.wilsoncenter.org/document/114840.
12. Dennis Kux, *Disenchanted Allies: The United States and Pakistan, 1947–2000* (Johns Hopkins University Press, 2001), 157–158.
13. Small, *The China-Pakistan Axis*, 24.
14. National Security Archives, Informal Memorandum on Policy Problems with Pakistan, Bureau of Intelligence and Research, US Department of State, July 21, 1965, declassified and approved for release May 29, 2003.
15. Hillman, *The Emperor's New Road*, 135.
16. Wilson Center Digital Archive, Record of Conversation Between Chen Yi and Zulfikar Ali Bhutto, February 25, 1964, History and Public Policy Program Digital Archive, PRC FMA 203-00635-01, 85–86, obtained and translated by Christopher Tang, http://digitalarchive.wilsoncenter.org/document/121574.
17. Kux, *Disenchanted Allies*, 163.
18. Gohar Ayub Khan, *Glimpses Into the Corridors of Power* (Oxford University Press, 2007), 320.
19. Kux, *Disenchanted Allies*, 167–168.
20. Kux, 170.
21. CIA Reading Room, Implications of Chinese Military Aid to Pakistan, Intelligence Memorandum, Directorate of Intelligence, Central Intelligence Agency, August 16, 1966, sanitized copy approved for release February 8, 2007.
22. National Archives, UK, FCO/37/194, Pakistan—Political relations with China (Folder 2), 1967–1968.
23. National Archives, UK, FCO/37/693, Pakistan—Political relations with China, 1970.
24. CIA Reading Room, Implications of Chinese Military Aid to Pakistan, Intelligence Memorandum, Directorate of Intelligence, Central Intelligence Agency, August 16, 1966, sanitized copy approved for release February 8, 2007.

25. CIA Reading Room, Chinese Aid in the Third World, Special Report Weekly Review, Directorate of Intelligence, Central Intelligence Agency, June 30, 1972, sanitized copy approved for release August 24, 2012; National Archives, UK, FCO/37/693, Pakistan—Political relations with China, 1970.
26. CIA Reading Room, Implications of Chinese Military Aid to Pakistan, Intelligence Memorandum, Directorate of Intelligence, Central Intelligence Agency, August 16, 1966, sanitized copy approved for release February 8, 2007; Telegram from the Embassy in Pakistan to the Department of State, September 19, 1980, Document 457, *FRUS, 1977–1980*, vol. 19, *South Asia* (US Government Printing Office, 2019).
27. Wilson Center Digital Archive, Intelligence Note 506 from Thomas L. Hughes to the Secretary, "Will Communist China Give Nuclear Aid to Pakistan?," August 12, 1966, History and Public Policy Program Digital Archive, RG 59, UD-UP 131, Bureau of Intelligence and Research, Reports Coordination and Review Staff, Intelligence Reports, 1961, 1963–1967, box 2, IN-500-579, http://digitalarchive.wilsoncenter.org/document/134064.
28. National Archives, UK, FCO/37/988, Chinese policy toward South Asia, 1972.
29. National Archives, UK, FCO/37/693, Pakistan—Political relations with China, 1970.
30. Sultan M. Khan, *Memories & Reflections of a Pakistani Diplomat* (Alden Press, 1998), 162–163.
31. Rabia Akhtar, "Pakistan's US Problem: The First Betrayal," *Express Tribune*, May 26, 2017.
32. Kux, *Disenchanted Allies*, 169–170.
33. National Archives, UK, FCO/37/903, Political relations between Pakistan and China, 1971.
34. National Archives, UK, FCO/37/903, Political relations between Pakistan and China, 1971.
35. Author interview with Ambassador Ali Sarwar Naqvi, director of the Center for International Strategic Studies, Islamabad, Pakistan, December 18, 2018.
36. National Security Archives, Pakistan and Communist China Strengthen Cooperation, Intelligence Note, Bureau of Intelligence and Research, US Department of State, December 4, 1968, declassified and approved for release February 20, 2004.
37. CIA Reading Room, Pakistan, Memorandum, Office of the Director of Central Intelligence, Central Intelligence Agency, November 19, 1982, declassified and approved for release April 4, 2007.
38. CIA Reading Room, Pakistan-China-US: Arms Technology Transfer, Memorandum, Directorate of Intelligence, Central Intelligence Agency, September 14, 1983, sanitized copy approved for release February 27, 2008.
39. National Archives, UK, FCO/37/193, Pakistan—Political relations with China (Folder 1), 1967.
40. CIA Reading Room, Communist Aid Activities in Non-Communist Less Developed Countries, 1980, Research Paper, National Foreign Assessment Center, Central Intelligence Agency, May 1981, sanitized copy approved for release April 6, 2012; National Archives, UK, FCO/37/693, Pakistan—Political relations with China, 1970.

41. State Department Reading Room, C05360287, Pakistan's Response to the Indian Nuclear Explosion, Intelligence Note, Bureau of Intelligence and Research, US Department of State, June 3, 1974, declassified and approved for release June 6, 2013.
42. Small, *The China-Pakistan Axis*, 31.
43. Wilson Center Digital Archive, Secretary of Defense Harold Brown to Ambassador-at-Large Gerard C. Smith, enclosing excerpts from memoranda of conversations with Geng Biao and Deng Xiaoping, January 31, 1980, History and Public Policy Program Digital Archive, FOIA release, obtained and contributed by William Burr and included in NPIHP Research Update #6, http://digitalarchive.wilsoncenter.org /document/114227.
44. Wilson Center Digital Archive, Deputy Director for National Foreign Assessment, Central Intelligence Agency, Enclosing Report "A Review of the Evidence of Chinese Involvement in Pakistan's Nuclear Weapons Program," December 7, 1979, History and Public Policy Program Digital Archive, obtained and contributed by William Burr and included in NPIHP Research Update #11, http://digitalarchive.wilsoncenter.org /document/116891.
45. National Security Archives, Proliferation Issues: The View from Beijing Looks Grim, Diplomatic Cable, US Department of State, April 1991, sanitized copy approved for release October 6, 2003.
46. Wilson Center Digital Archive, Defense Intelligence Agency cable to [excised location], "Pakistan-China: Nuclear Weapons Production and Testing," December 7, 1985, History and Public Policy Program Digital Archive, Defense Intelligence Agency FOIA release, obtained and contributed by William Burr and included in NPIHP Research Update #6, http://digitalarchive.wilsoncenter.org/document /114315; National Security Archives, The Pakistani Nuclear Program, Intelligence Report, US Department of State, June 23, 1983, sanitized copy approved for release February 7, 1991.
47. National Security Archives, US-PRC Nuclear Cooperation—Or the Lack of It, Diplomatic Cable, US Department of State, December 1982, declassified and approved for release January 14, 1998.
48. State Department Reading Room, 9703700, China's Foreign Policy: A Five-Year Review, Diplomatic Cable, US Department of State, December 16, 1983, declassified and approved for release January 14, 1998.
49. World Bank, *Poverty in Pakistan: Vulnerabilities, Social Gaps, and Rural Dynamics*, Report No. 24296-PAK (World Bank, October 28, 2002), 2–3, https://openknowledge .worldbank.org/handle/10986/15335?show=full&locale-attribute=en.
50. World Bank, 5.
51. State Department Reading Room, C17641538, Deflated Expectations: Pakistan One Year After the Coup, Diplomatic Cable, US Department of State, October 14, 2000, sanitized copy approved for release May 13, 2013.
52. State Department Reading Room, C06694945, Deputy Secretary's Meeting with Pakistani President Leghari, Diplomatic Cable, US Department of State, April 11, 1994, declassified and approved for release July 25, 2019; "Northridge Earthquake,

January 17, 1994," California Department of Conservation, accessed July 16, 2025, https://www.conservation.ca.gov/cgs/earthquakes/northridge.

53. Jane Perlez, "Rebuffed by China, Pakistan May Seek I.M.F. Aid," *New York Times*, October 18, 2008.
54. "General Pervez Musharraf's Address to the Nation," *Dawn*, October 18, 1999.
55. Pervez Musharraf, *In the Line of Fire: A Memoir* (Simon and Schuster, 2006), 181.
56. "General Pervez Musharraf's Address to the Nation."
57. State Department Reading Room, C17641382, Musharraf Speech: Little Give on Kashmir or Taliban in Overview of Foreign Policy, Diplomatic Cable, US Department of State, June 26, 2000, declassified and approved for release May 13, 2013.
58. State Department Reading Room, C06327510, Pakistani Public Sees US as Anti-Islamic, Opinion Analysis, Office of Research, US Department of State, September 18, 2001, declassified and approved for release November 3, 2017; State Department Reading Room, C06327516, Pakistani Views of Good Relations with US at Record High," Opinion Analysis, Office of Research, US Department of State, March 26, 2002, declassified and approved for release November 3, 2017.
59. "Beijing: Pervez Musharraf Meets Zhu Rongji [January 17, 2000]," posted July 25, 2015, by Associated Press, YouTube, 2 min., 20 sec., https://www.youtube.com/watch?v=cMvKp4rWKzQ.
60. Small, *The China-Pakistan Axis*, 98.
61. Filippo Boni, "Civil-Military Relations in Pakistan: A Case Study of Sino-Pakistani Relations and the Port of Gwadar," *Commonwealth & Comparative Politics* 54, no. 4 (2016): 504; Markey, *China's Western Horizon*, 159.
62. R. Hughes-Buller, *Baluchistan District Gazetteer Series: Volume VII, Makran* (Times Press, 1906), iv, 282, 285.
63. National Archives, 1973KARACH01804, Prime Minister Bhutto Concludes Tour of Baluchistan, Diplomatic Cable, US Consulate Karachi, September 10, 1973, declassified and approved for release June 30, 2005.
64. Hillman, *The Emperor's New Road*, 138.
65. National Archives, UK, FCO/37/2362, Pakistan—the Baluchistan problem, 1980.
66. Small, *The China-Pakistan Axis*, 100.
67. Akbar Ahmed, "Is Pakistan Heading for Disaster in Balochistan?," *Al Jazeera*, January 15, 2012, https://www.aljazeera.com/opinions/2012/1/15/is-pakistan-heading-for-disaster-in-balochistan.
68. William Branigin, "Baluchi Harbor a Lure to Soviets," *Washington Post*, February 9, 1980.
69. Markey, *China's Western Horizon*, 48.
70. Markey, 101.
71. Small, *The China-Pakistan Axis*, 101.
72. International Crisis Group, *China-Pakistan Economic Corridor: Opportunities and Risks*, Asia Report No. 297 (International Crisis Group, June 29, 2018), 18, https://www.crisisgroup.org/asia/south-asia/pakistan/297-china-pakistan-economic-corridor-opportunities-and-risks.

73. "Time to Broaden Ties with China: President," *Dawn*, April 28, 2006.
74. "Nawaz to Set Up 'China Cell' for Projects' Supervision," *Dawn*, July 7, 2013.
75. Boni, "Civil-Military Relations in Pakistan."
76. Boni, 499.
77. Perlez, "Rebuffed by China, Pakistan May Seek I.M.F. Aid"; Small, *The China-Pakistan Axis*, 112.
78. " 'Pakistan's Relations with China Will Never Fray': Asad Umar Responds to US Concerns Over CPEC," *Dawn*, November 24, 2019.
79. "Net Inflow of Foreign Private Investment (Archive)," State Bank of Pakistan, accessed July 17, 2025, https://www.sbp.org.pk/ecodata/NIFP_Arch/index.asp.
80. US Institute of Peace, *China's Influence on Conflict Dynamics in South Asia*, Senior Study Group Report No. 4 (US Institute of Peace, December 2020), https://www.usip.org/publications/2020/12/chinas-influence-conflict-dynamics-south-asia, 28.
81. Saeed Shah and Jeremy Page, "China Readies $46 Billion for Pakistan Trade Route," *Wall Street Journal*, April 16, 2015.
82. Government of Pakistan, *Long Term Plan for China-Pakistan Economic Corridor (2017–2030)* (Ministry of Planning, Development and Reform, November 2017), 6, http://cpec.gov.pk/long-term-plan-cpec.
83. Markey, *China's Western Horizon*, 48.
84. Government of Pakistan, *Long Term Plan for China-Pakistan Economic Corridor (2017–2030)*, 14–22.
85. Government of Pakistan, 14.
86. Government of Pakistan, 16.
87. Government of Pakistan, 24–25.
88. Peer Muhammad, "Pakistan to Hand Over 2,281 Acres of Gwadar's Free Trade Zone to China," *Express Tribune*, November 9, 2015.
89. " 'Today Marks Dawn of New Era': CPEC Dreams Come True as Gwadar Port Goes Operational," *Dawn*, November 13, 2016.
90. Government of Pakistan, *Long Term Plan for China-Pakistan Economic Corridor (2017–2030)*, 5.
91. Boni and Adeney, "The Impact of the China-Pakistan Economic Corridor on Pakistan's Federal System," 454–455.
92. "Eastern Route for CPEC May Foster Enmity Between Provinces, Warns Imran," *Express Tribune*, September 30, 2015.
93. Ishrat Husain, *CPEC & Pakistani Economy: An Appraisal* (Centre of Excellence for CPEC, 2017), 7, https://ir.iba.edu.pk/cgi/viewcontent.cgi?article=1039&context=faculty-research-books
94. Maria Abi-Habib, "China's 'Belt and Road' Plan in Pakistan Takes a Military Turn," *New York Times*, December 19, 2018.
95. Filippo Boni and Katharine Adeney, "The Impact of the China-Pakistan Economic Corridor on Pakistan's Federal System: The Politics of CPEC," *Asian Survey* 60, no. 3 (2020): 443–444; Jonathan E. Hillman et al., "The China-Pakistan Economic Corridor at Five," *CSIS Briefs*, Center for Strategic and International Studies, April 2020, 1–2, https://www.csis.org/analysis/china-pakistan-economic-corridor-five.

96. "'Pakistan's Relations with China Will Never Fray.'"
97. Frankopan, *The New Silk Roads*, 232.
98. "Joint Statement of PM Imran Khan's China Visit: 'Strengthening Strategic Cooperative Partnership,'" *News*, November 4, 2018.
99. Author attendance at International Conference on Conflict and Cooperation in South Asia, Islamabad Policy Research Institute, Islamabad, Pakistan, December 11–12, 2018.
100. International Crisis Group, *China-Pakistan Economic Corridor*, 9.
101. Author interview with Imtiaz Gul, Pakistani journalist, Islamabad, Pakistan, December 18, 2018.
102. Robert D. Kaplan, *The Return of Marco Polo's World: War, Strategy, and American Interests in the Twenty-First Century* (Random House, 2019), 28.
103. "Moody's Reaffirms Pakistan's Rating, but Vulnerabilities Remain," *Dawn*, May 22, 2018.
104. Author interview with Malik Siraj Akbar, journalist, Washington, DC, October 1, 2018.
105. Adnan Aamir, "$385bn of China's Belt and Road Lending Kept Undisclosed: Report," *Nikkei Asia*, September 29, 2021, https://asia.nikkei.com/Spotlight/Belt-and-Road/385bn-of-China-s-Belt-and-Road-lending-kept-undisclosed-report.
106. Katharine Houreld, "Pakistan Should Be More Transparent on $46 bn China Deal, State Bank Head Says," Reuters, December 4, 2015, https://www.reuters.com/article/pakistan-china/pakistan-should-be-more-transparent-on-46-bn-china-deal-state-bank-head-says-idUSL3N13T4SK20151204.
107. Abi-Habib, "China's 'Belt and Road' Plan in Pakistan Takes a Military Turn."
108. International Crisis Group, *China-Pakistan Economic Corridor*, 10.
109. Boni and Adeney, "The Impact of the China-Pakistan Economic Corridor on Pakistan's Federal System," 450–451.
110. Boni and Adeney, 449.
111. Afshan Subohi, "What Are Provinces Pitching at Seventh JCC? Sindh Makes Efforts, and Excuses," *Dawn*, November 20, 2017.
112. Syed Irfan Raza, "'CPEC Could Become Another East India Company,'" *Dawn*, October 18, 2016.
113. Author interview with Muhammad Amir Rana, president of the Pak Institute of Peace Studies, Islamabad, Pakistan, December 13, 2018.

5. CPEC AND THE BALOCH INSURGENCY

1. John F. Kennedy Presidential Library, JFKNSF-320-025-p0005, Staff Memoranda: Kissinger, Henry, February 1962: 13–28, February 1962, declassified and approved for release December 2003.
2. Selig S. Harrison, *In Afghanistan's Shadow: Baloch Nationalism and Soviet Temptations* (Carnegie Endowment for International Peace, 1981), 1.
3. "Punjabis Talk About Balochistan," posted November 17, 2014, by BBC Urdu, YouTube, 10 min., 26 sec., https://www.youtube.com/watch?v=fDWXQdlJqT8.

4. Akbar Ahmed, foreword to *Ethno-Political Conflict in Pakistan: The Baloch Movement*, by Rizwan Zeb (Routledge, 2020), xii.
5. Matthew Parris and Andrew Bryson, *Parting Shots: Undiplomatic Diplomats—the Ambassadors' Letters You Were Never Meant to See* (Penguin, 2011), 65.
6. Selig S. Harrison, "Nightmare in Balochistan," *Foreign Policy* 32 (1978): 142; Anatol Lieven, *Pakistan: A Hard Country* (Allen Lane, 2011), 339.
7. *Frontier and Overseas Expeditions from India*, vol. 3, *Baluchistan and the First Afghan War* (Superintendent Government Printing, 1910), 44.
8. *Administration Report of the Baluchistan Agency for 1886* (Superintendent of Government Printing, India, 1886), 11; Tripodi, "'Good for One but Not the Other,'" 776.
9. *Papers Relating to the Treaty Concluded Between the Government of India and the Khan of Khelat, on the 8th December 1876* (Her Majesty's Stationery Office, 1877), 3; Tripodi, *Edge of Empire*, 56.
10. *Papers Relating to the Treaty Concluded Between the Government of India and the Khan of Khelat*, 358, 362.
11. *Administration Report of the Baluchistan Agency for 1886–1887* (Superintendent of Government Printing, India, 1888), 45.
12. Balochistan Archives, File No. 7-B, D.B. Jamiat Rai, C.I.E., Note on the Marri-Bugti tribe, A.G.G. in Baluchistan, 1926, http://www.balochistanarchives.gob.pk/dcollections/introview/116#27.
13. Balochistan Archives, File No. 7-B, D.B. Jamiat Rai, C.I.E., Note on the Marri-Bugti tribe, A.G.G. in Baluchistan.
14. Peter Hopkirk, *On Secret Service East of Constantinople: The Plot to Bring Down the British Empire* (John Murray, 1994), 203–208.
15. Hopkirk, 208.
16. Hopkirk, 203.
17. National Archives, UK, FCO/37/1496, White Paper on Baluchistan, Government of Pakistan, October 19, 1974.
18. Syed Fazl-e-Haider, "Higher Poverty in Balochistan," *Dawn*, February 6, 2006.
19. Fazl-e-Haider.
20. Author interview with Malik Siraj Akbar.
21. "Balochistan Special," *Policy Matters with Nasim Zehra*, Dunya News TV Pakistan (Urdu), November 12, 2010.
22. "We Are Not Pakistani: Mazdak Baloch," posted September 7, 2016, by BBC Hindi, 6 min., 34 sec., https://www.youtube.com/watch?v=G5IU7PR5hnM.
23. Rahul Tripathi, "Call Me a Dog, but Not a Pakistani: Baloch Refugee," *Economic Times* (India), August 20, 2016.
24. James W. Spain, "Political Problems of a Borderland," in *Pakistan's Western Borderlands: The Transformation of a Political Order*, ed. Ainslie T. Embree (Royal Book Company, 1979), 8.
25. Akbar, *The Redefined Dimensions of Baloch Nationalist Movement*, 325.
26. Mahvish Ahmad, "Balochistan Beyond," in *Dispatches from Pakistan*, ed. Madiha R. Tahir et al. (University of Minnesota Press, 2014), 150–167.

27. Minutes of Viceroy's Twenty Fifth Miscellaneous Meeting, August 4, 1947, in *Quaid-i-Azam Mohammad Ali Jinnah Papers*, vol. 9, ed. Z. H. Zaidi (Quaid-i-Azam Papers Project, National Archives of Pakistan, 2003), 192.
28. Zeb, *Ethno-Political Conflict in Pakistan*, 72.
29. Harrison Akins, *Conquering the Maharajas: India's Princely States and the End of Empire, 1930–50* (Manchester University Press, 2023), 214–241.
30. Akins, 225–226, 233–234; Harrison, *In Afghanistan's Shadow*, 25.
31. Farhan Hanif Siddiqi, *The Politics of Ethnicity in Pakistan: The Baloch, Sindhi, and Mohajir Ethnic Movements* (Routledge, 2012), 61.
32. Paul Titus and Nina Swidler, "Knights, Not Pawns: Ethno-Nationalism and Regional Dynamics in Post-Colonial Balochistan," *International Journal of Middle East Studies* 32 (2000): 50.
33. Manzoor Ahmed, "The Dynamics of (Ethno) Nationalism and Federalism in Postcolonial Balochistan, Pakistan," *Journal of Asian and African Studies* 55, no. 7 (2020): 980.
34. Zeb, *Ethno-Political Conflict in Pakistan*, 83.
35. Ahmed, *The Thistle and the Drone*, 139–140; Zeb, *Ethno-Political Conflict in Pakistan*, 86.
36. Harrison, *In Afghanistan's Shadow*, 29.
37. Gary J. Bass, *The Blood Telegram: Nixon, Kissinger, and a Forgotten Genocide* (Alfred A. Knopf, 2013).
38. "Bhutto Urges Constituent Assembly Members to Keep Tryst with Destiny," *Dawn*, February 23, 1973.
39. Zeb, *Ethno-Political Conflict in Pakistan*, 100.
40. Malik Siraj Akbar, *The Redefined Dimensions of Baloch Nationalist Movement* (Xlibris, 2011), 39.
41. Akbar, 170, 207.
42. National Archives, UK, FCO/37/1139, Political situation in Baluchistan, 1972.
43. National Archives, UK, FCO/37/1139, Political situation in Baluchistan, 1972.
44. Association for Diplomatic Studies and Training, Foreign Affairs Oral History Project, Interview of George G. B. Griffin, April 30, 2002, https://adst.org/OH%20TOCs/Griffin,%20George%20G.B.toc.pdf.
45. Harrison, "Nightmare in Baluchistan," 155; Hussain Haqqani, *Pakistan: Between Mosque and Military* (Carnegie Endowment for International Peace, 2005), 169.
46. Haqqani, *Pakistan*, 169
47. Akbar, *The Redefined Dimensions of Baloch Nationalist Movement*, 313.
48. Titus and Swidler, "Knights, Not Pawns," 60.
49. National Archives, 1973ISLAMA07390, Deployment of US-Origin Helicopters in Logistic Support of Pak Army, Diplomatic Cable, US Embassy Islamabad, September 4, 1973, declassified and approved for release June 30, 2005; National Archives, 1973ISLAMA08925, Tikka Khan on Army in Baluchistan, Diplomatic Cable, US Embassy Islamabad, October 15, 1973, declassified and approved for release June 30, 2005; Harrison, "Nightmare in Balochistan," 138.

50. Harrison, *In Afghanistan's Shadow*, 37.
51. National Archives, UK, FCO/37/1336, Political situation in Baluchistan, province of Pakistan, 1973.
52. Harrison, "Nightmare in Balochistan," 139.
53. National Archives, UK, FCO/37/2362, Pakistan—the Baluchistan problem, 1980; Leake, "At the Nation-State's Edge," 527.
54. Leake, "At the Nation-State's Edge," 527.
55. National Archives, 1973ISLAMA07390, Deployment of US-Origin Helicopters in Logistic Support of Pak Army, Diplomatic Cable, US Embassy Islamabad, September 4, 1973, declassified and approved for release June 30, 2005; Harrison, "Nightmare in Baluchistan," 139; Titus and Swidler, "Knights, Not Pawns," 61; Zeb, *Ethno-Political Conflict in Pakistan*, 105.
56. National Archives, UK, FCO/37/1496, Internal political situation in Baluchistan Province of Pakistan, 1974.
57. National Archives, UK, FCO/37/1336, Unreported Speech of Baluchistan Governor Mohammad Akbar Khan Bugti, November 29, 1973.
58. National Archives, UK, FCO/37/1496, White Paper on Baluchistan, Government of Pakistan, October 19, 1974.
59. Ahmed, "The Dynamics of (Ethno) Nationalism and Federalism in Postcolonial Balochistan, Pakistan"; Zeb, *Ethno-Political Conflict in Pakistan*.
60. Harrison, *In Afghanistan's Shadow*, 156.
61. National Archives, UK, FCO/37/1788, Political situation in Baluchistan, Province of Pakistan, 1976.
62. Zeb, *Ethno-Political Conflict in Pakistan*, 103.
63. "Army's Service in Baluchistan Helpful, People Tell Bhutto," *Dawn*, July 29, 1974; Zeb, *Ethno-Political Conflict in Pakistan*, 107.
64. National Archives, UK, FCO/37/1496, White Paper on Baluchistan, Government of Pakistan, October 19, 1974.
65. National Archives, UK, FCO/37/1496, Internal political situation in Baluchistan Province of Pakistan, 1974.
66. Harrison, "Nightmare in Balochistan," 144.
67. Harrison, *In Afghanistan's Shadow*, 162.
68. National Archives, UK, FCO/37/2362, Pakistan—the Baluchistan problem, 1980.
69. Harrison, *In Afghanistan's Shadow*, 164.
70. Zeb, *Ethno-Political Conflict in Pakistan*, 124.
71. Harrison, "Nightmare in Balochistan," 139.
72. Harrison, *In Afghanistan's Shadow*, 45, 64.
73. Harrison, 150–151.
74. Telegram From the Embassy in Pakistan to the Department of State, March 28, 1979, Document 332, *FRUS, 1977–1980*, vol. 19, *South Asia* (US Government Printing Office, 2019).
75. Harrison, *In Afghanistan's Shadow*, 67.
76. National Archives, UK, FCO/37/2362, Pakistan—the Baluchistan problem, 1980.

77. Mahnaz Z. Ispahani, *Roads and Rivals: The Political Uses of Access in the Borderlands of Asia* (Cornell University Press, 1989), 58–81.
78. Harrison, *In Afghanistan's Shadow*, 154.
79. National Archives, UK, FCO/37/2362, Special Development Plan for Baluchistan, Planning Commission, Government of Pakistan, August 1980.
80. National Archives, UK, FCO/37/2362, Pakistan—the Baluchistan problem, 1980.
81. Harrison, *In Afghanistan's Shadow*, 47.
82. Harrison, 149.
83. "MCC Mining Project Winning Hearts and Minds of Families in Pakistan," *China Daily*, May 21, 2021, https://epaper.chinadaily.com.cn/a/202105/21/WS60a6fcao a31099a234356470.html.
84. Lieven, *Pakistan*, 367.
85. Muhammad Akbar Notezai, "The Saindak Files," *Dawn*, January 7, 2018, https://www .dawn.com/news/1381378.
86. "Chinese Mining Firm Gets 15-Year Lease for Copper, Gold Exploration in Saindak," *Arab News*, July 2, 2020, https://www.arabnews.pk/node/1698416/pakistan.
87. Shakoor Ahmad Wani, "The Changing Dynamics of the Baloch Nationalist Movement in Pakistan," *Asian Survey* 56, no. 5 (2016): 810; "MCC Mining Project Winning Hearts and Minds of Families in Pakistan," *China Daily*, May 21, 2021.
88. Notezai, "The Saindak Files."
89. Adnan Aamir, "China's Belt and Road Plans Dismay Pakistan's Poorest Province," *Financial Times*, June 14, 2018, https://www.ft.com/content/c4b78fe0-5399-11e8-84f4 -43d65af59d43.
90. "Balochistan Being Neglected in CPEC, Says Bizenjo," *Dawn*, April 12, 2018, https://www.dawn.com/news/1401117/balochistan-being-neglected-in-cpec-says -bizenjo.
91. International Crisis Group, *China-Pakistan Economic Corridor*, 20.
92. Akbar, *The Redefined Dimensions of Baloch Nationalist Movement*, 241–242.
93. Author interview with Dr. Abdul Basit Mujahid, Balochistan Intellectual Forum, Islamabad, Pakistan, December 14, 2018.
94. CIA Reading Room, Chinese Aid in the Third World, Special Report Weekly Review, Directorate of Intelligence, Central Intelligence Agency, June 30, 1972, sanitized copy approved for release August 24, 2012.
95. Frankopan, *The New Silk Roads*, 120–121.
96. Hillman, *The Emperor's New Road*, 4.
97. Reuters, "China Is Investing $57 Billion Into Pakistan," *Yahoo! Finance*, August 26, 2017, https://www.yahoo.com/news/china-investing-57-billion-pakistan-041502706 .html; Fakhar Durrani, "Will Coronavirus Affect CPEC and Pak Economy?," *News*, February 7, 2020, https://www.thenews.com.pk/print/610253-will-coronavirus-affect -cpec-and-pak-economy.
98. "'Chinese-Only Colony' in Pakistan to House 5 Lakh Workers," *Business Today*, August 21, 2018, https://www.businesstoday.in/latest/world/story/chinese-colony-in -pakistan-international-port-city-cpec-gwadar-109196-2018-08-21.

99. "Chinese to Outnumber Baloch Natives by 2048," *Nation*, December 29, 2016, https://www.nation.com.pk/29-Dec-2016/chinese-to-outnumber-baloch-natives-by-2048.
100. International Crisis Group, *Pakistan: The Forgotten Conflict in Balochistan*, Asia Briefing No. 69 (International Crisis Group, October 22, 2007), 10, https://www.crisisgroup.org/asia/south-asia/pakistan/pakistan-forgotten-conflict-balochistan.
101. Kiyya Baloch, "Locals Fear Investors in Chinese Trade Hub Are Pushing Them Out of Gwadar," *Gandhara*, January 26, 2021, https://www.rferl.org/a/gwadar-china-pakistan-cpec-investment-balochistan/31070269.html.
102. International Crisis Group, *China-Pakistan Economic Corridor*, 19.
103. The Land Acquisition Act, Government of Pakistan, accessed July 22, 2025, https://www.ma-law.org.pk/pdflaw/THE%20LAND%20ACQUISITION%20ACT%201894.pdf.
104. International Crisis Group, *China-Pakistan Economic Corridor*, 19.
105. Michael Kovrig, "National Ambitions Meet Local Opposition Along the China-Pakistan Economic Corridor," International Crisis Group, July 24, 2018, https://www.crisisgroup.org/asia/north-east-asia/china/national-ambitions-meet-local-opposition-along-china-pakistan-economic-corridor.
106. Khawar Abbas, "Socio-Economic Impacts of China-Pakistan Economic Corridor (CPEC) at Community Level: A Case Study of Gwadar Pakistan" (PhD diss., University of Agder, 2019), https://uia.brage.unit.no/uia-xmlui/bitstream/handle/11250/2616202/Abbas,%20Khawar.pdf?sequence=1; Naimat Khan, "'No Food Left in the Sea': Pakistani Fishermen Fearful as Chinese Trawlers Dock at Karachi Port," *Arab News*, October 19, 2020, https://www.arabnews.com/node/1751146/pakistan.
107. Abdul Hai Kakar and Abubakar Siddique, "Pakistan's Invisible Baluch Displacement Crisis," *Gandhara*, February 24, 2016, https://gandhara.rferl.org/a/pakistan-balochistan-displacement/27571358.html.
108. International Crisis Group, *China-Pakistan Economic Corridor*, 18.
109. Rina Saeed Khan, "Thirsty to Thriving? Parched Pakistani Port Aims to Become a New Dubai," Reuters, April 23, 2018, https://www.reuters.com/article/us-pakistan-port-water/thirsty-to-thriving-parched-pakistani-port-aims-to-become-a-new-dubai-idUSKBN1HV07K.
110. Khan.
111. Ijaz Kakakhel, "Gwadar Desalination Plant Enquiry Sent to NAB for Investigation," *Daily Times*, January 4, 2019, https://dailytimes.com.pk/340420/gwadar-desalination-plant-enquiry-sent-to-nab-for-investigation/amp/.
112. Small, *The China-Pakistan Axis*, 100.
113. Khan, "Thirsty to Thriving?"
114. International Crisis Group, *China-Pakistan Economic Corridor*, 18.
115. Muhammad Akbar Notezai, "Gwadar Protests Highlight CPEC's Achilles' Heel," *Diplomat*, December 9, 2021, https://thediplomat.com/2021/12/gwadar-protests-highlight-cpecs-achilles-heel/.

116. Author interview with Baloch researcher, Islamabad, Pakistan, December 2018.
117. Author interview with Pakistani academic, Islamabad, Pakistan, December 2018.
118. Small, *The China-Pakistan Axis*, 102.
119. "Navy to Build Base in Gwadar," *Daily Times*, April 19, 2004.
120. "Suspicions on China's Taking Over of Gwadar Port Are Groundless," *People's Daily*, February 20, 2013.
121. International Crisis Group, *China-Pakistan Economic Corridor*, 4.
122. International Crisis Group, 9.
123. National Archives, 1974MANILA02542, Proposed ADB Loan for Sui-Karachi Gas Pipeline Project (Pakistan), Diplomatic Cable, US Embassy Manila, March 5, 1974, Declassified and Approved for Release June 30, 2005; Sylvia A. Matheson, *The Tigers of Baluchistan* (Oxford University Press, 1975), 44.
124. Declan Walsh, *The Nine Lives of Pakistan: Dispatches from a Precarious State* (W. W. Norton, 2020), 232.
125. Wani, "The Changing Dynamics of the Baloch Nationalist Movement in Pakistan," 818.
126. Walsh, *The Nine Lives of Pakistan*, 230; Zeb, *Ethno-Political Conflict in Pakistan*, 150.
127. "15-Point Demand Given to Tariq Aziz, Says Bugti," *Dawn*, September 23, 2004, http://beta.dawn.com/news/371485/15-point-demand-given-to-tariq-aziz-says-bugti.
128. Zeb, *Ethno-Political Conflict in Pakistan*, 157.
129. Lieven, *Pakistan*, 350.
130. Walsh, *The Nine Lives of Pakistan*, 230.
131. Ahmed Rashid, "Explosive Mix in Pakistan's Gas Province," *BBC News*, February 4, 2005, http://news.bbc.co.uk/2/hi/south_asia/4195933.stm.
132. Declan Walsh, "Pakistan's Gas Fields Blaze as Rape Sparks Threat of Civil War," *Guardian*, February 20, 2005, https://www.theguardian.com/world/2005/feb/21/pakistan.declanwalsh.
133. Walsh, *The Nine Lives of Pakistan*, 235–236.
134. "It Was an Attempt to Eliminate Me: Bugti," *Dawn*, March 31, 2005, https://beta.dawn.com/news/387173/it-was-an-attempt-to-eliminate-me-bugti.
135. "Saboteurs Will Fail, Says Musharraf: Rockets Fired During President's Kohlu Visit," *Dawn*, December 15, 2005, http://beta.dawn.com/news/170026/saboteurs-will-fail-says-musharraf-rockets-fired-during-president-s-kohlu-visit.
136. "Paramilitary Action in Kohlu Continues: Over 50 Killed, Says Tribesmen," *Dawn*, December 20, 2005, https://beta.dawn.com/news/170763/paramilitary-action-in-kohlu-continues-over-50-killed-say-tribesmen.
137. "PM Rules Out Amnesty in Balochistan," *Dawn*, July 14, 2006, https://www.dawn.com/news/201406/pm-rules-out-amnesty-in-balochistan.
138. Zeb, *Ethno-Political Conflict in Pakistan*, 158.
139. Walsh, *Nine Lives of Pakistan*, 237.
140. Pervez Musharraf, "Understanding Balochistan Part-I," *News*, March 14, 2012; Pervez Musharraf, "Understanding Balochistan Part-II," *News*, March 15, 2012.
141. Walsh, *The Nine Lives of Pakistan*, 233.

142. Musharraf, "Understanding Balochistan Part-I"; Musharraf, "Understanding Balochistan Part-II."
143. Akbar, *The Redefined Dimensions of Baloch Nationalist Movement*, 52.
144. Zeb, *Ethno-Political Conflict in Pakistan*, 181.
145. Akbar, *The Redefined Dimensions of Baloch Nationalist Movement*, 260.
146. "BLA Claims Attack on Jinnah Residency in Ziarat," *Express Tribune*, June 14, 2013, https://tribune.com.pk/story/563531/one-official-killed-in-attack-on-quaid-e-azam-residency-in-balochistan.
147. "Global Terrorism Database (GTD)," National Consortium for the Study of Terrorism and Responses to Terrorism, accessed December 15, 2020, http://www.start.umd.edu/gtd.
148. Ahmed, *The Thistle and the Drone*, 137.
149. Akbar, *The Redefined Dimensions of Baloch Nationalist Movement*, 26.
150. Alok Bansal, "Factors Leading to Insurgency in Balochistan," *Small Wars & Insurgencies* 19, no. 2 (2008): 189.
151. Akbar, *The Redefined Dimensions of Baloch Nationalist Movement*, 95.
152. Malik Siraj Akbar, "Punjabi Settlers Biggest Victims of Bugti Aftermath," *Daily Times*, September 7, 2009.
153. "Settlers—Caught in Crossfire," *Dawn*, June 28, 2011.
154. Author interview with Malik Siraj Akbar.
155. "2021 Human Rights Report: Pakistan," US Department of State, accessed July 22, 2025, https://www.state.gov/reports/2021-country-reports-on-human-rights-practices/pakistan/.
156. Jon Boone and Kiyya Baloch, "A New Shenzhen? Poor Pakistan Fishing Town's Horror at Chinese plans," *Guardian*, February 3, 2016, https://www.theguardian.com/world/2016/feb/04/pakistan-new-shenzhen-poor-gwadar-fishing-town-china-plans.
157. Ahmed, "Is Pakistan Heading for Disaster in Balochistan?"; "Balochistan War: Pakistan Accused Over 1,000 Dumped Bodies," *BBC News*, December 28, 2016, https://www.bbc.com/news/world-asia-38454483.
158. Akbar, *The Redefined Dimensions of Baloch Nationalist Movement*, 47.
159. Akbar, 33.
160. "Eid in Balochistan: Families Protest at Quetta Press Club, Demand Recovery of Missing Relatives," *Balochwarna*, August 3, 2020, https://balochwarna.com/2020/08/03/eid-in-balochistan-families-protest-at-quetta-press-club-demand-for-recovery-of-missing-relatives/; "Protest Against 'Enforced Disappearances' During Eid al-Fitr Celebration in Balochistan," *WION News*, April 23, 2023, https://www.wionews.com/south-asia/protest-against-enforced-disappearances-during-eid-al-fitr-celebration-in-balochistan-585351.
161. Author interview with Malik Siraj Akbar; Pamela Constable, "Pakistani Journalist Given U.S. Asylum Tells of Threats, Disappearances in Baluchistan," *Washington Post*, November 14, 2011, https://www.washingtonpost.com/local/pakistani-journalist-given-us-asylum-tells-of-threats-disappearances-in-baluchistan/2011/11/09/gIQAtFufKN_story.html.

162. Abdul Hai Kakar and Abubakar Siddique, "The Human Cost of Balochistan's Separatist Conflict," *Gandhara*, February 17, 2021, https://www.rferl.org/a/balochistan-separatist-insurgency-karima-baloch-pakistan/31107566.html.
163. "KARACHI: Baloch Leaders Unimpressed by PPP Apology," *Dawn*, February 27, 2008, https://www.dawn.com/news/291143/karachi-baloch-leaders-unimpressed-by-ppp-apology.
164. "BLA Rejects Govt's Offer for Talks," *Dawn*, April 10, 2008, https://www.dawn.com/news/297522/bla-rejects-govt-s-offer-for-talks.
165. Akbar, *The Redefined Dimensions of Baloch Nationalist Movement*, 205.
166. A. R. Jerral, "The Balochistan Plan," *Nation*, October 3, 2012, https://www.nation.com.pk/03-Oct-2012/the-balochistan-plan.
167. "Text of the SC Order in Balochistan Case," *News*, October 16, 2012.
168. Anwer Abbas, "Apologies Cannot Appease the Baloch: Akhtar Mengal," *Pakistan Today*, September 30, 2012.
169. Raoof Hasan, "Mengal's Initiative," *Pakistan Today*, October 6, 2012.
170. "BNP Might Participate in Upcoming Polls: Mengal," *Pakistan Today*, April 20, 2013.
171. Walsh, *The Nine Lives of Pakistan*, 246.
172. "Pakistan Car Bomb Kills Chinese," *BBC News*, May 3, 2004, http://news.bbc.co.uk/2/hi/south_asia/3679533.stm.
173. "6 Rockets Fired Near Gwadar Airport," *Dawn*, May 22, 2004, https://www.dawn.com/news/394288/6-rockets-fired-near-gwadar-airport.
174. "Chinese Come Under Attack Again," *Dawn*, July 20, 2007, https://beta.dawn.com/news/257197/chinese-come-under-attack-again.
175. Small, *The China-Pakistan Axis*, 102.
176. Hassan, "To Protect Chinese Investment, Pakistan Military Leaves Little to Chance."
177. International Crisis Group, *China-Pakistan Economic Corridor*, 21.
178. Saleem Shahid, "Three Chinese Engineers Among Five Injured in Dalbandin Suicide Attack," *Dawn*, August 12, 2018, https://www.dawn.com/news/1426550; Farhan Zahid, "BLA's Suicide Squad: Majeed Fidayeen Brigade," *Terrorism Monitor* 17, no. 2 (January 2019), https://jamestown.org/program/blas-suicide-squad-majeed-fidayeen-brigade/.
179. Asad Hashim, "Gunmen Attack Chinese Consulate in Karachi," *Al Jazeera*, November 23, 2018, https://www.aljazeera.com/news/2018/11/23/gunmen-attack-chinese-consulate-in-karachi.
180. "Pakistan Attack: Gunmen Storm Five-Star Hotel in Balochistan," *BBC News*, May 12, 2019, https://www.bbc.com/news/world-asia-48238759.
181. Salman Masood, "Gunmen Wage Deadly Battle at Pakistan Stock Exchange," *New York Times*, June 29, 2020, https://www.nytimes.com/2020/06/29/world/asia/pakistan-stock-exchange-shooting.html#:~:text=Armed%20with%20assault%20rifles%20and,killed%20the%20attackers%2C%20officials%20said.
182. Vivek Sinha, "Exclusive Interview: Basheer Zeb, Chief Balochistan Liberation Army (BLA)," *News Intervention*, July 31, 2020, https://www.newsintervention.com/exclusive-interview-basheer-zeb-chief-baloch-liberation-army-bla/.

183. "Militant Attack in Pakistan's Balochistan Targets Chinese Engineers," *RFE/RL*, August 13, 2023, https://www.rferl.org/a/pakistan-balochistan-militants-attack-chinese-engineers/32546082.html.
184. Mushtaq Ali, "Six Killed in Suicide Attack on Chinese Engineers in Pakistan," Reuters, March 26, 2024, https://www.reuters.com/world/asia-pacific/five-chinese-nationals-killed-suicide-bomb-attack-pakistan-2024-03-26/.
185. Syed Fazl-e-Haider, "Pakistan: The Dangerous Reality of Working on China's Megaprojects," *Interpreter*, April 5, 2024, https://www.lowyinstitute.org/the-interpreter/pakistan-dangerous-reality-working-china-s-megaprojects.
186. Small, *The China-Pakistan Axis*, 99.
187. Saira H. Basit, "Terrorizing the CPEC: Managing Transnational Militancy in China-Pakistan Relations," *Pacific Review* 32, no. 4 (2019): 700.
188. Small, *The China-Pakistan Axis*, 115.
189. Tom Wright and Jeremy Page, "China Pullout Deals Blow to Pakistan," *Wall Street Journal*, September 30, 2011, https://www.wsj.com/articles/SB10001424052970203405504576600671644602028?gaa_at=eafs&gaa_n=ASWzDAhFZwck26mcqh1RRFpTL_IA-qbbY1eNZW5ZtVib8mhrk9pfOtV4gUWA70DdJ28%3D&gaa_ts=6892a5ce&gaa_sig=7jDBdq2s1BvoXz7w603E73hEyNtA3coO1UUEVj3VK_i4vNoaiLpH4zIRyFNlh1WtHb_DeH_OKnTegjTurWvOTw%3D%3D.
190. Small, *The China-Pakistan Axis*, 115.
191. Basit, "Terrorizing the CPEC."
192. Farhan Bokhari, Lucy Hornby, and Christian Shepherd, "China Urges Pakistan to Give Army Lead Role in Silk Road Project," *Financial Times*, July 21, 2016, https://www.ft.com/content/5eea66c0-4ef9-11e6-8172-e39ecd3b86fc.
193. Markey, *China's Western Horizon*, 62.
194. "New Garrisons in Balochistan to Ensure Safety of Key Installations: ISPR," *News*, September 26, 2004.
195. Small, *The China-Pakistan Axis*, 111–112.
196. International Crisis Group, *China-Pakistan Economic Corridor*, 7.
197. Adnan Aamir, "Pakistan to Fence Off Gwadar to Shield China's Belt and Road Port," *Nikkei Asia*, December 14, 2020, https://asia.nikkei.com/Spotlight/Belt-and-Road/Pakistan-to-fence-off-Gwadar-to-shield-China-s-Belt-and-Road-port.
198. Syed Raza Hassan, "To Protect Chinese Investment, Pakistan Military Leaves Little to Chance," Reuters, February 7, 2016, https://www.reuters.com/article/pakistan-china-security-gwadar/to-protect-chinese-investment-pakistan-military-leaves-little-to-chance-idUSKCN0VH06F.
199. Syed Raza Hassan, "Attacks Have Killed 44 Pakistanis Working on China Corridor Since 2014," Reuters, September 8, 2016, https://www.reuters.com/article/us-pakistan-china/attacks-have-killed-44-pakistanis-working-on-china-corridor-since-2014-idUSKCN11E1EP; "China's State-Owned MCC to Operationalize Juzzak Airstrip in Balochistan, Pakistan," *Janes IntelTrak*, September 2, 2021, https://www.rwradvisory.com/chinas-state-owned-mcc-to-operationalize-juzzak-airstrip-in-balochistan-pakistan/; "Balochistan's Juzzak Airport made operational," *Pakistan Today*,

September 13, 2021, https://profit.pakistantoday.com.pk/2021/09/13/balochistans-juzzak-airport-made-operational/.

200. "Raheel Vows to Complete CPEC at All Costs," *Dawn*, July 26, 2015, http://www.dawn.com/news/1196440.

201. Mateen Haider, "Army Aware of Hostility Against CPEC, Will Protect It at Any Cost: Gen Raheel," *Dawn*, June 2, 2016, https://www.dawn.com/news/1262298.

202. Mehreen Zahra-Malik, "New Council Puts Pakistan Army Chief in Economic Driving Seat," *Arab News*, June 20, 2019, https://www.arabnews.com/node/1513691/pakistan.

203. Aamir Yasin, "Asim Bajwa Made Chairman of Newly Created CPEC Authority," *Dawn*, November 27, 2019; F. M. Shakil, "China's Belt and Road Going Nowhere Fast in Pakistan," *Asia Times*, November 11, 2020, https://asiatimes.com/2020/11/chinas-belt-and-road-going-nowhere-fast-in-pakistan/.

204. "China Looks Forward to 'Jointly Promote' CPEC with Its New Civilian Chief," *Express Tribune*, August 5, 2021; Adnan Aamir, "Pakistan Replaces Its Belt and Road Chief with Beijing Favorite," *Nikkei Asia*, August 8, 2021, https://asia.nikkei.com/Spotlight/Belt-and-Road/Pakistan-replaces-its-Belt-and-Road-chief-with-Beijing-favorite.

205. Khurram Husain, "Exclusive: CPEC Master Plan Revealed," *Dawn*, June 21, 2017, https://www.dawn.com/news/1333101.

206. Khaleeq Kiani, "Power Consumers to Pay Security Cost of CPEC Projects," *Dawn*, August 4, 2017, https://www.dawn.com/news/1349492.

207. Government of Pakistan, *Long Term Plan for China-Pakistan Economic Corridor (2017–2030)* (Ministry of Planning, Development, and Reform, November 2017), 7, 26, http://cpec.gov.pk/long-term-plan-cpec.

208. "Pak–China Joint Statement on Prime Minister Imran's Meetings with President Xi & Premier Li," *Pakistan in the World*, February 6, 2022, https://pakistanintheworld.pk/live/pak-china-joint-statement-on-prime-minister-imrans-meetings-with-president-xi-premier-li/?fbclid=IwAR3KrkBEUKKAcBsjqmVh9RW79zg7NLg_Bq-jnEr-zhk5jeyBDL44nJ8YG6M.

209. "Foreign Ministry Spokesperson's Remarks on the Dasu Bomb Attack in Pakistan," Ministry of Foreign Affairs of the People's Republic of China, March 27, 2024, https://www.mfa.gov.cn/eng/xwfw_665399/s2510_665401/202403/t20240327_11271358.html; Adnan Aamir, "China Wants Own Security Company to Protect Assets in Pakistan," *Nikkei Asia*, June 28, 2022, https://asia.nikkei.com/Politics/International-relations/China-wants-own-security-company-to-protect-assets-in-Pakistan; Adnan Aamir, "Pakistan Beefing Up Security After Deadly Attacks on Chinese Workers," *Nikkei Asia*, June 3, 2024, https://asia.nikkei.com/Politics/Terrorism/Pakistan-beefing-up-security-after-deadly-attacks-on-Chinese-workers.

210. Raza Khan, "15,000 Troops of Special Security Division to Protect CPEC Projects, Chinese Nationals," *Dawn*, August 12, 2016, http://www.dawn.com/news/1277182/15000-troops-of-special-security-division-to-protect-cpec-projects-chinese-nationals.

211. Kiani, "Power Consumers to Pay Security Cost of CPEC Projects."

212. "Pakistan, China to Foil Conspiracies Against CPEC," *Nation*, September 16, 2017, https://www.nation.com.pk/16-Sep-2017/pakistan-china-to-foil-conspiracies-against-cpec.
213. International Crisis Group, *China-Pakistan Economic Corridor*, 20.
214. "CPEC an Existential Threat to Baloch: Khan of Kalat," *Financial Express*, May 27, 2017, https://www.financialexpress.com/world-news/cpec-an-existential-threat-to-baloch-khan-of-kalat/688331/.
215. Author interview with Malik Siraj Akbar.
216. "Embassy Condemns Suicide Attack Targeting Chinese Nationals in Pakistan, Two Children Killed," *Global Times*, August 21, 2021, https://www.globaltimes.cn/page/202108/1232063.shtml.
217. "Pakistan Attack: Chinese Tutors Killed in Karachi University," *BBC News*, April 26, 2022, https://www.bbc.com/news/world-asia-61229589; Sophia Saifi, Saleem Mehsud, and Azaz Syed, "Female Suicide Bomber Behind Karachi Attack That Killed 3 Chinese Citizens: Police," *CNN*, April 7, 2022, https://www.cnn.com/2022/04/27/asia/pakistan-karachi-blast-chinese-nationals-killed-intl-hnk/index.html.
218. Syed Fazl-e-Haider, "Pakistani Separatists Turn Their Sights on China," *Interpreter*, May 16, 2022, https://www.lowyinstitute.org/the-interpreter/pakistani-separatists-turn-their-sights-china.
219. Ajeyo Basu, "Pakistan: Insurgents Destroy Several Chinese Mobile Towers Along CPEC Route in Balochistan," *Firstpost*, April 19, 2023, https://www.firstpost.com/world/pakistan-insurgents-destroy-several-chinese-mobile-towers-along-cpec-route-in-balochistan-12477762.html.
220. "If PDM Comes to Rawalpindi, We'll Offer Them Tea: DG ISPR," *Dawn*, January 11, 2021, https://www.dawn.com/news/1600950/if-pdm-comes-to-rawalpindi-well-offer-them-tea-dg-ispr.
221. Hillman et al., "The China-Pakistan Economic Corridor at Five," 2.
222. Khaleeq Kiani, "Joint Cooperation Committee Agrees to Revive Mega Projects Under CPEC," *Dawn*, October 28, 2022, https://dawn.com/news/1717242.
223. Shahjahan Khurram, "Pakistan Says 'CPEC 2.0' to Attract More Chinese Companies and Investment," *Arab News*, January 23, 2025, https://www.arabnews.com/node/2586996/pakistan.
224. "Protestors to Be Charged Under Anti-Terrorism Laws: Pak on CPEC Row," *Business Insider*, August 18, 2016, https://www.business-standard.com/article/international/protestors-to-be-charged-under-anti-terrorism-laws-pak-on-cpec-row-116081800623_1.html.
225. Frankopan, *The New Silk Roads*, 120; Hillman, *The Emperor's New Road*, 147.
226. Hillman, *The Emperor's New Road*, 125.

CONCLUSION

1. Ahmed, *The Thistle and the Drone*, 173.
2. Wilson Center Digital Archive, "Speech Made by Pham Van Dong," September 5, 1978, S-0442-0365-03, United Nations Archives and Records Management Section, obtained

for CWIHP by Charles Kraus, https://digitalarchive.wilsoncenter.org/document/118418; Wilson Center Digital Archive, "Letter Dated 2 November 1979 from the Permanent Representative of Viet Nam to the United Nations addressed to the Secretary-General," November 2, 1979, United Nations General Assembly, A/34/648; United Nations Security Council, S/13606, 2 November 1979, via UN Official Document System, https://digitalarchive.wilsoncenter.org/document/290750.

3. Kevin Klose, "Soviets and Vietnamese Sign Treaty, Warn Chinese," *Washington Post*, November 3, 1978.
4. Wilson Center Digital Archive, "Cable from the Foreign Ministry, 'Vice Premier Deng Xiaoping Discusses the Vietnam Issue with a Foreign Guest,'" February 21, 1979, Fujian Provincial Archives, 222-12-287, 1–3, translated by David Cowhig, https://digitalarchive.wilsoncenter.org/document/290999.
5. Wilson Center Digital Archive, "Chinese Government Delegation Leader's Statement at 8th Session of Sino-Vietnamese Negotiations," October 5, 1978, S-0442-0365-03, United Nations Archives and Records Management Section, obtained for CWIHP by Charles Kraus, https://digitalarchive.wilsoncenter.org/document/118420.
6. "Chinese Government Delegation Leader's Statement at 8th Session of Sino-Vietnamese Negotiations."
7. Wilson Center Digital Archive, "Statement of the Ministry of Foreign Affairs of the People's Republic of China on the Expulsion of Chinese Residents by Viet Nam," June 12, 1978, S-0442-0365-01, United Nations Archives and Records Management Section, obtained for CWIHP by Charles Kraus, https://digitalarchive.wilsoncenter.org/document/118404; Wilson Center Digital Archive, "Four Notes Transmitted by the Socialist Republic of Viet Nam," June 20, 1978, S-0442-0365-01, United Nations Archives and Records Management Section, obtained for CWIHP by Charles Kraus, https://digitalarchive.wilsoncenter.org/document/118405; Wilson Center Digital Archive, "Record of Meeting Between Prime Minister Fukuda and Vice Premier Deng (First Meeting)," October 23, 1978, Diplomatic Archives of the Ministry of Foreign Affairs of Japan, 01-935-1, 001–015, contributed by Robert Hoppens and translated by Stephen Mercado, https://digitalarchive.wilsoncenter.org/document/120018.
8. "Four Notes Transmitted by the Socialist Republic of Viet Nam"; "Chinese Government Delegation Leader's Statement at 8th Session of Sino-Vietnamese Negotiations."
9. Xiaoming Zhang, *Deng Xiaoping's Long War: The Military Conflict Between China and Vietnam, 1979–1991* (University of North Carolina Press, 2015).
10. George E. Dooley, *Battle for the Central Highlands: A Special Forces Story* (Ballantine Books, 2000), 254–255.
11. Wilson Center Digital Archive, "Những Vấn Đề Trọng Yếu Trong Công Tác Đấu Tranh Chống Gián Điệp Trung Quốc, Gián Điệp Mỹ và Chống Địch Phá Hoại Tư Tưởng" [Key issues in the struggle against Chinese spies and American spies and in the struggle against the enemy's ideological attacks] (People's Public Security Forces Document, printed by the People's Security University, Hanoi, 12 September 1981), 1–38, contributed and translated by Merle Pribbenow, https://digitalarchive.wilsoncenter.org/document/tran-dong-key-issues-struggle-against-chinese-spies-and-american-spies-and-struggle.

12. Enze Han, "Myanmar's Internal Ethnic Conflicts and Their Implications for China's Regional Grand Strategy," *Asian Survey* 60, no. 3 (2020): 466–489.
13. "Genocide, Crimes Against Humanity and Ethnic Cleansing of Rohingya in Burma," US Department of State, March 21, 2022, https://2021-2025.state.gov/burma-genocide/.
14. Harrison Akins, "The Two Faces of Democratization in Myanmar: A Case Study of the Rohingya and Burmese Nationalism," *Journal of Muslim Minority Affairs* 38, no. 2 (2018): 229–245; Azeem Ibrahim, *The Rohingyas: Inside Myanmar's Hidden Genocide* (C. Hurst & Co., 2016); Andrew Nachemson and Lun Min Mang, "Rakhine: The New Front in Myanmar's Violent Ethnic Conflicts," *Al Jazeera*, January 7, 2020, https://www.aljazeera.com/news/2020/1/7/rakhine-the-new-front-in-myanmars-violent-ethnic-conflicts.
15. Skylar Lindsay, "A Chinese Special Economic Zone Is Deepening Conflict in Myanmar's Rakhine State," *ASEAN Today*, May 17, 2019, https://www.aseantoday.com/2019/05/a-chinese-special-economic-zone-is-deepening-conflict-in-myanmars-rakhine-state/.
16. Si Yang and Lin Yang, "Leaked Documents Suggest Fraying of China-Myanmar Ties," *Voice of America*, March 12, 2021, https://www.voanews.com/a/east-asia-pacific_leaked-documents-suggest-fraying-china-myanmar-ties/6203234.html.
17. Aung Zaw, "With the Bear and the Dragon, Myanmar Military Plays Safe," *Irrawaddy*, May 2, 2019, https://www.irrawaddy.com/opinion/commentary/bear-dragon-myanmar-military-plays-safe.html.
18. "Myanmar Coup: China Blocks UN Condemnation as Protest Grows," *BBC News*, February 3, 2021, https://www.bbc.com/news/world-asia-55913947.
19. "Myanmar Military Airstrike: More than 100 people Feared Dead," *BBC News*, April 12, 2023, https://www.bbc.com/news/world-asia-65238250.
20. Frederick Kempe, "Xi Is Positioning China as the World's Indispensable Economy—and Biden's Greatest Challenge," *CNBC*, January 24, 2021, https://www.cnbc.com/2021/01/24/op-ed-xi-is-positioning-china-as-the-worlds-indispensable-economy-and-bidens-greatest.html.
21. Frankopan, *The New Silk Roads*, 152.
22. Richard A. Boucher, "U.S. Policy in Central Asia: Balancing Priorities (Part II)," statement to the House International Relations Committee, Subcommittee on the Middle East and Central Asia, April 26, 2006, https://2001-2009.state.gov/p/sca/rls/rm/2006/65292.htm.
23. Akins, *The Terrorism Trap*, 59–90.
24. Mike Allen, "America's First Pacific President," *Politico*, November 13, 2009, https://www.politico.com/story/2009/11/americas-first-pacific-president-029511.
25. Frankopan, *The New Silk Roads*, 89.
26. Author interview with Cameron Munter, former US ambassador to Pakistan, New York, NY, January 23, 2019.
27. Nick Gass, "Trump: 'We Can't Continue to Allow China to Rape Our Country,'" *Politico*, May 2, 2016, https://www.politico.com/blogs/2016-gop-primary-live-updates-and-results/2016/05/trump-china-rape-america-222689.

28. "Memorandum on Withdrawal of the United States from the Trans-Pacific Partnership Negotiations and Agreement," White House, January 23, 2017, https://www.govinfo.gov/content/pkg/DCPD-201700064/html/DCPD-201700064.htm.
29. "How China Won Trump's Trade War and Got Americans to Foot the Bill," *Bloomberg News*, January 11, 2021, https://financialpost.com/news/economy/how-china-won-trumps-trade-war-and-got-americans-to-foot-the-bill.
30. Scott Neuman, "In Military Name Change, U.S. Pacific Command Becomes U.S. Indo-Pacific Command," *NPR*, May 31, 2018, https://www.npr.org/sections/thetwo-way/2018/05/31/615722120/in-military-name-change-u-s-pacific-command-becomes-u-s-indo-pacific-command.
31. Humeyra Pamuk, David Brunnstrom, and Michael Martina, "'Tough' U.S.-China Talks Signal Rocky Start to Relations Under Biden," Reuters, March 19, 2021, https://www.reuters.com/article/uk-usa-china-alaska-idUKKBN2BB2DE.
32. "Uighurs: Western Countries Sanction China Over Rights Abuses," *BBC News*, March 22, 2021, https://www.bbc.com/news/world-europe-56487162.
33. "Blinken Tells NATO Allies They Don't Need to Choose US or China," *Al Jazeera*, March 24, 2021, https://www.aljazeera.com/news/2021/3/24/blinken-to-tell-nato-allies-they-dont-need-to-choose-us-or-china.
34. "Transcript: Secretary of Defense Lloyd J. Austin III Press Conference in New Delhi," Department of Defense, March 20, 2021, https://www.defense.gov/Newsroom/Transcripts/Transcript/Article/2544454/secretary-of-defense-lloyd-j-austin-iii-press-conference-in-new-delhi/.
35. *National Security Strategy* (White House, October 2022), ii, 24, 38, https://bidenwhitehouse.archives.gov/wp-content/uploads/2022/10/Biden-Harris-Administrations-National-Security-Strategy-10.2022.pdf.
36. Refael Kubersky, "What Trump Has Promised on China in a Second Term," *PBS Frontline*, November 27, 2024, https://www.pbs.org/wgbh/frontline/article/trump-china-second-term/.
37. Bahot (@bahot_baluch), "The Karachi attack was carried out by BLA units, Majeed Brigade, and ZIRAB," X, October 7, 2024, https://x.com/bahot_baluch/status/1843322262189232134.

BIBLIOGRAPHY

ARCHIVES

Balochistan Archives, Government of Balochistan, http://balochistanarchives.gob.pk

Central Intelligence Agency Reading Room, McLean, VA

Chughtai Library, Lahore, Pakistan, https://www.chughtailibrary.com
  Reports Archive

Foreign Affairs Oral History Project, Association for Diplomatic Studies and Training, https://adst.org

John F. Kennedy Presidential Library, https://www.jfklibrary.org/archives/search-collections/browse-digitized-collections

National Archives, College Park, MD
  Central Foreign Policy Files

National Archives, London, UK
  Dominion Office Papers
  Foreign and Commonwealth Office Papers

National Archives of India, New Delhi, India
  Foreign Department Papers
  Ministry of External Affairs Papers
  Ministry of Home Affairs Papers
  Ministry of States Papers
  Private Papers of Sardar Patel

National Security Archives, George Washington University, Washington, DC

Nehru Memorial Museum and Library, New Delhi, India

State Department Reading Room, Washington, DC

Woodrow Wilson Center Digital Archive, https://digitalarchive.wilsoncenter.org

PUBLISHED PRIMARY SOURCES AND DOCUMENT COLLECTIONS

Administration Report of the Baluchistan Agency for 1886. Superintendent of Government Printing, 1886.

Administration Report of the Baluchistan Agency for 1886–1887. Superintendent of Government Printing, 1888.

Baluchistan Agency Administration Report for 1945–46, Agent to the Governor General in Baluchistan. Government of India Press, 1948.

Foreign Relations of the United States, 1952–1954. Vol. 11, pt. 2, *Africa and South Asia*. US Government Printing Office, 1983.

Foreign Relations of the United States, 1961–1963. Vol. 19, *South Asia*. US Government Printing Office, 1996.

Foreign Relations of the United States, 1964–1968. Vol. 30, *China*. US Government Printing Office, 1998.

Foreign Relations of the United States, 1977–1980. Vol. 29, *South Asia*. US Government Printing Office, 2019.

Frontier and Overseas Expeditions from India. Vol. 3, *Baluchistan and the First Afghan War*. Superintendent Government Printing, 1910.

Lord Curzon in India: Being a Selection from His Speeches as Viceroy & Governor-General of India, 1898–1905. Macmillan and Co., 1906.

Lord Curzon of Kedleston. *The Romanes Lecture 1907: Frontiers*. Clarendon Press, 1907.

Nehru, Jawaharlal. *Letters for a Nation: From Jawaharlal Nehru to His Chief Ministers, 1947–1963*. Edited by Madhav Khosla. Penguin Books, 2014.

Papers Relating to The Treaty Concluded Between the Government of India and the Khan of Khelat, on the 8th December 1876. Her Majesty's Stationery Office, 1877.

Quaid-i-Azam Mohammad Ali Jinnah Papers, vols. 1–18. Edited by Z. H. Zaidi. Quaid-i-Azam Papers Project, National Archives of Pakistan, 1993–2012.

Selected Works of Jawaharlal Nehru. 2nd ser., vol. 25. Edited by S. Gopal. Jawaharlal Nehru Memorial Fund, 1999.

MEDIA OUTLETS

Al Jazeera, Arab News, ASEAN Today, Asia Times, Associated Press, Balochwarna, BBC News, Bloomberg News, Business Today, Business Insider, China Daily, Christian Science Monitor, The Citizen, CNBC, CNN, Colombo Page, Daily Times, Dawn, The Diplomat, Dunya News TV Pakistan, Economic Times, Express Tribune, Financial Express, Financial Times, Firstpost, Foreign Affairs, Foreign Policy, Gandhara, Global Times, The Guardian, The Hindu, Hindustan Times, Huffington Post, Indian Defence Review, The Interpreter, The Irrawaddy, Jane's IntelTrak, Los Angeles Review of Books, Militant Wire, The Nation, New York Times, The News, News Intervention, Nikkei Asia, Pakistan in the World, Pakistan Today, PBS Frontline, People's Daily, Politico, Reuters, RFE/RL, Scroll.in, The Statesman, Times of India, Voice of America, Wall Street Journal, Washington Post, WION News, The Wire

SECONDARY SOURCES

Abbas, Khawar. "Socio-Economic Impacts of China-Pakistan Economic Corridor (CPEC) at Community Level: A Case Study of Gwadar Pakistan." PhD diss., University of Agder, 2019. https://uia.brage.unit.no/uia-xmlui/bitstream/handle/11250/2616202/Abbas,%20 Khawar.pdf?sequence=1.

Ahmed, Akbar S. *Pakistan Society: Islam, Ethnicity and Leadership in South Asia.* Oxford University Press, 1986.

Ahmed, Akbar S. *Jinnah, Pakistan, and Islamic Identity: The Search for Saladin.* Routledge, 1997.

Ahmed, Akbar. *The Thistle and the Drone: How America's War on Terror Became a Global War on Tribal Islam.* Brookings Institution Press, 2013.

Ahmed, Manzoor. "The Dynamics of (Ethno) Nationalism and Federalism in Postcolonial Balochistan, Pakistan." *Journal of Asian and African Studies* 55, no. 7 (2020): 979–1006.

Akbar, Malik Siraj. *The Redefined Dimensions of Baloch Nationalist Movement.* Xlibris, 2011.

Akins, Harrison. "Between Allies and Enemies: Explaining the Volatility of the U.S.-Pakistan Relationship, 1947–2018." Policy Brief 7:18, Howard H. Baker Jr. Center for Public Policy, March 2018. https://bakercenterdev.utk.edu/images/brief6.pdf.

Akins, Harrison. "Mashar Versus Kashar in Pakistan's FATA: Intra-Tribal Conflict and the Obstacles of Reform." *Asian Survey* 58, no. 6 (2018): 1136–1159.

Akins, Harrison. "The Two Faces of Democratization in Myanmar: A Case Study of the Rohingya and Burmese Nationalism." *Journal of Muslim Minority Affairs* 38, no. 2 (2018): 229–245.

Akins, Harrison. "The Assam Rifles and India's North-East frontier policy." *Small Wars & Insurgencies* 31, no. 6 (2020): 1373–1394.

Akins, Harrison. "Violence on the Home Front: Interstate Rivalry and Pro-Government Militias." *Terrorism and Political Violence* 33, no. 3 (2021): 466–488.

Akins, Harrison. *Conquering the Maharajas: India's Princely States and the End of Empire, 1930–50.* Manchester University Press, 2023.

Akins, Harrison. *The Terrorism Trap: How the War on Terror Escalates Violence in America's Partner States.* Columbia University Press, 2023.

Ambedkar, B. R. *History of the Frontier Areas Bordering on Assam.* Assam Government Press, 1942.

Atzili, Boaz, and Min Jung Kim. "Buffer Zones and International Rivalry: Internal and External Geographic Separation Mechanisms." *International Affairs* 99, no. 2 (2023): 645–665.

Bansal, Alok. "Factors Leading to Insurgency in Balochistan." *Small Wars & Insurgencies* 19, no. 2 (2008): 182–200.

Baruah, Sanjib. *In the Name of the Nation: India and Its Northeast.* Stanford University Press, 2020.

Basit, Saira H. "Terrorizing the CPEC: Managing Transnational Militancy in China-Pakistan Relations." *Pacific Review* 32, no. 4 (2019): 694–724.

Bass, Gary J. *The Blood Telegram: Nixon, Kissinger, and a Forgotten Genocide.* Alfred A. Knopf, 2013.

Benton, Lauren. "Colonial Law and Cultural Differences: Jurisdictional Politics and the Formation of the Colonial State." *Comparative Studies in Society and History* 41, no. 3 (1999): 563–588.

Bhattacherjee, Kallol. *The Great Game in Afghanistan: Rajiv Gandhi, General Zia and the Unending War.* HarperCollins, 2017.

Bhaumak, Subir. *Insurgent Crossfire: North-East India.* Lancer Publishers, 1996.

Boni, Filippo. "Civil-Military Relations in Pakistan: A Case Study of Sino-Pakistani Relations and the Port of Gwadar." *Commonwealth & Comparative Politics* 54, no. 4 (2016): 498–517.

Boni, Filippo, and Katharine Adeney. "The Impact of the China-Pakistan Economic Corridor on Pakistan's Federal System: The Politics of CPEC." *Asian Survey* 60, no. 3 (2020): 441–465.

Brautigam, Deborah. *The Dragon's Gift: The Real Story of China in Africa.* Oxford University Press, 2009.

Bruce, Richard. *The Forward Policy and Its Results or Thirty-Five Years' Work Amongst the Tribes on Our North-Western Frontier of India.* Longmans, Green, and Co., 1900.

Bueno de Mesquita, Bruce, and Randolph M. Siverson. "War and the Survival of Political Leaders: A Comparative Study of Regime Types and Political Accountability." *American Political Science Review* 89, no. 4 (1995): 841–855.

Carey, Sabine C., Michael P. Colaresi, and Neil J. Mitchell. "Governments, Informal Links to Militias, and Accountability." *Journal of Conflict Resolution* 59, no. 5 (2015): 850–876.

Chatzky, Andrew, and James McBride. "Backgrounder: China's Massive Belt and Road Initiative." Council on Foreign Relations, January 28, 2020. https://www.cfr.org/backgrounder/chinas-massive-belt-and-road-initiative.

Cheema, Pervaiz Iqbal. *Pakistan's Defense Policy, 1947–58.* St. Martin's Press, 1990.

Clarke, Michael. "Beijing's Pivot West: The Convergence of *Innenpolitik* and *Aussenpolitik* on China's 'Belt and Road?'" *Journal of Contemporary China* 29, no. 123 (2020): 336–353.

Clary, Christopher. *The Difficult Politics of Peace: Rivalry in Modern South Asia.* Oxford University Press, 2022.

Cohen, Stephen Philip. *The Idea of Pakistan.* Brookings Institution Press, 2004.

Condos, Mark. "'Fanaticism' and the Politics of Resistance Along the North-West Frontier of British India." *Comparative Studies in Society and History* 58, no. 3 (2016): 717–745.

Copland, Ian. "The Princely States, the Muslim League, and the Partition of India in 1947." *International History Review* 13, no. 1 (1991): 38–69.

Das, Debojyoti. "Understanding Margins, State Power, Space and Territoriality in the Naga Hills." *Journal of Borderland Studies* 29, no. 1 (2014): 63–80.

Dasgupta, Jyotirindra. "Community, Authenticity, and Autonomy: Insurgence and Institutional Development in India's Northeast." *Journal of Asian Studies* 56, no. 2 (1997): 345–370.

Dooley, George E. *Battle for the Central Highlands: A Special Forces Story.* Ballantine Books, 2000.

Dunham, Mike. *Buddha's Warriors: The Story of the CIA-Backed Tibetan Freedom Fighters, the Chinese Invasion, and the Ultimate Fall of Tibet.* Penguin, 2004.

Dzuvichu, Lipokmar. "Roads and the Raj: The Politics of Road Building in Colonial Naga Hills, 1860s–1910s." *Indian Economic and Social History Review* 50, no. 4 (2013): 473–494.

Eaton, Richard M. "Conversion to Christianity Among the Nagas, 1876–1971." *Indian Economic and Social History Review* 21, no. 1 (1984): 1–44.

Elwin, Verrier. *A Philosophy for NEFA*. North-East Frontier Agency, 1957.

Elwin, Verrier. *Nagaland*. Assam Government Research Department, Adviser's Secretariat, 1961.

Embree, Ainslie T., ed. *Pakistan's Western Borderlands: The Transformation of a Political Order*. Royal Book Company, 1979.

Fearon, James D. "Domestic Political Audiences and the Escalation of International Disputes." *American Political Science Review* 88, no. 3 (1994): 577–592.

Fleming, Peter. *Bayonets to Lhasa: The British Invasion of Tibet*. Harper, 1961.

Fingar, Thomas, ed. *The New Great Game: China and South and Central Asia in the Era of Reform*. Stanford University Press, 2016.

Frankopan, Peter. *The New Silk Roads: The Present and Future of the World*. Bloomsbury Publishing, 2018.

French, Howard. *Everything Under the Heavens: How the Past Helps Shape China's Push for Global Power*. Vintage Books, 2017.

Fulton, Jonathan. "Domestic Politics as Fuel for China's Maritime Silk Road Initiative: The Case of the Gulf Monarchies." *Journal of Contemporary China* 29, no. 122 (2020): 175–190.

Gardner, Kyle J. *The Frontier Complex: Geopolitics and the Making of the India-China Border, 1846–1962*. Cambridge University Press, 2021.

Geertz, Clifford. *The Interpretation of Cultures*. Basic Books, 1973.

Ghosh, Arunabh. "Before 1962: The Case for 1950s China-India History." *Journal of Asian Studies* 76, no. 3 (2017): 697–727.

Gilmour, David. *The British in India: A Social History of the Raj*. Picador, 2018.

"Global Terrorism Database (GTD)." National Consortium for the Study of Terrorism and Responses to Terrorism. Accessed December 15, 2020. http://www.start.umd.edu/gtd.

Goldstein, Melvyn C. *A History of Modern Tibet, 1913–1951: The Demise of the Lamaist State*. University of California Press, 1989.

Gott, Richard. *Britain's Empire: Resistance, Repression and Revolt*. Verso, 2011.

Gourevitch, Peter. "The Second Image Reversed: The International Sources of Domestic Politics." *International Organization* 32, no. 4 (1978): 881–912.

Government of Pakistan. *Long Term Plan for China-Pakistan Economic Corridor (2017–2030)*. Ministry of Planning, Development and Reform, November 2017. http://cpec.gov.pk/long-term-plan-cpec.

Guha, Ramachandra. *India After Gandhi: The History of the World's Largest Democracy*. Ecco, 2008.

Guha, Ramachandra. *Savaging the Civilized: Verrier Elwin, His Tribals, and India*. Penguin Press, 2014.

Guite, Jangkhomang. "Colonialism and Its Unruly?—the Colonial State and Kuki Raids in Nineteenth Century Northeast India." *Modern Asian Studies* 48, no. 5 (2014): 1188–1232.

Guite, Jangkhomang. "Colonial Violence and Its 'Small Wars': Fighting the Kuki 'Guerillas' During the Great War in Northeast India, 1917–1919." *Small Wars & Insurgencies* 30, no. 2 (2019): 447–478.

Guite, Jangkhomang, and Thongkholal Haokip, eds. *The Anglo-Kuki War, 1917–1919: A Frontier Uprising Against Imperialism During the First World War.* Routledge, 2019.

Gungwu, Wang, and Zheng Yongnian. *China and the New International Order.* Routledge, 2008.

Gupta, Sonika. "Frontiers in Flux: Indo-Tibetan Border: 1946–1948." *India Quarterly* 77, no. 1 (2021): 42–58.

Guyot-Rechard, Berenice. *Shadow States: India, China and the Himalayas, 1910–1962.* Cambridge University Press, 2017.

Han, Enze. "Myanmar's Internal Ethnic Conflicts and Their Implications for China's Regional Grand Strategy." *Asian Survey* 60, no. 3 (2020): 466–489.

Hansen, Thomas Blom, and Finn Stepputat, eds. *Sovereign Bodies: Citizens, Migrants, and States in the Postcolonial World.* Princeton University Press, 2005.

Haqqani, Hussain. *Pakistan: Between Mosque and Military.* Carnegie Endowment for International Peace, 2005.

Harrison, Selig S. *In Afghanistan's Shadow: Baloch Nationalism and Soviet Temptations.* Carnegie Endowment for International Peace, 1981.

Hillman, Jonathan E. *The Emperor's New Road: China and the Project of the Century.* Yale University Press, 2020.

Hillman, Jonathan E., Maesea McCalpin, and Kendra Brock. "The China-Pakistan Economic Corridor at Five." *CSIS Briefs.* Center for Strategic and International Studies, April 2020. https://www.csis.org/analysis/china-pakistan-economic-corridor-five.

Hoffman, Steven A. *India and the China Crisis.* University of California Press, 1990.

Hopkins, Benjamin D. *Ruling the Savage Periphery: Frontier Governance and the Making of the Modern State.* Harvard University Press, 2020.

Hopkirk, Peter. *The Great Game: On Secret Service in High Asia.* Oxford University Press, 1991.

Hopkirk, Peter. *On Secret Service East of Constantinople: The Plot to Bring Down the British Empire.* John Murray, 1994.

Hughes-Buller, R. *Baluchistan District Gazetteer Series: Volumes VII, Makran.* Times Press, 1906.

Hunt, Michael H. *The Genesis of Chinese Communist Foreign Policy.* Columbia University Press, 1996.

Husain, Ishrat. *CPEC & Pakistani Economy: An Appraisal.* Centre of Excellence for CPEC, 2017. https://cpec-centre.pk/wp-content/uploads/2018/04/CPEC-and-Pakistani-Economy_An-Appraisal.pdf.

Ibrahim, Azeem. *The Rohingyas: Inside Myanmar's Hidden Genocide.* C. Hurst and Co., 2016.

International Crisis Group. *China-Pakistan Economic Corridor: Opportunities and Risks.* Asia Report No. 297. International Crisis Group, June 29, 2018. https://www.crisisgroup.org/asia/south-asia/pakistan/297-china-pakistan-economic-corridor-opportunities-and-risks.

Ispahani, Mahnaz Z. *Roads and Rivals: The Political Uses of Access in the Borderlands of Asia.* Cornell University Press, 1989.

Jaffrelot, Christophe. *The Pakistan Paradox: Instability and Resilience.* C. Hurst and Co., 2015.

Jain, Romi. "Pitfalls or Windfalls in China's Belt and Road Economic Outreach?" *Asian Survey* 60, no. 4 (2020): 685–709.

Jervis, Robert. *Perception and Misperception in International Politics.* Princeton University Press, 1976.

Johri, Major Sitaram. *Where India, China, and Burma Meet.* Thacker Spink and Co., 1963.

Joshi, Manoj. *Understanding the India-China Border: The Enduring Threat of War in High Himalaya.* Oxford University Press, 2022.

Kaplan, Robert D. *The Return of Marco Polo's World: War, Strategy, and American Interests in the Twenty-First Century.* Random House, 2019.

Keith, Ronald C. *Deng Xiaoping and China's Foreign Policy.* Routledge, 2018.

Khan, Gohar Ayub. *Glimpses Into the Corridors of Power.* Oxford University Press, 2007.

Khan, Sultan M. *Memories & Reflections of a Pakistani Diplomat.* Alden Press, 1998.

Kipling, Rudyard. *Rudyard Kipling's Verse: Inclusive Edition, 1885–1918.* Doubleday, Page and Co., 1920.

Koenig, Peter. "China—the Belt and Road Initiative—the Bridge That Spans the World." Global Research, November 24, 2019. https://www.globalresearch.ca/china-belt-road-initiative-bridge-spans-world/5695727.

Korf, Benedikt, and Isabel Lavadenz. "Sri Lanka: Land and Conflict in the North and East." Policy note, World Bank, July 2007. https://openknowledge.worldbank.org/handle/10986/12721?show=full&locale-attribute=en.

Knight, Edward F. *Where Three Empires Meet: A Narrative of Recent Travel in Kashmir, Western Tibet, Gilgit, and the Adjoining Countries.* Longmans, Green, and Co., 1893.

Kux, Dennis. *Disenchanted Allies: The United States and Pakistan, 1947–2000.* Johns Hopkins University Press, 2001.

Laruelle, Marlene, Jean-Francois Huchet, Sebastien Peyrouse, and Bayram Balci, eds. *China and India in Central Asia: A New "Great Game"?* Palgrave Macmillan, 2010.

Lauridsen, Laurids S. "Drivers of China's Regional Infrastructure Diplomacy: The Case of the Sino-Thai Railway Project." *Journal of Contemporary Asia* 50, no. 3 (2020): 380–406.

Leake, Elisabeth. "At the Nation-State's Edge: Centre-Periphery Relations in Post-1947 South Asia." *Historical Journal* 29, no. 2 (2016): 509–539.

Le Corre, Philippe, and Alain Sepulchre. *China's Offensive in Europe.* Brookings Institution Press, 2016.

Lieven, Anatol. *Pakistan: A Hard Country.* Allen Lane, 2011.

Lin, Hsiao-ting. *Tibet and Nationalist China's Frontier: Intrigues and Ethnopolitics, 1928–1949.* University of British Columbia Press, 2006.

Lintner, Bertil. *Great Game East: India, China, and the Struggle for Asia's Most Volatile Frontier.* Yale University Press, 2015.

Lintner, Bertil. *China's India War: Collision Course on the Roof of the World.* Oxford University Press, 2018.

Longkumer, Arkotong. "The Power of Persuasion: Hindutva, Christianity, and the Discourse of Religion and Culture in Northeast India." *Religion* 47, no. 2. (2017): 203–227.

Longkumer, Arkotong. " 'Along Kingdom's Highway': The Proliferation of Christianity, Education, and Print Amongst the Nagas in Northeast India." *Contemporary South Asia* 27, no. 2 (2019): 160–178.

Longkumer, Arkotong. *The Greater India Experiment: Hindutva and the Northeast.* Stanford University Press, 2021.

Mackenzie, Alexander. *History of the Relations of the Government with the Hill Tribes of the North-East Frontier of Bengal.* Home Department Press, 1884.

Mahoney, James. "Strategies of Causal Assessment in Comparative Historical Analysis." In *Comparative Historical Analysis in the Social Sciences*, edited by James Mahoney and Dietrich Rueschemeyer. Cambridge University Press, 2003.

Malik, Mohan. *China and India: Great Power Rivals.* First Forum, 2011.

Markey, Daniel S. *China's Western Horizon: Beijing and the New Geopolitics of Eurasia.* Oxford University Press, 2020.

Matheson, Sylvia A. *The Tigers of Baluchistan.* Oxford University Press, 1975.

McKinney, Jared. "How Stalled Global Reform Is Fueling Regionalism: China's Engagement with the G20." *Third World Quarterly* 39, no. 4 (2018): 709–726.

Mehta, Ved. *Portrait of India.* Yale University Press, 1993.

Mullik, B. N. *My Years with Nehru, 1948–1964.* Allied Publishers, 1972.

Musharraf, Pervez. *In the Line of Fire: A Memoir.* Simon and Schuster, 2006.

Nag, Sajal. "*Expanding Imaginations:* Theory and Praxis of Naga Nation Making in Post Colonial India." *South Asian History and Culture* 3, no. 2 (2012): 177–196.

Naseemullah, Adnan. *Patchwork States: The Historical Roots of Subnational Conflict and Competition in South Asia.* Cambridge University Press, 2022.

Naseemullah, Adnan, and Paul Staniland. "Indirect Rule and Varieties of Governance." *Governance* 29, no. 1 (2016): 13–30.

Nehru, B. K. *Nice Guys Finish Second: Memoirs.* Penguin India, 2000.

Otorbaev, Djoomart. *Central Asia's Economic Rebirth in the Shadow of the New Great Game.* Routledge, 2023.

Palit, Major General D. K. *Sentinels of the North-East: The Assam Rifles.* Palit and Palit, 1984.

Pant, Harsh V. "Rising China in India's Vicinity: A Rivalry Takes Shape in Asia." *Cambridge Review of International Affairs* 25, no. 3 (2013): 1–18.

Parris, Matthew, and Andrew Bryson. *Parting Shots: Undiplomatic Diplomats—the Ambassadors' Letters You Were Never Meant to See.* Penguin, 2011.

Paul, T. V. "Why Has the India-Pakistan Rivalry Been So Enduring? Power Asymmetry and an Intractable Conflict." *Security Studies* 15, no. 4 (2006): 600–630.

Paul, T. V., ed. *The China-India Rivalry in the Globalization Era.* Georgetown University Press, 2018.

Pottinger, Henry. *Travels in Beloochistan and Sinde: A Geographical and Historical Account of Those Countries, With a Map*. London, 1816.

Putnam, Robert D. "Diplomacy and Domestic Politics: The Logic of Two-Level Games." *International Organizations* 42, no. 3 (1988): 427–460.

Rashid, Ahmed. *Taliban: Islam, Oil and the New Great Game in Central Asia*. I. B. Tauris, 2002.

Reardon-Anderson, James, ed. *The Red Star and the Crescent: China and the Middle East*. Oxford University Press, 2018.

Reid, Robert. *History of the Frontier Areas Bordering on Assam from 1883–1941*. Assam Government Press, 1942.

Reid, Robert. "The Excluded Areas of Assam." *Geographical Journal* 103, nos. 1–2 (1944): 18–29.

Rustomji, Nari. *Imperilled Frontiers: India's North-Eastern Borderlands*. Oxford University Press, 1983.

Scott, James C. *The Art of Not Being Governed: An Anarchist History of Southeast Asia*. Yale University Press, 2009.

Scott, James C. *Against the Grain: A Deep History of the Earliest States*. Yale University Press, 2017.

Sewell, William. "Three Temporalities: Toward an Eventful Sociology." In *The Historic Turn in the Human Sciences*, edited by Terrence J. McDonald. University of Michigan Press, 1996.

Shah, Abdur Rehman. "China's Belt and Road Initiative: The Way to the Modern Silk Road and the Perils of Overdependence." *Asian Survey* 59, no. 3 (2019): 407–428.

Shakespear, L. W. *History of the Assam Rifles*. Cultural Publishing House, 1929.

Shinn, David H., and Joshua Eisenman. *China and Africa: A Century of Engagement*. University of Pennsylvania Press, 2012.

Shinn, David H., and Joshua Eisenman. *China's Relations with Africa: A New Era of Strategic Engagement*. Columbia University Press, 2023.

Siddiqi, Farhan Hanif. *The Politics of Ethnicity in Pakistan: The Baloch, Sindhi, and Mohajir Ethnic Movements*. Routledge, 2012.

Silvius, Ray. "China's Belt and Road Initiative as Nascent World Order Structure and Concept? Between Sino-Centering and Sino-Deflecting." *Journal of Contemporary China* 30, no. 121 (2021): 314–329.

Simpson, Thomas. "Bordering and Frontier-Making in Nineteenth-Century British India." *Historical Journal* 58, no. 2 (2015): 513–542.

Simpson, Thomas. *The Frontier in British India: Space, Science, and Power in the Nineteenth Century*. Cambridge University Press, 2021.

Sivaramakrishnan, K. *Modern Forests: Statemaking and Environmental Change in Colonial Eastern India*. Stanford University Press, 1999.

Small, Andrew. *The China-Pakistan Axis: Asia's New Geopolitics*. Oxford University Press, 2020.

Strangio, Sebastian. *In the Dragon's Shadow: Southeast Asia in the Chinese Century*. Yale University Press, 2020.

Styan, David. "China's Maritime Silk Road and Small States: Lessons from the Case of Djibouti." *Journal of Contemporary China* 29, no. 122 (2020): 191–206.

Thong, Tezenlo. "'To Raise the Savage to a Higher Level': The Westernization of Nagas and Their Culture." *Modern Asian Studies* 46, no. 4 (2012): 893–918.

Thornton, Thomas Henry. *Colonel Robert Sandeman: His Life and Work on Our Indian Frontier.* John Murray, 1895.

Titus, Paul. "Honor the Baloch, Buy the Pushtun: Social Organization and History in Western Pakistan." *Modern Asian Studies* 32, no. 3 (1998): 657–687.

Titus, Paul, and Nina Swidler. "Knights, Not Pawns: Ethno-Nationalism and Regional Dynamics in Post-Colonial Balochistan." *International Journal of Middle East Studies* 32 (2000): 47–69.

Toukan, Mark. "International Politics by Other Means: External Sources of Civil War." *Journal of Peace Research* 56, no. 6 (2019): 812–826.

Tripodi, Christian. "'Good for One but Not the Other': The 'Sandeman System' of Pacification as Applied to Baluchistan and the North-West Frontier, 1877–1947." *Journal of Military History* 73, no. 3 (2009): 767–802.

Tripodi, Christian. *Edge of Empire: The British Political Officer and Tribal Administration on the North-West Frontier, 1877–1947.* Ashgate, 2011.

US Institute of Peace. *China's Influence on Conflict Dynamics in South Asia.* Senior Study Group Report No. 4. US Institute of Peace, December 2020. https://www.usip.org/publications/2020/12/chinas-influence-conflict-dynamics-south-asia.

Uzonyi, Gary. "Interstate Rivalry, Genocide, and Politicide." *Journal of Peace Research* 55, no. 4 (2018): 476–490.

Vajpeyi, Ananya. "Resenting the Indian State: For a New Political Practice in the Northeast." In *Beyond Counterinsurgency: Breaking the Impasse in Northeast India*, edited by Sanjib Baruah. Oxford University Press, 2009.

Vijayan, Suchitra. *Midnight's Borders: A People's History of Modern India.* Melville House, 2021.

Walsh, Declan. *The Nine Lives of Pakistan: Dispatches from a Precarious State.* W. W. Norton, 2020.

Wani, Shakoor Ahmad. "The Changing Dynamics of the Baloch Nationalist Movement in Pakistan." *Asian Survey* 56, no. 5 (2016): 807–832.

Wolpert, Stanley. *A New History of India.* 6th ed. Oxford University Press, 2000.

World Bank. *Poverty in Pakistan: Vulnerabilities, Social Gaps, and Rural Dynamics.* Report No. 24296-PAK. World Bank, October 28, 2002.

Yadav, Anil. *Is That Even a Country, Sir!: Journeys in Northeast India by Train, Bus and Tractor.* Translated by Anurag Basnet. Speaking Tiger, 2017.

Zahid, Farhan. "BLA's Suicide Squad: Majeed Fidayeen Brigade." *Terrorism Monitor* 17, no. 2 (January 2019). https://jamestown.org/program/blas-suicide-squad-majeed-fidayeen-brigade/.

Zeb, Rizwan. *Ethno-Political Conflict in Pakistan: The Baloch Movement.* Routledge, 2020.

Zhang, Xiaoming. *Deng Xiaoping's Long War: The Military Conflict Between China and Vietnam, 1979–1991.* University of North Carolina Press, 2015.

Zhao, Suisheng. "A Neo-Colonialist Predator or Development Partner? China's Engagement and Rebalance in Africa." *Journal of Contemporary China* 23, no. 90 (2014): 1033–1052.

Zou, Yizheng, and Lee Jones. "China's Response to Threats to Its Overseas Economic Interests: Softening Non-Interference and Cultivating Hegemony." *Journal of Contemporary China* 29, no. 121 (2021): 92–108.

INDEX

GPSR Authorized Representative: Easy Access System Europe, Mustamäe tee 50, 10621 Tallinn, Estonia, gpsr.requests@easproject.com

www.ingramcontent.com/pod-product-compliance
Lightning Source LLC
Chambersburg PA
CBHW032117020426
42334CB00016B/981

* 9 7 8 0 2 3 1 2 2 1 8 2 5 *